Festive Revolutions

Performance Studies
Expressive Behavior in Culture

Sally Harrison-Pepper, General Editor

Festive Revolutions

The Politics of Popular Theater and the San Francisco Mime Troupe

Claudia Orenstein

University Press of Mississippi/Jackson

Manufactured in the United States of America

01 00 99 98 4 3 2 1

The paper in this book meets the guidelines for permanence and durability of the Committee on Production Guidelines for Book Longevity of the Council on Library Resources.

Library of Congress Cataloging-in-Publication Data
Orenstein, Claudia.
Festive revolutions : the politics of popular theater and the San Francisco Mime Troupe / Claudia Orenstein.
p. cm.—(Performance studies)
Includes bibliographical references and index.
ISBN 1-57806-063-X (cloth : alk. paper).—ISBN 1-57806-079-6 (pbk. : alk. paper)
1. Workers' theater. 2. San Francisco Mime Troupe—History. 3. Theater—Political aspects. I. Title. II. Series: Performance studies (Jackson, Miss.)
PN3305.074 1999
792′.022—dc21 98-28413
CIP

British Library Cataloging-in-Publication Data available

Contents

Acknowledgments

I would like to thank the many people whose help and encouragement made it possible for me to bring this project to fruition. First and foremost, of course, I owe a great debt of gratitude to all the members of the San Francisco Mime Troupe itself, past and present. Their exciting productions and dedication to creating political theater has been the main inspiration for this research. The Troupe's generosity in opening their rehearsals to me during the winter of 1989 and allowing me to help on their revival of *Secrets in the Sand* gave me a great deal of insight into the day-to-day running of the company and all the work that goes on behind the scenes. I am especially grateful to Ellen Callas and to Marieville Sales for the time they took sending me scripts, getting photo reprints, and answering all my questions.

Many people helped me work out my ideas through discussions on the topics I cover here and by reading the manuscript at various stages. I am grateful for their time and input. Sandra Richards, Martin Esslin, and Jean-Marie Apostilides all helped in the preliminary stages of my work. Alice Rayner, Harry Elam, Bill Eddelman, and Carl Weber of Stanford University gave me copious comments and insightful suggestions on early drafts of the manuscript, when I worked on it as my dissertation. Professor Rayner in particular was extremely supportive and helpful throughout that process. The comments and suggestions of two anonymous readers helped guide my revisions.

I would also like to thank the many people who helped me gather information and resources for the book. Jim Mayer and Ideas in Motion in San Francisco graciously let me spend hours in front of their video monitors looking at tapes of old San Francisco Mime Troupe shows. The material collected on the Mime Troupe at the University of California-Davis Library Department of Special Collections was very useful, and the librarians there were extremely helpful. Jean Ashton, director of the Rare Book and

Manuscript Library at Columbia University, sorted through the puppets in the Dramatic Museum Collection so I could see them and take their pictures. Amy Trompetter lent me her Punch and Judy puppets, Jonathan Bell directed me to other puppet resources, Steve Friedman read and commented on an earlier draft of the manuscript, and Ruth Wikler was generous in sharing her Mime Troupe experiences with me. I am also grateful to the editors at the University Press of Mississippi for all the time and effort they have put into this book.

Finally, I would like to thank my family for their encouragement and patience as I saw this project through to its completion. My mother, Gloria Orenstein, first exposed me to alternative theater at an early age, and it has always been a joy sharing my ideas with her. Thanks also to my father, Stephen Orenstein, my sister, Nadine Orenstein, and my in-laws Grace, Rod, and Sean Carman. Most of all, I am grateful to my husband, Taylor Carman, who has supported and inspired me at every step. Without his help the book would not have been possible.

Introduction

Every summer, city parks throughout the San Francisco Bay Area play host to a familiar sight, so familiar in fact that some have come to regard it as a yearly ritual. Early in the day a long white truck with a big red star emblazoned on its side pulls up to a grassy lawn in the park. Soon platforms, flats, wires, and step units are unloaded. Working as a team over the course of the morning, a small band of techies deftly assembles the pieces into a raised outdoor stage, complete with amplification and brightly colored backdrops. When they're done, the colorful cloth drops rustle gently in the breeze, illuminated by the sun. Costume racks, props, chairs, and musical instruments gather about the set, giving the impression of a garage sale at the home of some eccentric neighbor. Onlookers stop by to watch the lively work that disrupts the otherwise lazy weekend afternoon, and the company members urge them to stick around for the show.

What had once been a bare, green lawn is transformed into a theatrical space. The workers have metamorphosed as well. Some don wigs and costumes while others pick up instruments and start to play. The upbeat music attracts and entertains the gathering crowd. Many arrive planning to attend the performance, and, children and dogs in tow, they spread out blankets and unpack picnic lunches. Others, caught unawares by the day's events, watch standing up or leaning against a tree. A booth hawking T-shirts, posters, and tapes, and political activists who work the crowd, handing out flyers and pamphlets, soon round out the festive atmosphere. When the crowd is sufficiently filled out, the actors costumed, and programs distributed, a company member takes the stage and welcomes those gathered to another San Francisco Mime Troupe performance.

This scene's familiarity to many, both in the Bay Area and beyond, is testimony to the Mime Troupe's widespread impact and longevity. Founded in 1959 by R. G. Davis, the Mime Troupe boasts a history of more than thirty-five years of performing politically engaged theater in parks,

1. Portable stage for *Killing Time* viewed from the back (summer 1997). Photograph by Taylor Carman.

2. The Mime Troupe's portable stage and backstage dressing area (summer 1997). Photograph by Taylor Carman.

3. Ed Holmes and Keiko Shimosato, backstage, put on makeup for *Killing Time* (1997). Photograph by Taylor Carman.

4. Audience members picnic and chat as they await the beginning of the Mime Troupe show *Killing Time* to begin (Live Oak Park, Berkeley, 1997). Photograph by Taylor Carman.

theaters, and meeting halls across the country and abroad. In the late 1960s the Troupe came to national attention with original productions like *The Minstrel Show, or Civil Rights in a Cracker Barrel* and *L'Amant Militaire* that openly and provocatively addressed the most volatile issues of their day: the civil rights movement and the Vietnam War. In that era the Troupe found, both on college campuses and in the counterculture of which they were a part, audiences eager to hear the call to revolution that their shows put forth. During this period of their greatest national prominence, the Mime Troupe's work was fresh and provocative, comfortably in sync with both the political and aesthetic climate of the day.

In the years since then, however, the Troupe has had to adjust their work to an ever-changing political environment. In the seventies the advent of feminism caused the Troupe to rethink its political orientation, while in the eighties neoconservatism brought new challenges from the political right. Although in the early nineties the Mime Troupe optimistically ended every show with a statement like "The 90's, it looks like a promising decade" (Holden, Callas, and Barthol 43), in comparison to the sixties, the nineties may be said to be marked by political apathy, especially on the left. Because of the changes in the political environment that the Mime Troupe has had to confront, some contemporary critics have questioned the continued relevance of the Troupe's work. While they still claim a strong following, the Troupe no longer seems to challenge the status quo in ways that are threatening enough to lead to arrests, as they had in the past, and they are often accused of merely preaching to the converted.

One of the reasons the Troupe has garnered the kind of criticism that they have is that, since the sixties, the Troupe has continued to define itself by a unique performance style that blends popular theatrical traditions, including mime, commedia dell'arte, vaudeville, minstrel shows, and melodrama, with a firm leftist political agenda. In conjunction with both their broad theatrical style and their political ideals, the Troupe has made a point whenever possible of performing for free in the parks in order to take their message to the people. The outdoor venues combine with the Troupe's lively, comic performance style to create a festive atmosphere that helps to bring their audiences together.

However, it is precisely the use of a theatrical style that embraces a grassroots counterculture that makes the Troupe's work seem, to some, outdated, trapped in the aesthetic fashions of the sixties. The communal atmosphere of their outdoor performances, defiantly unmediated by corporate, bureaucratic institutions, is reminiscent of the often utopian attempts of that period to nurture alternative cultural models. The Troupe's longevity, which brands them as the "most established anti-establishment theatre"[1] in the country, is thus both a blessing and a curse. To some it speaks to the ongoing relevance of their work, while to others it is evidence of the Mime Troupe's inability to adapt to the needs of new social and political circumstances and consequently serves only to confirm the fact that their work is moribund, living on only through its nostalgic appeal.

The primary concern of this book is not specifically to assess the ongoing relevance of the Mime Troupe's present work, although I will address this issue at some length. Nor is it to do a complete history of the Mime Troupe by recounting the stories of those who have been a part of it, and thoroughly contextualizing it within the turbulent times that gave birth to it, though this would indeed be a worthy and welcome project. My intention in this book is rather to come to a better understanding of the general possibility of using popular traditions in an ongoing project of creating politically engaged, radical theater. By "radical" I do not mean that which necessarily endorses extreme or violent action but rather a theatrical project that looks to unravel and express the root causes of social and political ills. The conclusions I draw from my analysis and research will in the end reflect back on the Mime Troupe and help both to evaluate the current state of their endeavors as well as to suggest whether or not they, and other similar-minded groups, can continue to promote a progressive political agenda through such performance techniques.

This project takes the San Francisco Mime Troupe as a point of departure. From the Mime Troupe's body of work I attempt to define the nature of popular theater more generally. I analyze closely the Troupe's productions, the traditional forms they draw on in creating those productions, and the origins and histories of those forms. Throughout the book, examples from thirty-five years of Mime Troupe performances show how popular theater forms can be used both successfully and unsuccessfully. They also serve to illustrate specific theoretical ideas. Again, however, the main objective of this research is to conceptualize in general both the possibilities and the limits popular theater forms present in creating actively engaged political theater, not to evaluate the potential of popular forms solely in relation to the Mime Troupe's use of them. It is my contention, however, that Mime Troupe productions work best in instances when the Troupe has been able to use popular forms to their best advantage. A deep understanding of the nature of popular forms, combined with careful implementation of them, can allow socially minded theater practitioners like the Mime Troupe to keep pace with an ever-changing political climate while staying true to a progressive social and political agenda.

Finally, while this work is not concerned solely with the San Francisco Mime Troupe, I hope that the Troupe's theatrical oeuvre will be seen in a new light within the context of the present discussion. Scholars and historians generally, and understandably, look at the Mime Troupe within the context of alternative theater movements of the sixties, and place them side by side with companies like the Living Theatre, the Bread and Puppet Theatre, El Teatro Campesino, and the Open Theatre. There is of course much to be gained by seeing the Mime Troupe in this way, within their own historical and aesthetic milieu. I will be referring to some of the theater groups mentioned above from time to time as well as reviewing the Troupe's work from the sixties in my final chapter and throughout. However, this book attempts to reposition the Mime Troupe as a contemporary example of a long historical tradition of popular theatrical endeavors with a political orientation. The eruption of theatrical fervor of which the Mime Troupe was a part was not unique to the sixties but was rather a modern example of an intermingling of political issues and popular performance practices that has recurred throughout Western history. It is important to remember that theatrical performance has historically played a pivotal role in giving voice to popular concerns. It is equally important to pay attention to the forces that have both facilitated and impeded that expression.

In the first chapter I attempt to characterize the multifaceted term "popular" as it relates to performance practices. What is popular theater? What understanding of the popular unites the disparate forms that seem to comprise the Mime Troupe's theatrical heritage? How can popular theater, so often thought of as mere entertainment, be politically engaged? For my purposes it is useful to use the term "festive-revolutionary" to set apart a unique type of popular performance that unites a festive atmosphere with revolutionary aspirations. This performance tradition defines a lineage that links the Mime Troupe with many of the forms they choose to draw on in their work. I use the theoretical works of anthropologists like Victor Turner, critics like Mikhail Bakhtin, and theater practitioners like Tom Leabhart to help identify some of the features unique to festive-revolutionary forms and common to traditions as diverse as mime and minstrel shows.

Behind the visible particulars of these disparate theatrical forms, there is a shared sense of optimism linked to patterns of rejuvenation that positions revolutionary change as a joyous moment of social and political renewal. The unique blend of optimism within a structure that is both cyclical and progressive shapes the political perspective of festive-revolutionary forms. I propose that this type of theater not only adapts easily to changing political circumstances but carries with it a latent political potential that constantly tends toward revolution. I use "revolution" in the strict sense of a total inversion or conversion of existing social conditions through disruption and chaos. Such disruptive action need not necessarily be violent or coercive; nevertheless popular forms are revolutionary insofar as they prompt one to envision radical change by challenging or undermining established forms of power and authority. Festive-revolutionary forms are therefore not just useful tools with which performers like the Mime Troupe can convey their political message but, to some extent, embodiments of a certain ideal of liberation itself.

While a theoretical discussion of the attributes of popular forms argues for their political potential, critics are quick to point out that what is revolutionary in theory does not always equal revolution in practice. A form may have supposed revolutionary potential and yet may never have concrete political effects. For this reason I turn to the history of the forms the Mime Troupe uses to determine the political orientation they had in their origins: Was their political import revolutionary in the salient sense? Has that political import been preserved in any way in the forms themselves?

The historical origin and development of many European festive-revolutionary forms suggests that the link between these forms and a revolutionary political perspective is very strong, and has been since their inception. Tracing the broad historical development of popular theater within a single cultural context brings this to light. The political origin and legacy of popular forms, as well as the role popular theater has played as part of an alternative culture, comes into vivid relief when set against the background of a traditional history of theatrical and political development.

Chapter 2 of this study focuses on the development of popular theater within the single cultural context of France and French theater in order to bring out the contrast between the development of popular and "elite" theater forms. The French context serves as a good example since commedia dell'arte, circus, and other popular forms all found a home in France. It was also in France that the art of pantomime, cousin to the Mime Troupe's form of mime, developed. A broad perspective on the history of theater in France shows an ongoing dynamic in which popular forms emerge and reemerge in continuous opposition to the power structure. Originating as a voice for the common people, popular forms continue to play this role. Their historical challenge to established authority leads them to become irrevocably associated with a resistance to oppression. The historical development of popular forms in France suggests that there exists not only a theoretical link between popular forms and revolutionary politics but an actual historical link between the practices and occasions of festivals on the one hand, and the real threat of revolution, on the other. The resulting association between festival and revolution is played out in French theater right up to the present era, as evidenced by the Théâtre du Soleil's 1970 production, *1789: The Revolution Must Continue to the Perfection of Happiness.* While not all popular European forms will have developed identically with those in France, the exploration presented here suggests a pattern that in one form or another may have been common to the popular theater of Europe generally, for throughout Europe theater developed in circumstances where similar economic, political, and social conditions prevailed.

Chapter 3 also presents evidence that at least one popular form, the puppet show Pulcinella (known to English audiences in its counterpart "Punch and Judy") functioned similarly in different countries throughout Europe. I use the study of Pulcinella to address a further question about the nature of popular forms. It might be agreed that a general sense of something called "popular theater" with a distinctly festive-revolutionary character, historically spoke for the common people of Europe, situating itself in opposition to authority. However, within the diverse offerings of popular performance there existed distinct theatrical traditions that evolved with their own unique characters and structures. How then was the political position of the popular translated into distinct theatrical practices? This question is best answered by focusing on how the distinct features of a single popular form like Pulcinella fit themselves to the general revolutionary function of popular theater as a whole.

The choice of Pulcinella as the subject for this study is owing partly to its great popularity throughout Europe and partly to the Mime Troupe's resurrection of the character Punch in one of their most successful antiwar plays, *L'Amant Militaire.* Once again we find that looking at the history of the forms the Troupe uses reveals the rich political-theatrical tradition of which they are a part. The Pulcinella tradition answers the questions above about the true revolutionary character of popular traditions by suggesting that the distinct characteristics of individual popular forms coalesced as a variety of tactics used to discredit and ridicule power structures, to evade or avoid repression, and to propose possibilities for liberation and retaliation. The historical facts of the Pulcinella tradition belie the childish facade of this and many other popular forms. A powerful voice for the common people throughout Europe, Pulcinella's trademark violence lies somewhere between slapstick antic and revolutionary threat.

Yet even a theatrical form as antagonistic to the status quo as Pulcinella still partakes of many of the popular moral prejudices of its day. The victims of Pulcinella's violence are not only figures of authority but also representatives of traditionally oppressed groups such as women, blacks, and Jews. Pulcinella's own oppression of the oppressed brings into question the revolutionary nature of this puppet show, and perhaps of all popular forms. A distinctly lower-class, white, Christian, male perspective shaped Pulcinella's antiauthoritarian message, and therefore Pulcinella reflects not only that group's desire for change but also their own position of dominance over other groups. On the other hand, as a series of tactics that counter authoritarian structures, the form itself seems to be flexible enough to shape its revolutionary message to any number of causes. The Mime Troupe's use of Punch in a play about the Vietnam War is evidence for the form's continuing adaptability. Yet the prejudicial aspect of the form still remains in question. To raise this point is not to demand a "politically correct" point of view by today's standards from a sixteenth-century puppet but rather to ask whether such a form, grown in a specific cultural setting, can transcend the prejudices of the environment that created it. In other words, it is to pose the dramaturg's question of how to translate Punch to the present cultural environment while maintaining the artistic integrity of his decidedly anarchic character.

Chapter 4 addresses this question in regard to a form that foregrounds the prejudices of a particular cultural and historical period. While Pulcinella shows have historically played on prejudices against women, blacks, and Jews, they do not depend on this antagonism for their distinctive character (a show can be and often has been created that simply avoids involving these figures and any reference to them). The American minstrel show tradition, by contrast, grew out of the historical context of slavery in America and has since its beginnings fulfilled its self-imposed mandate of exhibiting and subsequently denigrating black Americans. Can such an apparently reactionary form have any genuine revolutionary import?

The minstrel show, like all popular forms, relies heavily on the use of stereotypes. In this form the stereotypes are particularly incriminating, for while the content of the shows may vary widely, the stereotypes always highlight the black man (and sometimes woman) as a clown. While an integral part of American popular culture, minstrel shows grew not out of the oppressed community that they represented but out of white America's vision of that community. Minstrel shows, therefore, enjoy a curious position in the field of popular theater. Yet there is evidence that in the hands of blacks the form was turned around and, like other clown masks, minstrel blackface could give performers license to challenge the status quo. The true revolutionary power of a form like the minstrel show, however, could only be engaged when performers used the stereotypes that defined the form to transform those images themselves, replacing them with new, positive ones. The Mime Troupe's use of the minstrel show form in their own production, *The Minstrel Show, or Civil Rights in a Cracker Barrel,* shows one attempt at playing out stereotypes in order to transform them. In this production the use of stereotypes was central to the piece's political project of questioning, destroying, and redefining cultural prejudices. The present work does not offer any definite conclusions about the political role of stereotypes in all popular forms but rather tries to show some evidence of the positive value in the self-conscious reliance on and manipulation of stereotypes. The questions concerning the possibilities and limitations of using stereotypes in the theater extend beyond this study, specifically to the use of stereotypes of women in popular traditions.

Having explored some of the byways in the subject of popular forms and their political positions, we are brought back to issues concerning the Mime Troupe's work. Popular forms, as I have suggested, are a powerful resource for political theaters. The question remains whether the Mime Troupe has been able to continue to take advantage of the political potential of popular forms. How has the change in political environment affected the Troupe's ability to capitalize on their theatrical style? More generally, what role does the historical context play in determining the political success of any popular theater?

The final chapter of the book therefore focuses solely on the Mime Troupe's work and their struggle to fit their theatrical style to changing times. By looking back at how popular forms worked for the Troupe in the sixties and how the social and political environment has changed, we can better understand how the Troupe's theatrical style does or does not work for them today. An understanding of the nature of popular forms and how they interact with historical circumstances suggests that the Mime Troupe's work is in no way simply out of date. While the political climate may not be ripe for revolutionary change, the type of popular theater practiced by the Mime Troupe still holds the potential to enlighten audiences about political struggles and possibly to engage them in political action as well.

Scholars have long neglected the field of popular theater owing both to the stigma attached to it as "low art" and to the ephemeral nature of the traditions themselves, which makes evidence hard to come by. It is only in recent years that so-called low art has opened up as an area of wide study and interest. This book owes a great debt to the work of current scholars like Joel Schechter and Robert C. Toll, to contemporary performers like Dario Fo, and of course to the Mime Troupe, all of whom are seriously addressing the history and practice of popular forms. While many more scholars have now taken up the project of looking at popular theater forms, there no doubt still remains a great deal of work to be done in this area. At the outset of my research I posed the simple question: Why are popular forms often so good for doing political theater? In order to answer it I have covered fairly extensive terrain. Even so, this study only scratches the surface of a vast field that awaits much more research and discussion. In the process of my work, however, I hope that I have contributed to an understanding of popular forms and, more important, to a greater curiosity about their nature, history, and the possibilities they offer theater practitioners today.

San Francisco Mime Troupe Chronology

1959 *Mime and Words*
1960 *11th Hour Mime Show*
1961 *Act Without Words II*; *Purgatory*; *Krapp's Last Tape*; Event I
1962 *The Dowry*
1963 Film: *Plastic Haircut*; Event II; *The Root*; *Ruzzante's Maneuvers*; *Ubu King*
1964 Event III; *Tartuffe*; *Chorizos*; *Mimes and Movie*
1965 *Tartuffe*; *The Exception and the Rule*; *A Minstrel Show, or Civil Rights in a Cracker Barrel*; *Candelaio*; *Chronicles of Hell*; Appeal I; Appeal II
1966 Appeal III; *What's That a Head?*; *Jack Off!*; Film: *Mirage and Centerman*; *Olive Pits*; *Search and Seizure*; *The Miser*; *Out Put You*
1967 *The Minstrel Show, or Civil Rights in a Cracker Barrel*; *The Condemned*; *The Vaudeville Show*; Appeal IV; *L'Amant Militaire*
1968 *Ruzzante, or The Veteran*; Gorilla Marching Band is formed; Gutter Puppets: *Meter Maid, Little Black Panther, Meat*; *The Farce of Patelin*; Radical Theater Festival; Children's Xmas play
1969 Women's Drill Team; Bookmobile puppets; *The Third Estate*; *Congress of the Whitewashers, or Turandot*
1970 *The Independent Female, or A Man Has His Pride*; *Ecoman*; *Telephone Man, or Ripping Off Ma Bell*; *Los Siete*; *Seize the Time*
1971 *The Dragon Lady's Revenge*; *Clown Show*; *Highway Robbery; Soledad*
1972 *The Dragon Lady's Revenge*; *Highrises*; *Frozen Wages*; *American Dreamer*
1973 *San Francisco Scandals of 1973*; *The Mother*
1974 *The Great Air Robbery*
1975 *Frijoles or Beans to You*; *Power Play*

1976 *False Promises/Nos Engañaron*
1977 *Hotel Universe*
1978 *Electrobucks*
1979 *Squash*; *T.V. Dinner*; *We Can't Pay We Won't Pay*
1980 *Factperson*
1981 *Americans, or Last Tango in Huahuatenango*; *Ghosts*; *Factwino Meets the Moral Majority*
1982 *Factwino vs. Armageddonman*
1983 *Secrets in the Sand*; *The Uprising at Fuente Ovejuna*
1984 *Steeltown*; *1985*
1985 *Factwino: The Opera*; *Crossing Borders (A Domestic Farce)*
1986 *Spain/36*; *Hotel Universe*; *The Mozamgola Caper*
1987 *The Dragon Lady's Revenge*
1988 *Ripped Van Winkle*
1989 *Seeing Double*; *Secrets in the Sand*
1990 *Rats!*; *Uncle Tom's Cabin*
1991 *Back to Normal*; *I Ain't Yo' Uncle: The New Jack Revisionist "Uncle Tom's Cabin"*
1992 *Social Work*; *I Ain't Yo' Uncle: The New Jack Revisionist "Uncle Tom's Cabin"*
1993 *Offshore*
1994 *Escape to Cyberia*; *Offshore*; *Big Wind*; *Revenger Rat Meets the Merchant of Death*
1995 *Coast City Confidential*; *Escape to Cyberia*
1996 *Gotta Getta Life*; *13 Dias/13 Days*; *Soul Suckers from Outer Space*
1997 *Killing Time*

Note: This list includes theater productions and special events presented by the San Francisco Mime Troupe since 1959. Some of the productions are from original Mime Troupe scripts while others are of well-known plays, adaptations of well-known plays, or plays written by non-Mime Troupe members in collaboration with the Mime Troupe.

Festive Revolutions

1 What Is Festive-Revolutionary Theater?

Red streamers flutter out from behind the backdrop of the makeshift stage in San Francisco's Alamo Square. Fire! Whistles blow. Characters run to and fro in a frenzy, to the accompaniment of fast-paced music from the band. A tall, thin man in a sailor suit rushes on stage carrying a bucket. Drunk, he spins off balance. Although he intends, heroically, to throw the contents of the bucket onto the burning building, he somehow ends up facing the audience. He sways back and forth, ready to swing the bucket. A moment of suspense. The audience giggles and squirms in anticipation. Finally, he hurls the contents of the bucket and the audience is doused with confetti.

A ragged black cloth spreads down across the backdrop from behind. Thanks to this low-budget special effect the painted building on the drop now appears charred. This burned-out structure is the Hotel Universe where a group of earnest but clownish senior citizens—a thin white woman in a polka-dot dress, a Mexican-American man in baggy trousers, a large black woman in a tiny white hat, and an emotionally high-strung Russian prima ballerina—make their home.

The true buffoons of the piece, however, are not these tenants but their landlord and his partner in crime, the mayor. Each wears a large false nose held on by a conspicuous elastic strap. The landlord struts about in a top hat and tails, while the mayor sports a banner across his chest that says, "MAYOR." The oversized yellow flower in the lapel of his green suit will, of course, squirt water in the face of anyone who gets too close. The landlord and the mayor have conspired to set the hotel on fire so they can then condemn it, evict the tenants, and sell the property to developers. Before the play is over, the landlord—doing double-duty as judge—will get a pie in the face.

5. A landlord (Barry Levitan) evicts tenants (Deb'bora Gilyord and Eduardo Robledo), who fight back in *Hotel Universe* (1977). Photograph by Angus MacKenzie.

In spite of the pie, and although the residents barricade themselves in the hotel to avoid forcible removal, the tenants lose their fight. The backdrop that depicted the inside of their homes lowers to reveal another scene, a solid line of policemen, armed and expressionless, coming to force them out. This new drop moves forward, engulfing the hotel residents. It then turns around, throwing them to the front of the small stage. The motley crew now looks back to see a new image on the backside of the drop: the outside of their hotel, boarded up with a sign reading "CONDEMNED."

The Mime Troupe's *Hotel Universe,* created and performed in 1977, made free use of the techniques and conventions of circus clowning to expose the joint corruption of land developers and urban politicians. The piece addressed the controversy surrounding the International Hotel in San Francisco, home to about fifty-five mostly retired, low-income Filipino and Chinese men. These residents were facing forced eviction for the benefit of developers hoping to build a parking lot on the site of their home. The piece itself, along with the closing speech delivered after the show by a cast member, focused voter attention on a ballot measure, Proposition

U, that would stop demolition of the hotel and force the city to maintain and repair low-rent housing. In reality, as in the play, the building was torn down. Development never occurred, and the site remained unused for nearly twenty years. By 1996 plans for a new construction project were again under discussion, this one to provide low-income housing and a Philippine Cultural Center.

The Mime Troupe have relied time and again on conventions drawn from circus clowning, vaudeville, carnival, puppet shows, and other supposedly "frivolous" entertainments to address serious social and political issues. What motivates this choice? Why jeopardize drawing serious attention to a cause by embedding it in a comic theatrical framework? Are such popular forms mere palliatives, putting a kind of sugarcoating on unsettling political issues to render them more palatable and easier to digest, or do they have political content and value beyond their merely strategic usefulness as light entertainment? How can political theater groups enlisting these forms maintain a balance between comic style on the one hand, and the gravity of the issues on the other? In what ways, if any, are comic and highly theatrical forms of entertainment advantageous for the Mime Troupe or any politically minded theater as a means of communicating serious political ideas?

In this book I will try to answer these questions and show that it is no accident that clowning and other popular traditions are good vehicles for political theater. Popular forms were themselves born of social struggle, and even in contemporary contexts they continue to reflect their origins by offering theatrical strategies for confronting social and political oppression in a way that empowers performers and their audiences.

Why do theater companies like the Mime Troupe rely so heavily on political clowning? Critic Joel Schechter offers one compelling answer and also describes the ways in which performers avoid some of the pitfalls involved in mixing the serious and the comic. In *Durov's Pig: Clowns, Politics, and Theatre,* he discusses the work of a number of twentieth-century performers who have successfully managed to combine antic styles with genuine political content. Schechter draws a sharp distinction, however, between these twentieth-century performers and the fools, clowns, and jesters he sees as their ancestors. While acknowledging that "fools and clowns have long practiced symbolic resistance to the status quo," he stresses that "the temporary nature of these upheavals was agreed upon in advance by those at the top of the social order" (10). Though he concedes that these earlier performers may have had antiestablishment intentions no less than their contemporary counterparts, he maintains that the political effects of their performances, if they had any at all, were temporary and inconsequential.

Those arguing against the political relevance and efficacy of clowning and related popular forms often recur to the "safety-valve" theory to support their position. In this view, the traditional entertainments in question encourage and enact resistance to the status quo in the same way a safety-valve reduces pressure by letting off steam, in effect avoiding—and possibly even preventing—any significant change. Small theatrical transgressions thus express, but at once defuse, brewing political unrest, perhaps even undermining the prospect of real and effective political action.

However, unlike those who apply the safety-valve theory across the board, Schechter believes that many contemporary performers do possess the kind of political consciousness that actively gears their work toward political and social change. What makes twentieth-century performers unique, he says, is that "their modern political consciousness comes from Marx, Brecht and Mayakovsky" (viii). Modern political clowns consciously break away from the subordinate social position clowns have traditionally maintained. Instead of confining their antics to times officially sanctioned as "holiday," they continue to play the role of political and cultural critic on an everyday basis. Although the redistribution of power these clowns effect is also only "temporary," the work they do has some very real consequences. Their daring is communicated to the audience, inciting it to action: "Much as clowns destroy stage conventions, the audience for its part is invited—by direct address—to consent to the rebellion, join it, celebrate its utopian goals and speak out against injustice and oppression after the play ends" (16).

Schechter's discussion of clowning accurately pinpoints the issue that seems to plague debates about the viability of clowning as a form of social protest and political practice. The question is whether such techniques can have any permanent effect on the real world. Schechter concedes the possibility of genuine political impact, but only in a limited number of cases, specifically post-Marxian performance.

One of the issues that underlies the opposition between the safety-valve theory and Schechter's position is whether the theatrical models political clowns represent and embody are essentially cyclical or progressive, that is to say, whether their structure allows the status quo continually to return at the end of the performance or instead envisions change and urges spectators toward a radically different future. For Schechter, a political consciousness derived from a progressive Marxian theory of history is what makes all the difference as to whether political clowning is an effective or an ineffective form of protest.

But is it fair to say that no clowning was really politically relevant or efficacious prior to the influence of Marx? How is it that these forms, whose traditions reach so far back in our history, could become effective only with a contemporary political understanding? Is there anything in the forms themselves that might incline them to this type of perspective, with or without Marx? Are cyclical and progressive models of change the only factors determining the efficacy of political clowning, and are they really at odds with each other?

The Mime Troupe's work is indeed politically informed. They acknowledge the decisive influence of Marx's theories and Bertolt Brecht's theatrical ideas on their own work. Yet in spite of the Troupe's obvious political self-consciousness, even Schechter remains skeptical of the political potential of their recent work: "The feeling of being 'the good minority' can too easily become self-congratulatory and encourage complacency rather than activism among its adherents . . . Revolutionary posturing suits the Mime Troupe's broad, exaggerated style of acting . . . Such stiff rhetorical poses are more removed from American life today than they were in the 1960s, when 'revolutionary' was a term used to describe new cars as well as radical political plans. It may well be that the Mime Troupe's style was better suited to the sixties than it is to the present" (172–73). Here Schechter's argument shifts from political consciousness and ideological structure to a question of style. He argues that the Mime Troupe's style no longer engages today's audiences and he is not alone in thinking that their work is out of date or a nostalgic throwback to the sixties.

Joan Holden, the Mime Troupe's principal playwright, has responded to these concerns. She agrees that the Troupe needs to change its work to keep pace with the changes taking place in the world at large, but she prefers changes in content rather than style: "The politics of the sixties and our politics of the seventies were very programmatic. We knew what the issues were, we were Marxists, the message was clear, the foreign models were clear. We're still Marxists, but the models aren't clear anymore" (Kleb 60).

So, whereas Schechter points to a stylistic problem in the Mime Troupe's contemporary work, Holden proposes that the problem lies in the lack of substantive political models to put on the stage. Both emphasize the Troupe's need to adapt to changing times. Both agree that clowns can only represent a revolutionary political agenda by imbuing their work with concrete political content and that that content itself needs to change along with the changing historical context of performance. Their views raise further questions about the ways in which different types of political clowning can be politically effective. Are popular forms politically viable only in special, isolated situations, or do they have revolutionary import that can serve them well regardless of the immediate social circumstances?

The argument I would like to make goes beyond Schechter in recuperating popular theater practices for progressive political work and supports Holden's emphasis on changing content over style. My view attributes to popular theater forms the ability to unite a cyclical and a progressive understanding of history, a festive style and a revolutionary perspective. Schechter is certainly right that Marx's political theories and Brecht's and Vladimir Mayakovsky's theatrical models have given focus to the political goals and strategies of theater companies like the Mime Troupe. However, I believe that what renders certain popular theatrical traditions politically viable is not their attachment to a theory but their connection to a long tradition of what I shall call "festive-revolutionary" practices. These practices are both cyclical and progressive in that they emphasize renewal and rebirth on the one hand while focusing on altering the material and social conditions of life on the other. Both perspectives—the cyclical-festive and the progressive-revolutionary—have characterized certain popular theatrical forms long before Marx. It is the way popular forms combine their festive and revolutionary impulses that makes popular traditions useful for creating theatre for social change.

This is not to deny, of course, that in the final analysis the political efficacy of any theatrical work ultimately depends on the political climate in which it is performed. No theater production could possibly take responsibility for inspiring apolitical audiences in a complacent era to concrete political action. The Mime Troupe's social and historical environ-

6. The lively, rambunctious character of seventeenth-century fairs is depicted in this Dusart print. In the background a troupe of traveling players vies for the crowd's attention with their acrobatic feats. *Village Fair* (Dutch 17th-century engraving) by Cornelis Dusart, courtesy of the Metropolitan Museum of Art, Purchase, Joseph Pulitzer Bequest, 1917 (17.50.15–340).

ment has indeed changed, yet their best work still has political import in part because of its connection to festive-revolutionary traditions.

What, then, are the salient features of the festive-revolutionary style of popular theater, and how do cyclical and progressive models of change figure within it? Theodore Shank gives a fairly comprehensive list of the multiplicity of forms the Mime Troupe has drawn on in their work when he states that "in keeping with other political theatres of the last twenty years they have used *commedia dell'arte,* circus, puppet shows, music hall, vaudeville, parades, magicians, carnival side-shows, buskers, brass bands, comic strips, melodrama, minstrel shows and other means of exhilarating entertainment" (*American Alternative Theater* 59). As this list indicates, the Mime Troupe's influences go well beyond clowning to a whole variety of theatrical entertainments. What do these forms have in common? And what, if anything, is distinctively political about them?

7. Hogarth's engraving of a raucous village fair depicts a number of competing popular entertainments, including (in the background) a rope-dancer, a Harlequin show, and a Punch and Judy play. *Southwark Fair* (British 18th-century engraving) by William Hogarth, courtesy of the Metropolitan Museum of Art, Harris Brisbane Dick Fund, 1932 [32.35 (27)].

In trying to define these forms of "exhilarating entertainment," one is tempted simply to classify them as "popular." But I want to suggest instead "festive-revolutionary" as a term to designate the kind of popular tradition that specifically lends itself to politically engaged theater. This term will facilitate the discussion by denoting a category of performance that links the joyous spirit that seems to be so large a part of that "exhilarating entertainment" with a political agenda that pushes for change in a particularly progressive way. What kinds of performance, then, qualify as festive-revolutionary, and how do they work?

Granted, the term "festive-revolutionary" itself already assumes a connection between festive and revolutionary practices, an assumption I hope at least to explain in what follows. Moreover, the term deliberately conflates cyclical and progressive conceptions of historical change. Festivals, which belong to Schechter's category of essentially temporary "holiday" entertainments, tend toward a reaffirmation of the status quo once the festival is over, whereas "revolutionary" seems to imply total, permanent change and progress. What I have called "festive-revolutionary" forms, however, manage to mix these two structural ideas in a way that lends itself to precisely the kind of political theatrical enterprise in which the Mime Troupe is engaged. For such forms combine familiar and recurrent patterns of change with a vision of a new and unpredictable future, while always conceiving of progress itself as a kind of renewal.

This mixing of the cyclical and the progressive seems less paradoxical if one keeps in mind that the word "revolution" itself means revolving and returning. The point of appealing to terms such as "cyclical" and "progressive" in this case lies not so much in determining whether history actually follows a linear or a circular course, but rather in characterizing how people perceive or envision change. If the object of politically engaged theater is at some level to move its spectators to concrete action, it is crucial to understand how it conceives of the present moving into the future in general.

The term "festive-revolutionary" also serves to exclude some notions of the "popular" that, for a variety of reasons, I do not intend to deal with in what follows. The first sense of "popular" that I exclude from my discussion has to do with mass, technological entertainment. Much of what we refer to today as "popular theater" is anything but revolutionary; instead, it is typically either reactionary or apolitical. But such cases are the exception rather than the rule for popular theater forms at large and owe their currency to a new meaning the term "popular" has taken on in our technological age and the fact that we now identify the word "popular" with technological forms of entertainment such as movies and television. Max Horkheimer and Theodor Adorno describe the system that creates these entertainments as the "culture industry" (121). What fuels the production of culture in such a system is a technological rationale rather than a creative impulse. The culture industry produces goods for the greatest number of consumers by appealing to the lowest common denominator of audience interest. The result is a leveling and a homogenization of cultural artifacts: "A technological rationale is the rationale of domination itself . . . It has made the technology of the culture industry no more than the achievement of standardization and mass production, sacrificing whatever involved a distinction between the logic of the work and that of the social system" (121). The products of the culture industry claim to be popular art in virtue of their appeal to a large number of people. But a large following is only one element of popular entertainment. Important aspects of popular theater are not represented in a system that is so far removed from the lives of ordinary people and whose raison d'être is simply to sell commercial products. Moreover, a system whose cultural products seem apolitical because they avoid active engagement with political issues in fact supports conservative, big-business politics in the name of the status quo. Contemporary popular entertainment could therefore be said to be not merely apolitical but positively reactionary.

Horkheimer and Adorno's critique of the culture industry proposes a dialectic between mass culture and the Kantian concept of a work of art. In so doing, it contrasts mass culture with elite art. However, it fails to address past, nontechnological forms of popular theater that are instances neither of mass culture nor of elite art. The Mime Troupe draws on forms such as commedia dell'arte and clowning, which have traditionally had broad appeal but were not propagated through a technological medium. These forms developed in popular venues through direct contact with their audiences. They were not industrialized and were, as we shall see, antielitist, embodying a distinctive revolutionary ideal.

The content of the Mime Troupe's work is no doubt influenced by the popular media. This is evidenced by the specific references to, stylistic quotations from, and campy or parodic plays on pop music stars, television sitcoms, and blockbuster movies in their productions. Furthermore, Mime Troupe members are always as up-to-date and well-informed on the latest breaking scandals and celebrity gossip to be found in popular tabloids like *People Magazine* as they are on substantive political issues. Topical references and allusions from the mainstream popular culture that are immediately familiar allow the Troupe's work to speak directly to their audiences. These references provide a vocabulary for Mime Troupe shows as much as any political education, and this vocabulary is the cultural currency the Troupe shares with their audiences. It is also evident, conversely, that many stylistic features of mass media entertainment reveal the debt they owe to popular theatrical traditions such as vaudeville and clowning.

Nonetheless there are fundamental differences between the project of the Mime Troupe and their peers and that of the mass media, and I believe it is important to distinguish these two realms rather than lump them all together under the single category of "the popular." While both claim to be appealing on some level to a mass audience, in one case artistic creation is shaped by ongoing and immediate live audience response, in the other case by a corporate system serving the needs and perceptions of sponsors and administrative boards. The mass media is thus always kept at a distance from its true audience. Its entertainment cannot be shaped in the moment of performance by viewer response. Through its association with and dependence on corporations it is fundamentally conservative, and it cannot elect to be otherwise. The mass media therefore cannot in fact freely respond to its audience if their tastes and desires should run to more radical perspectives.

A second type of popular theater that I have excluded from the present discussion is agitational propaganda, or "agit-prop," a form of mass didactic theater. The twenties and thirties was a fertile era for political theatre across Europe, Russia, and the United States. One style of presentation that emerged from this flowering became known as agit-prop. Agit-prop offered a different cultural response to industrial society from that provided by the culture industry. Like the culture industry, agit-prop addressed itself to a mass audience. Yet it had as its main goal the task of educating the working class concerning their situation in industrialized, capitalist society. Its further purpose was to inspire workers to fight to improve their condition. Unlike the products of the culture industry that Horkheimer and Adorno describe, agit-prop theaters were primarily revolutionary, specifically devoted to fostering communist revolution. Their means of achieving that goal, however, were often extremely didactic and on the whole diverged sharply from the "frivolous" or playful elements of popular theater.[1]

The Mime Troupe has adopted some extremely useful techniques from agit-prop theater, one example being their use of "actos," short didactic pieces, patterned after the work of the Teatro Campesino. Like the early agit-prop groups the Mime Troupe also tries to educate audiences to a progressive perspective and to inspire them to political action. However, the didacticism that characterizes much of agit-prop is only one aspect of the Mime Troupe's work. Agit-prop can make for very effective political theatre. Nonetheless, my discussion here will not go into depth in this area. Agit-prop does not capture, for me, those elements that are most effective and most characteristic of popular forms, and therefore I don't believe this area of inquiry is able to provide the best answer to the question of whether contemporary theater practitioners can use popular forms effectively for political purposes. There is a fundamental difference between the aesthetic of festive-revolutionary theatre and that of agit-prop, and it is in this difference that the popular element of the Mime Troupe's work most strongly resides.

Finally, I shall exclude the sense of "popular" as it applies to the aesthetic discourse of postmodernism. There is an ever-growing body of criticism that discusses and debates myriad aspects of postmodern culture. My intent here is not to enter into that debate but merely to distinguish a discussion of postmodernism from an account of popular forms as such. Although theories of postmodernity do not claim to define the popular, one typical characteristic of postmodern art, especially in contrast to modernism, is the way in which it mixes high and low, elite and popular forms. This mixture of forms seems to mimic the mixture of the serious and the frivolous that has characterized much of the Mime Troupe's work.

A postmodern aesthetic, however, is very different from a popular one, especially in the way it addresses political issues. Postmodern thought mixes the serious and the frivolous in order to deny and flatten familiar hierarchies. The intent is to create the sense of a world without anchoring points, in which all meaning is relative. Festive-revolutionary theater, as I hope to define it, by contrast, derives meaning from depicting inequalities and prejudices that do exist, as they exist. Like postmodern forms, it attempts to disrupt our adherence to hierarchies, yet it does so first by acknowledging their existence. While also displaying a myriad of images, popular theater of the festive-revolutionary variety assumes that there are truths or anchoring points underlying the disparate images that compose our everyday world. In these forms, an understanding of power structures as they really exist is the first step toward taking concrete action to change the world. Postmodern works of art often leave the viewer feeling powerless in a bewildering world of relative meanings. Festive-revolutionary works of art, on the contrary, educate the viewer and empower her to change the world by exposing inequalities and injustices as they really exist.

The Mime Troupe's brand of popular theater, then, is neither the technological popular of contemporary television and movies nor the political didacticism of agit-prop. Its incorporation of serious subjects in a festive format reflects a more intricate marriage of two realms than the familiar postmodern mixture of high and low forms. The Mime Troupe's brand of theater derives from the many popular theatrical forms of the past that they draw on and blend together in their productions. Their work amounts to a kind of theater whose joyous spirit, spontaneity, and freedom embody both the spirit of festivity and the ideals of revolution.

While the Mime Troupe's work draws on many sources, Schechter is perhaps correct to focus on clowns as a central rallying point for these different forms. John Towsen also proposes clowns as a common ground among popular traditions, and in doing so reveals an important aspect of festive-revolutionary theater. A historical more than a theoretical work, his book *Clowns* groups together a wide variety of traditions through the figure of the clown and its manifestations in cultures throughout history.[2] In its many forms, the clown is often a kind of mascot or representative of the popular, even when it appears in performances or traditions that do not exhibit a popular aesthetic. Clown figures echo one another as variations on a single theme. The clown is "perpetually rediscovered by society" because "he meets compelling needs." He spans history, the globe, and generations and "represents a vision of the world that both intellectual and so-called primitive cultures have valued highly, a sense of the comic meaningful to children and adults alike, and a dynamic form of acting based on startling technique and inspired improvisation" (4–5).

What has continually attracted such widely different audiences to the clown and comparable figures is his joyful irreverence, his ability gleefully to transcend social norms free of the inhibitions and restrictions that structure our daily lives. In exploring these uncharted territories, clowns forge a path that follows our own hidden desires and in turn lead us to discover our possible alternative selves. In defining "the fool" Towsen observes: "Unimpressed with sacred ceremonies or the power of rulers, he is liable to be openly blasphemous and defiant; uninhibited in sexual matters, he often delights in obscene humor . . . Society may ostracize those it considers to be fools, but it also has shown an abiding interest in them. On one level, this paradox reflects man's recognition of folly as an unavoidable part of his life . . . On another level, the fool represents the free spirit, the unconventional thinker whose example encourages others to view the world in new and extraordinary ways" (5–6). The idea of impurity in expressive movement is central to popular traditions and is a reflection of the clown's general social nonconformity. Clowns are "blasphemous," "defiant," "obscene." Because of their foolishness, whether owing to true madness, divine inspiration, or cunning disguise, they are given license to say and do things that are ordinarily proscribed by social norms. These qualities excite both love and hatred, hatred particularly in those occupying positions of power who are responsible for maintaining the status quo that clowns are constantly undermining. The license granted these foolish characters often puts them in the unique position of being able to make radical political statements with impunity. Towsen points out the many traditions where clowns take up the role of cultural critic, including those of rural Chinese clowns and European court jesters (34, 29).

However, in spite of the apparent similarities among disparate clown traditions, the license accorded them, and their transgression of norms and conventions, there seems to be a dichotomy within the general category. While some clowns and their supposed foolishness are enjoyed or merely tolerated, other clowns are viewed as sacred and form an important part of a society's cosmological conception. This distinction between secular and sacred clowns may be drawn along Western and non-Western lines, though not exclusively so. Some non-Western clowns, often referred to as "tricksters," such as the figures in African and Native American cultures, while showing the same disrespect for authority, rationality, and social convention as Western clowns, are nonetheless sacred, and as such are respected for their eccentricities and accorded an important place within their respective cultures. Their actions are often interpreted as embodying a meaning that can only be expressed in an unconventional manner, but which is nonetheless connected to a sacred understanding of the cosmos. These tricksters may disturb and overthrow, but their actions are sanctioned by their relation to a cosmology that transcends their specific time and place. Their presence contradictorily preserves and renews order.

Robert Pelton's study of the trickster figure Ananse in the West African tradition tries to make the function of one of these complex, comic figures comprehensible to Westerners, who are often confused by the seemingly paradoxical idea of a "clown-god." Pelton emphasizes how Ananse's tricks have a very specific social function. In summing up one of the Ananse tales, he says:

> The aim of this story is to show that Ananse creates a social intercourse by disclosing, plunging into, heightening or even embodying the raw forces out of which human life is made. He renews by the power of antistructure. His relentless willfulness is not some archaic version of laissez-faire, but a passionate entry into the rawness of pre-cultural relationships to reclaim and restore their potencies, to make them available for new patterns of order . . . Furthermore, the social order molded by that dealing has an abiding potential for renewal, for in rejecting pure stasis as the ideal social life and the apparent enemies of that life, Ananse transforms disruption from a destructive into a creative force. (50–51)

Kathy Foley's work shows that the West Javanese clown-god, Semar, one of the main characters of a West Javanese puppet tradition, performs a function in Javanese culture similar to the function Ananse performs in West African culture. Foley articulates Semar's role by contrasting him to the apparently similar clown puppet, Punch, of western European tradition: "Where figures like Punch play havoc with the social order, slaughtering wives, judges, and hangmen both verbally and literally, the Southeast Asian clown tests ideas of social order in more fundamental ways. Though originally a high god, he willingly serves a mere man—the hero of whichever tale is told on that particular night. Though his utterances can refer to scatology, sex, or political scandal, they may be felt by the audience to contain truths that go beyond such subject matters to hint at a comedy divine" (65). It is surprising to most westerners that Semar, like Ananse, is a god. Foley goes on to explain that Semar fits into a cosmological understanding in Javanese thought and that he plays a role in the complex relationship of individuals to their ancestors. In Javanese thought, Semar represents one part of the whole self.

While Semar sometimes offers political commentary, he is not socially marginalized but is rather an integral part of a religious tradition. Foley, however, notes—and mourns—the decline of traditional belief systems in Java: "Changing ideas of the self and the social order are being ushered in by education. Belief in a spirit world is fading, at the same time that migration to the city is snapping the conceptual cords that bind one villager to another" (76). In light of these changes, she writes, "it is the more rational, class interpretation of the clown that has come to predominate" (75). This class interpretation, which dissociates Semar from his religious origin and highlights his material condition as a lowly servant, is closer to the way we have come to view western European clown figures like Punch.

Asian, African, and Native American[3] traditions of course are multifaceted and all unique, but their clowns seem to occupy similar positions as sacred tricksters whose pranks somehow reflect or return people to an original cosmological order. Clowns from Western traditions, by contrast, are usually antagonistic to social structures. The official order regards them with distrust and, though on occasion may tolerate them patiently, may as easily seek to extirpate them. Western clowns are, at best, necessary evils. Only rarely does the culture acknowledge them as divine sources of wisdom, which is the position they frequently occupy in non-Western traditions. Having no investment in the established order, Western clowns may have greater potential to effect revolutionary political change than the tricksters whose presence is sanctioned by the divine forces mythically credited with creating the world as it is. While they may dabble in chaos, god-clowns advocate a specific kind of change, one that renews structures rather than destroys them. Western-modeled clowns, on the other hand, are free agents, free to sign on to and advocate for even the most disruptive forms of social reorganization should the opportunity arise.

This dichotomy between clown traditions, however, may be somewhat misleading. There are critics, like Anthony Caputi, who view Western clowns too as agents of social renewal. Caputi derives his views on theater and its function from the school of Cambridge anthropologists A. W. Pickard-Cambridge, Allardyce Nicoll, Gilbert Murray, and Jane Ellen Harrison, who claim that the roots of Western drama are to be found in rituals, especially spring rituals that marked the change of seasons, celebrating reflowering and rejuvenation. These rituals, they say, came to be acted out in folk dramas that represent an agon, or fight, between Winter and Spring. The triumph of Spring represents a sacred renewal that parallels the rejuvenation brought about by the trickster figures mentioned above. Although this theory of the evolution of theatre has never been substantiated by archeological evidence, this view provides Caputi with a compelling perspective on popular traditions and the thematic link that exists between rituals of renewal and clowning.[4]

Anthony Caputi defines a category of drama he calls "*buffo*," or vulgar comedy, which unites performers as far back as the Atellan farceurs with twentieth-century comics like Laurel and Hardy. Caputi starts by pointing to formal qualities that identify *buffo,* stating that: "It is a rule of thumb that characters in vulgar comedy are always rendered simply and boldly."

Vulgar comedy includes "songs, frequent asides," and "free use of the stage" (176–77); it "has been associated with dancers and acrobats" (179); it has "the kind of physical movement which fills out the picture of a flamboyant acting style"; and it "requires from the beholder no greater range of sensibility and no high order of intelligence" (181). Caputi's definition focuses on some of the same qualities of performance that Shank and Towsen discuss, and he identifies the "vulgar" (in several senses of the word), physical movement, and comic clowning as essential components of *buffo*.

In the final analysis, however, Caputi is less concerned with pointing out the discrete elements that identify *buffo* than with tracing its origins in spring ritual and seeing them reflected in all instances of *buffo*. "When the gestalt is right," he concludes, "we know we have to do with a particular kind of celebration, with a special way of seeing the world" (185). He thereby moves beyond the formal similarities of popular forms to find a common function or effect inherent in the performances themselves.

Caputi points out the themes that emerge from spring rituals,[5] then analyzes how they persist throughout the evolution of vulgar comedy in "religious holidays . . . processional practices . . . discrete dramatic exercises . . . primitive emergent plays . . . free-standing vulgar comedies" (23). He maintains that even in the later forms of vulgar comedy, in which ritual patterns from which they may have evolved are unknown to the audience, the performances still convey the celebration of life and renewal common to early fertility rites. Caputi elaborates on this, what he calls the true "genius of vulgar comedy," in passages such as this on eighteenth-century review plays:

> In all these examples, rebirth, whether literal or metaphorical, becomes a proof of the world's capacity to change unexpectedly for the better. If prominent enough, renewal, like wholesale transformations, beget a metamorphic sense of reality, a sense of a world not merely unstable and unfixed but seething with creativity . . . a structure designed to generate a frenzy, both in the world of the play and in the beholder . . . it reflects the pervasive purpose of the revels: to stir up and create agitation to prompt the revelers to lavish expenditures of energy—energy which itself becomes proof of the capacity of the revel to renew life. (139)

Caputi sums up his perspective by saying, "Very simply, *buffo* is this sense of mastery, this feeling of temporary but triumphant security in a perilous world" (196). Whether or not there is any actual link between fertility rites and the evolution of theatrical form seems less important than acknowledging the power that Caputi finds in "*buffo.*"

For Caputi, the exuberance that the revels inspire in the audience is their most powerful force, and this exuberance is true of *buffo* in all periods. The feeling of empowerment, of "security in a perilous world," is a very important element of popular forms and is part of what makes them appropriate for political theater. A feeling of optimism can give an audience the confidence it needs to face an otherwise overwhelming political situation. There is nothing in Caputi's analysis, however, that assumes that this exuberance will necessarily issue in political action.

In linking comic forms to spring rituals, Caputi attributes a cosmological function to Western clowns similar to that of their non-Western counterparts. Though their cosmologies are different, the *buffo* clowns also provide an opportunity for the social world to renew itself and reintegrate with the natural order, and in so doing these forms empower their spectators with courage and optimism. It may be, however, that Western societies do not incorporate this form of renewal into their worldview, and so remain steadfastly set against it. Western cultures often equate social renewal with linear, progressive change and consequently see it as necessarily at odds with the status quo. This Western perspective derives perhaps from the Christian conception of spiritual renewal in the hereafter, rather than in the present and in this world. Metaphors equating social renewal with the natural cycle of death in winter and rebirth in spring are instead tied to pagan traditions Christianity has always defined itself against. The invocation of a cyclical form of renewal can therefore look like an attack on Christian ideology, hence an attack on the dominant power structures in Western society itself.

Mikhail Bakhtin's view of popular forms and politics contrasts with Schechter's for, in examining Renaissance festive practices, he proposes that there has in the past been a link between popular forms and a revolutionary message whose political import did not rely on any explicit political theory.[6] Bakhtin shows that revolutionary content was an intrinsic part of what he calls "carnivalesque" folk traditions and was bound up with their imagery of renewal and their creation of what Victor Turner terms *communitas.*[7] Bakhtin's work, therefore, provides an alternative position—one that allows for political critique in a pre-Marxist setting.

In *Rabelais and His World* Bakhtin studies European folk humor through the work of the great sixteenth-century French author. In showing "the oneness and meaning of folk humor, its general ideological, philosophical and aesthetic essence" (58), Bakhtin finds reflected in European folk culture as a whole the same features of rebirth and renewal that Caputi found in the narrower world of European folk drama. Bakhtin, however, highlights the radical political potential underlying the folk forms.

He points out that popular humor represents the world in a comic mirror that distorts the status quo in two very important ways. First, folk humor distorts the world by turning it upside down. The language games, imagery, and action of folk festivals, feasts, carnivals, and theatrical events all work together to elevate what lies at the lower end of the social hierarchy and to debase what stands at the top. The result is a topsy-turvy world where madness and clowning prevail. Turning the world upside down in this way shows the arbitrariness of everything conventionally acceptable in normal circumstances. The status quo is momentarily reversed or completely destroyed, revealing endless possibilities latent in the world. This Saturnalian practice, as in Roman times, stresses radical change in the social and political order.

Bakhtin points out that folk imagery brings down whatever is elevated by associating it with the lower bodily stratum and with everything that has to do with procreation, thus echoing Towsen's emphasis on blasphemous clowns: "debasement is the fundamental artistic principle of grotesque realism; all that is sacred and exalted is rethought on the level of the material bodily stratum or else combined and mixed with its images . . . The material bodily stratum is productive. It gives birth, thus assuring mankind's immortality. All obsolete and vain illusions die in it, and the real future comes to life" (370–71, 378). Bakhtin goes beyond Caputi by linking the inversion of the hierarchy—a prevalent form of political lampooning—with the cycle of death and regeneration. Inverting the world creates a circular relationship between the top and the bottom of the social and political hierarchies by uniting the two ends. The elevated is brought down to the level of procreation, whence it is then reborn.

The carnivalesque mirror also distorts the world by revealing its doubleness, with old and new living side by side: "Carnival celebrates the destruction of the old and the birth of the new world—the new year, the new spring, the new kingdom. The old world that has been destroyed is offered together with the new world and is represented with it as the dying part of the dual body" (410). This imagery always focuses on the moment of transformation. The old is dying out, but not without a promising new world already present and waiting to be fully born. Picturing the moment of transformation generates great hope. In this moment death appears not negatively but ambivalently, as a necessary step in the life process, which will eventually lead to rebirth and to a new, abundant, fertile world.

Both Caputi and Bakhtin see the traditional forms they study as originating in spring rituals and find that the hope engendered by the arrival of spring carries over into the ritual's supposed theatrical descendants. Their view crucially sees the life cycle being played out on the level of the community rather than the individual,[8] thus evoking the political dimensions of these forms. For Bakhtin, the transformations that take place do so by being firmly grounded in the material world. In fact, the transformations rely on the materiality of human procreativity to produce a world that can and constantly does renew itself in the here and now, and on into the future. The new world thus promised is not a mythical one on a different plane or in a Christian heaven but one that can be perceived in the here and now in the procreative potential of the physical world. The individual may die, but the people can rejoice in the enduring life of the community. The inversion of the world, and the fall of the exalted into the lower bodily stratum, is a celebration of the material substance of the world and the promise of the community's future. Bakhtin puts it more emphatically when he says that this celebration is "not abstract thought about the future but the living sense that each man belongs to the immortal people who create history" (367). "Popular festive forms look into the future. They present the victory of this future, of the golden age, over the past. This is the victory of all the people's material abundance, freedom, equality, brotherhood. The victory of the future is insured by the people's immortality" (256). Though the imagery emphasizes a cyclical view of life, the historical perspective it offers is essentially future-directed. The image of the double world, in which the old and the new coexist side by side constitutes a moment of transformation and hope in the life cycle, revealing death at the very instant it reveals the future. The historical picture is thus future-looking, emphasizing the abundance that is constantly visible on the horizon and insured by the community's eternal replenishment. The change promised is cyclical but never a mere repetition.

One important feature of Bakhtin's carnivalesque is that the world created during carnival stands over against the established order. It is a festival that the people put on for themselves, an alternative to other official festivals organized by the dominant power structures. Embedded in this festive alternative is the idea that popular culture stands in opposition to an elite culture. This division seems to be a class division, but as Andrew Ross says, it is "categories of taste, which police the differential middle ground" between high and low culture, and these "are also categories of cultural power which play upon every suggestive trace of difference in order to tap the sources of dignity, on the one hand, and *hauteur,* on the other" (5). A class division is played out within a cultural form, and the imagery of the lower-class culture, representing death and rebirth and the triumph of the lower class as a community facing grave obstacles, puts the very essence of the popular in a revolutionary, adversarial stance vis-à-vis the status quo. Bakhtin's argument is that during the Renaissance there was something intrinsic in popular culture that reflected the attitudes and desires of the lower-class community and that gave it a revolutionary power, without the help of any explicit theory of class struggle.[9]

Giving us another way of approaching festive-revolutionary theatre is Thomas Leabhart, a theater critic and performer, who uses the term "mime" to categorize a wide variety of performance traditions, including those that appear on Shank's list as well as the work of the San Francisco Mime Troupe itself. For Leabhart, the important feature of mime is not that it is silent, for it need not be,[10] but that it relies on the body as the primary means of expression, on "a return to expressive movement" (1) and away from reliance on verbal communication.[11] Leabhart's definition of mime makes sense of the Mime Troupe's seemingly incongruous name (their performances not only include music and dialogue but are indeed "outspoken") by linking them, through the idea of "expressive movement," to a tradition of physically expressive theater forms, such as commedia dell'arte and clowning, going as far back as 270 B.C.[12]

Leabhart's category, however, also links the Mime Troupe's work with that of Jacques Copeau and Étienne Decroux, as wells as to postmodern and new vaudevillian performers. Many of the performances of these mimes are quite unrelated to popular theater in any sense. For instance, in describing the work of the contemporary performer Daniel Stein, Leabhart quotes Sylvia Drake from the *Los Angeles Times,* who says, "the presence of feeling in everything he does is what makes it so affecting. This marriage of craft and emotion, precision and pain, control and abandon is exceptional in this artist. The work is very pure, the variety of its physical compression seemingly infinite" (130). Speaking of a production of another contemporary group, the Canadian theater company, Carbonne 14, Leabhart says, "*Le Voyage immobile* was like a North American Noh play in its highly charged understatement" (138). Neither of these descriptions taps into any even intuitive notions of popular theatre, and both point more to some "elite" type of performance that can only be grasped through studied appreciation by a coterie of aficionados.

While expressive movement is a characteristic of most, if not all, of the theatrical forms that Shank mentions, it also extends beyond the world of the popular. It can easily be applied to performances that are close to modern dance or performance art, as well as to those whose abstractions and subtleties place them beyond the appreciation of general audiences. The fact that this kind of mime is unlike the traditions the Mime Troupe draws on tells us something important about the nature of expressive movement in festive-revolutionary theater, namely, that it has very little to do with the abstract, the "pure," and "understatement." It is, on the contrary, concrete and impure, both in the sense of mixing from a variety of sources and in the sense of being bawdy or raunchy. The popular, in this sense, is exaggeration and overstatement. Expressive movement is an essential aspect of popular forms, but it is an insufficient category for defining them. Popular theater requires a specific kind of expressive movement, one that is, again, concrete, impure, and exaggerated.

Many of the mime performers that Leabhart mentions have been influenced by the later work of Étienne Decroux,[13] in which Decroux explored the idea that metaphysical weights can produce effects on the body similar to those produced by physical weights. "Nonpopular" mime performers draw from this aspect of his work. While the focus of these artists is still on the human body, they seem to move beyond mere physicality to another—a metaphysical—dimension. In popular traditions, however, the performers remain firmly rooted in the material world.

The centrality of the body on the popular stage has implications for the political direction these forms often take. The human body is the locus of meaning in popular forms.[14] The performer develops the meaning of a piece through physical expression, physical transformation, and interac-

8. This print shows the characteristic outfit and physical posture of the commedia character Arlecchino. *Arlequin* (French 17th-century Intaglio print) by Dolivar, courtesy of the Metropolitan Museum of Art, the Elisha Whittelsey Collection, the Elisha Whittelsey Fund, 1954 (54.510.21).

9. In this etching from *Balli di Sfessania,* Callot depicts the very eccentric physical postures of popular masked entertainers associated with the commedia dell'arte. A portable commedia stage with actors appears in the background. *The Commedia Dell'Arte in Florence* (French 17th-century etching) by Jacques Callot, the Metropolitan Museum of Art, Gift of Edwin de T. Bechtel, 1957 [57.650.304 (4)].

tion with the environment. In these forms the human body is the locus of action in a wholly concrete, material world.[15] Popular forms emphasize interaction with the physical environment and encourage a recognition of the material conditions of life. Material conditions therefore frame the perspective popular forms take up on human relationships, institutions, and the political sphere.

More than conventional theater, popular performance highlights the body as something apparently common revealed to be extraordinary. The fabulous feats of acrobats or tightrope walkers, as well as the physicality of commedia actors striking the famous postures of their characters, are examples of this kind of transformation. At a further extreme are the displays of freaks at circuses and sideshows. Though in many cases the performer's body may simply be on display, it is nonetheless a positive aspect of popular forms that they demonstrate the wide range of physical and expressive potential of the human form. Moreover, the centrality of the body is empowering for performers, for it means that they themselves make up the most important element in their work. For spectators, too, the display of a wide range of physical expressivity and potential can be empowering, for they can perceive it as a field of possibility within themselves.

In all theatrical events there exists a tension between the planned course of the performance and the uncontrollable element of the actor, whose actions can drastically alter the set course of events. In the moment of performance an actor can improvise or react in unforeseen ways. This possibility always lurks behind the controlled expression that is the performer's craft. The tension between the controlled and the uncontrolled takes on greater significance in popular performances in which the live, human body, the unpredictable element of theatrical presentation, is the locus of action and meaning.

Popular forms are in fact structured to highlight the tension between controlled or patterned movement and the freedom of the uncontrolled body, for they create a space for improvisation. In the commedia dell'arte, for example, each character has a specific physical posture and a set of determined characteristics. Comic gags that are played out between performers are well rehearsed and often rely on precise timing. Yet commedia scripts are only sketchy scenarios on which the actors improvise dialogue, jokes, references to the audience, and topical allusions. They foreground the tension between the very precise structures that the performers must adhere to on the one hand and their freedom to display their individual wit on the other. The body is at once a spontaneous and a controlled element of the performance; the actor's body conforms to the norms of the theatrical production and yet goes beyond them.

In "Theatre History and the Ideology of the Aesthetic," Joseph Roach discusses the eighteenth century's use of classical statuary as a model for physical postures assumed on stage. This and other notation systems for movement lead, he says, to "the power to write movement, to authorize and control the activities of the body" (161). Though notation systems like the ones Roach describes lay out a pattern of controlled movement the way a script lays out a controlled pattern of speech, the body itself, in the moment of performance, is always at liberty to transgress these boundaries, especially in popular forms that rely on verbal and physical improvisation. Scripts, sets, notation systems, and the like, are all attempts to control the body and the meaning it creates on stage. Forms that focus on the body's expression apart from these outside forces leave the power to create meaning in the hands (and bodies) of the performers.

Popular forms not only allow for incidental improvisational moments, they also are well suited to adapt to changing contexts generally. They are porous structures that come to life in each new performance with the addition of improvisation and topical allusion. Popular forms, like sponges, are able to absorb the world around them. They can contain an ever-changing stream of contemporary references. Though each performance is essentially ephemeral, the structures themselves persist through time.[16] For, more than conventional theater, popular performances are tied to the specificities of their time and place. Consequently, scholars have looked down on popular performances because they feel that, unlike more textually based theater traditions, they express no "universal" truth. However, it is precisely by wedding themselves to their own ephemerality that popular forms retain their political potential. They continually reincarnate themselves to reveal the new truths of each specific time and place in which they are performed. Popular forms derive their value from the meaning created in each new instance of performance and in the persistence of traditions as a whole, rather than by the richness or longevity of any single text or production.

As I have said, popular theater relies on improvisation and other forms of interpolation to transform itself from moment to moment, from performance to performance. These interpolations are left up to the individual performers, and no trace of them remains when the shows are over. The popular theater's true trickster quality, then, is to appear, say the unsayable, and then disappear. Such performance makes no investment in its own future and is therefore wedded to no social or political structures that would preserve it.

These traditions operate in such a way that the structures, the forms that are developed to hold the improvisations, are passed on and remembered in the minds of the spectators and in the bodies of the performers. They are, as scholars like Robert Weimann have noted, part of an oral tradition, structured like oral forms, using simple, repeatable formulas, which render them memorable and reproducible. Yet it is not necessarily in these structures that the true radical nature of the popular resides. The most controversial elements of popular theater are those that are added to these structures. These additions are typically not preserved and so are not subject to outside control. They cannot be censored or appropriated beforehand precisely because they are ephemeral, hence uncontrollable. The tension between the controllable and uncontrollable elements of the theater, as I have said, is present in the body of the performer. This tension is reflected in other aspects of the traditions of the popular theater that, while being structured, remain open to transformation in the moment of performance.

Significantly, though these forms are similar to oral traditions, they can be more powerful than most oral forms because the actions and the world they create are not merely imagined but are made manifest on the stage. The anthropologist Clifford Geertz has pointed out how important it is for social groups to have a model to emulate in attempting to transform their communities. Popular theater can provide people with just such a model, one that is made visibly manifest before their eyes.

It is true, as both Schechter and Holden note, that popular forms need to keep addressing new political situations. While Schechter may or may not be correct about the Mime Troupe's current relevance and political effectiveness, the Troupe's chosen style not only is capable of adapting to changing circumstances but is nearly defined by the ability to do so. Whether the Mime Troupe is still able to tap the potential of popular forms, or whether changing circumstances have forever altered the political viability of their work, remains to be seen. But that question does not affect the essential adaptability of popular forms themselves.

* * *

The San Francisco Mime Troupe is certainly a theater whose "modern political consciousness comes from Marx, Brecht and Mayakovsky" (viii), as Schechter states. They were without question influenced by the social theories of their political and theatrical contemporaries like the Situationists, the Teatro Campesino, and the Bread and Puppet Theatre. These influences cannot be denied. However, I would like to stress the relationship between the Mime Troupe and the older inheritance of festive-revolutionary theatrical traditions and how these traditions can assist the work of any politically engaged theater company. As Bakhtin shows, the imagery and structures of popular forms already have latent within them a political perspective with revolutionary tendencies. The combination of Marxist ideals with popular forms is not a haphazard combination, nor are popular forms an indifferent vehicle for propounding a wholly detachable political message.

Popular forms rely on concrete and exaggerated expressive movement and are intimately bound up with the material conditions of life. They foreground the diversity and extraordinary potential of the human body as agent. They rely on comic clowning to bring a new vision, an outside perspective on situations, and thereby question and challenge the status quo. They instigate change and place it in a positive light by equating it with renewal and rebirth. They address their audience as a community and thereby create a sense of community. These qualities are essential to the type of popular theater that I have called "festive-revolutionary," as distinct from the productions of the culture industry, the didactic early agit-prop theater, and postmodern performance. A tendency toward revolutionary action is already latent within popular forms of this special kind. As demonstrated in *Hotel Universe,* where the Troupe used the tropes of circus clowns to plead a case for low-income housing, the Mime Troupe's Marxist politics work in concert with the popular style they have chosen, bringing to life the political potential already embodied in it and then marshaling that potential to meet historically specific issues.

Popular forms, as Bakhtin and Caputi observe, have grown out of festive practices, and a festive atmosphere still surrounds them. The exploration of the relationship between festivals and revolutions in the following chapter will explore some of the qualities they share, as well as the way in which they have come to be associated with one another.

2

Festivals, Revolutions, and the French Stage

In Paris, on May 15, 1968, Jean-Louis Barrault wrote, "On the now occupied roof, red flags, black ones and tricolours took turns in a lamentable ballet. The square outside had become a regular fairground: a man with a monkey, a man with a bear, guitarists, rubbernecks and more or less camouflaged ambulances. Slogans all over the wall. In the basement of the theatre, Molotov cocktails, petrol bombs, grenades—preparation for a siege" (316). One might suppose that, as a man of the theater, Jean-Louis Barrault was more inclined than most to see the occupation of the Odéon theater by militant protesters in terms of a theatrical metaphor, that of a fairground. But one did not need the eyes of an actor or a director to characterize the events of May 1968 as he did. Indeed, descriptions of political uprisings as festive celebrations are common. Moreover, the French protesters considered the cultural sphere to be deeply implicated in their own struggle. For them, suppressing the activities of Barrault's Théâtre de France—"an emblem of 'bourgeois culture' " (Barrault 314)—by taking over the Odéon where it was housed and turning that space into a forum for open debate was a significant political act.

Furthermore, the French New Left also described the changed world they wished to create through revolution as one of festivity. The Situationists, their spokesmen, wrote in a 1966 pamphlet that "revolutions will be festivals or they will not be, for the life they herald will itself be created in festivity" (Champagne 6). The Situationists were influenced by the sociologist Henri Lefebvre's critique of everyday life and by his vision of "total revolution" (Lefebvre 197). In his essay "Toward a Permanent Cultural Revolution" he sums up the goals of such a revolution: "*The festival rediscovered* and magnified by overcoming the conflict between everyday life and festivity and enabling these terms to harmonize in and through urban society, such is the final cause of the revolutionary plan" (206).

The convergence of radical politics and festive performance is neither accidental nor merely a rhetorical trope. Nor is it a union exclusive to the events described in France. Time and again, periods of political unrest and outbreaks of revolution have, on a metaphorical as well as a concrete level, taken on the trappings of traditional festive practice and a general spirit of festivity. This recurrent pattern is evident not only in the actions of May 1968 but also in the Revolution of 1789 itself, which many '68 protesters felt they were finally bringing to completion. The analogy between festivals and revolutions also holds for much of the unrest in the United States in the 1960s, in which the San Francisco Mime Troupe took part, and which was roughly contemporaneous with the protests in France. The Russian Revolution of 1917, too, exhibits the same thematic link between festival and revolution. And the list does not end there. In *Subversive Laughter* Ron Jenkins describes the antiapartheid struggles in South Africa in similar terms.

Conversely, many theater practitioners inspired by the power of revolution have used both revolt and festivity as theatrical models for creating politicized theater. The protests of May '68 helped to shape the theatrical work and commitment of fledgling French directors like Armand Gatti and the Théâtre du Soleil's Arianne Mnouchkine, just as the context of political unrest in the United States influenced the Mime Troupe. In 1789, French fairground theaters stifled by government regulations found liberation in the political turmoil surrounding them. In post-1917 Russia directors like Nikolai Evreinov staged mass spectacles that reenacted the revolution's most fervent moments.

A festive atmosphere underlies all the popular forms that I have called "festive-revolutionary," and I want to suggest that it is precisely that atmosphere of carefree abandon, so akin to chaos, that first gives these forms a revolutionary direction. It is a mistake, however, to suppose that the lack of an actual revolution brought on by a festive uprising in any way speaks against the political import of festive-revolutionary forms. Their open-endedness keeps them alive and aggressive but prevents them from taking on the kind of specific political content that could give shape to a new power structure. The impetus of popular forms is to overturn structures, not necessarily to create new ones. In this they are essentially and permanently revolutionary and, though they might not lead to actual political or social transformation, they nevertheless continually point in that direction.

This chapter will explore the link between festivals and revolutions, as well as the ways in which that link has evolved through the historical association of the two. In weighing this relationship I hope to develop a deeper understanding of how popular theater forms may or may not be useful in the service of revolutionary projects. At issue is the historic context of a production and its importance in determining the revolutionary potential of popular forms. The development of popular traditions from within a festive context—an environment that unleashes social disruption—in large part explains the revolutionary spirit of the forms the Mime Troupe and other popular political theaters have available to them. In practice those forms tend to reawaken both the festive and revolutionary energy that is their inheritance.

The focus of much of this chapter is on French theater. Popular performance in France has had a great impact on popular forms in America and elsewhere. The history of French theater uniquely highlights the social and political forces that influenced the development of popular traditions, as well as the role class consciousness and class struggle have played in shaping them. Moreover, in France theater has always stood at the center of political conflict. Throughout French history, whenever political power has changed hands, the locus of theatrical control has changed accordingly.[1] Popular forms reflect this struggle, and their genealogy bears the marks both of political history and of the history of festive practices. While of course not all the popular traditions a group like the Mime Troupe uses have passed through French hands (the Mime Troupe itself is notably influenced by American, English, Mexican, Russian, and German forms as well), in isolating the case of French theater this chapter delineates clear patterns of development and struggle that may be applicable to popular traditions elsewhere.

As we have seen, Bakhtin equated French Renaissance festivals with a revolutionary spirit. The connection between festivals and revolutions resides neither in the actual political content of the festival alone nor simply in the enactment of saturnalian reversals, however politically aggressive they may be. Festivals are theatrical events in which strictly speaking there are no spectators. Everyone is at once spectator and actor and may be involuntarily swept up in the mass frenzy. This mass movement of humanity in a festive context is analogous to the mass movement of a people in the midst of a political uprising. Bakhtin, who had lived through the mass uprisings of the Russian Revolution of 1917, was well aware of the similarity. As Hélène Iswolsky remarks in her introduction to *Rabelais and His World*, "The revolution gave a particularly Russian twist to Joyce's line, 'Here comes everybody' " (Bakhtin xiv).

But the relation between festival and revolution goes beyond mere analogy into concrete practice. The transformation of revolutionary action into a theatrical event seems to be a natural and not uncommon process. It draws on the powerful emotions and the great drama and spectacle of an uprising, which goes to the very heart of theater itself. For example, in 1920, on the third anniversary of the Russian Revolution, Nikolai Evreinov staged *The Taking of the Winter Palace*. This mass spectacle, which reconstructed the revolutionary events of October 1917, was a strange blend of festival, theater, and revolutionary uprising. "The performance began on specially constructed stages with a dramatization of the various events that had prepared for the Bolshevik uprising and culminated, as spectators and participants mingled freely, in the taking of the Winter Palace" (Bradby and McCormick 48). Here the reenactment of revolution itself became a festival, reflecting in turn the festive nature of the original revolutionary action. A commemoration thereby became a reenactment, not just a remembrance but a reliving, and perhaps, in a Bakhtinian sense, a renewing as well.

The Taking of the Winter Palace is a good example of how festivals are a unique type of performance. This celebration of the violent end of czarist rule in Russia was at once an orchestrated, theatrical re-creation and at the same time a performance that went beyond the conventional definition of theater. The sheer scope of the piece endowed it with one of the features Margaret Drewal attributes to some Yoruba rituals, which are also based on a festive model, namely a simultaneity of festive practices over a large area, such that each participant has only a partial and fragmented view of the event as a whole. The result, Drewal says, is that "even constructing a narrative description of what happens in ritual is in some sense faulty since no one could ever experience a ritual in its 'totality' " (24–25).

Drewal's description applies both to the Russian Revolution itself and to Evreinov's mass spectacle. There was no single vantage point from which to view the entirety of either event, so no individual could possibly participate in or observe all parts at once. By incorporating the spontaneous multiplicity of actions of an entire community, *The Taking of the Winter Palace* resisted the imposition of any external, totalizing, or controlling force. Thus, in spite of the organizational elements that mark it as a rehearsed piece of theater, there is also considerable room for free improvisation on the part of all participants, those who had been cast as performers as well as presumptive spectators. The performance therefore takes on its own shape in the moment of enactment over and beyond anything orchestrated in advance. In this way it captures the spirit of spontaneous action inherent in the original revolutionary event itself.

Drewal's observations of Yoruba rituals based on myths are also useful to the study of festivals and other commemorative-festive practices. She says that these performances have "a double dynamic" inasmuch as they refer backward in time to the events they commemorate even as "they simultaneously renegotiate the present" (94). The use of festive forms is a way of at once recalling a moment in the past and providing an opportunity to reconceive the present conditions of life. The commemorative festival thus recreates the "liminal," or in-between, space of a transformative time and in so doing opens up an opportunity for social re-creation—not mere recreation.

A good example of a historical moment when festive enactment was used to its full force was during the French Revolution. In that period both the politically powerful and the politically marginalized drew on the evocative power of festivals to commemorate past events and to affirm or renegotiate interpretations of the present. The enactment of festival became the site of struggle and resistance between two opposing revolutionary forces. On the one hand, there were the festivals sponsored by the newly dominant middle class, which accordingly embodied bourgeois values and reaffirmed the social and economic privileges of that sector of society. On the other hand, there were also the actions of the provincial peasant class who, seeing themselves denied the benefits of the Revolution, responded with festivals marked by an undertone of violence and a lack of closure. The middle class adopted a vision of the classical world as their own heritage, and their interpretation of that world reflected their own democratic ideals. For the people of the provinces, by contrast, the local, deeply rooted folk celebrations provided a symbolic language through which they could express their desire for further political transformation to their own advantage.

In hearkening back to republican models of antiquity, the Chapelier regime hoped to unite the people under the new secular faith of humanism. To this end they paraded representations of allegorical figures of Revolution, Virtue, Victory, and Youth through the streets of Paris. The sheer number of elaborate festivals they staged testifies to the faith the regime had in their ability to educate people to a new civic culture in this way. Mona Ozouf remarks on their abundance: "there seems to be no end to the number of festivals! And they were celebrated everywhere. In the smallest municipality, several times a year and sometimes even several times a month, the flags and drums were taken out, the joiners and painters summoned, songs rehearsed, and programs drawn up" (13). But Ozouf also shows that these festivals were more often a desperate attempt to represent a unified society than an effective means of creating real social unity. The festivals, she says, were "a camouflage, a facade plastered onto a gloomy reality that it was their mission to conceal" (11).

It was the nature of the Revolution, and much of the violence that accompanied it, to work against closure. However, the festivals of the French Republic tried to impose closure on the Revolution, that is to say, a consensus about the goals of the Revolution and an acknowledgment that they had in fact been achieved. But no such consensus or acknowledgment in fact existed. Both in their elaborate rhetorical displays and in the lack of a real counterpart to the ideals they represented, the festivals of the Revolution were identical to those presentations of power put on by the monarchy before them. These new lavish productions more mirrored than destroyed the excessive royal pageants, entrées, *tableaux vivants*, and other celebrations of the monarchy. As the Revolution replaced aristocratic with bourgeois values, so too it replaced images of royal power with those of republican order. But the structures of representation remained unchanged, as did the emphasis on maintaining a status quo in which the oppressed sectors of society, the lowest classes, remained disenfranchised.

The attempt to effect closure exemplified in the official celebrations contrasts sharply with the open-ended nature of the popular festivals of the period. As previously stated, an emphasis on improvisation and interpolation, along with the constant disenfranchisement of popular entertainment from the bastions of political power, has always kept popular forms open-ended. Bakhtin reiterates this point in his assessment of the grotesque body:

> The grotesque body . . . is a body in the act of becoming. It is never finished, never completed; it is continually built, created and builds and creates another body . . . This is why the essential role belongs to those parts of the grotesque body in which it outgrows its own self, transgressing its own body, in which it conceives its new, second body: the bowels and the phallus . . . the mouth, through which enters the world to be swallowed up. And next is the anus . . . Eating, drinking, defecation and other elimination . . . as well as copulation, pregnancy, dismemberment, swallowing up by another body . . . In all these events the beginning and end of life are closely linked and interwoven. (317)

The official revolutionary festivals, with their long orations, their solemn parades, and their allegories, were as far removed as possible from the lower classes and their culture. However, it was to the symbolic language of their own local practices, to a Bakhtinian carnivalesque, that the lower classes returned when, in response to the official festivals, unofficial actions erupted throughout the provinces. Drawing on local traditions, the people paraded effigies of political figures through villages and then burned them (Ozouf 217–62). They resisted the solemnity of republican chants with the din of raucous songs and music. They also resisted the imposition of the republican calendar by celebrating the traditional festivals of Carnival and the Pastoral Feast more vigorously than ever.

These unofficial events were often violent, but their violence was construed within the framework of familiar practices, so that they also seemed ritualized. Mona Ozouf describes how the disenfranchised folk of the provinces interpreted their own revolutionary goals through traditional festive forms, in some cases transforming the Republic's symbolic Liberty Tree into a traditional maypole, or *mai sauvage.* Enacting an organized ritual pattern of action, groups would march to a neighboring village in order to plant a tree, and "the erection of the maypole was always carried out during a riot or an armed expedition to a neighboring village, which was then forced to adopt the maypole whether or not it wanted to" (Ozouf 234). Folk customs were echoed in this ritual that unified a symbol of life with a threat of death: "There was never any question of letting it take root. In this, the maypole erected by the rioters is similar to the maypole of folklore, which could be a tall painted pole, or a crowned mast, or again a tree on which the topmost branches remained . . . In any case it was always a trimmed, painted, decorated tree" (237). Furthermore, these trees were often decorated with messages that helped to clarify their meaning, namely as expressions of dissatisfaction with the Revolution. In one case a maypole was left at a church door with a sign proclaiming it to be a "final discharge of rents" (238).

The common folk used festive forms to express their own desires concerning the final outcome of the Revolution. Indeed, their celebratory traditions, which embodied a lack of closure, were better suited than their bourgeois counterparts to the idea of a complete social revolution. But, as we have seen, these festive practices value not just change but constant change. Though they usually voice the concerns of the lower classes, they are not wedded to any concrete political program. The events of 1789 threw the country into flux and disorder, but this had not been the goal of the bourgeois revolutionaries. Their aim was rather to create a legal and political order. People who had wanted to transform the very structure of society soon found themselves fighting a new republic that the "revolutionaries" no longer wanted overturned.

The use of popular festivals as a way of manifesting discontent was not new at the time of the Revolution. Emmanuel Le Roy Ladurie shows how in 1579–80 the people of the city of Romans in France used the occasion of the annual celebration of Carnival to stage a masked revolt. Barber cites another example of festive practices turning into political action in England. He describes a case in Lincolnshire in which the Dymock family and their friends used a traditional holiday play to criticize the stinginess of the local earl and were eventually tried and sanctioned for the offense. Drawing on a different tradition, Drewal refers to an incident in Nigeria in 1982, just before the national elections, when an Egungun, a masked festival, was canceled because "it was rumored that the minority opposition political party in one southern town was going to use the outing of the warrior masks to riot" (98). A festival incorporating "warrior masks" might already seem to evoke a kind of violence, but in the ordinary course of events the Egungun only enacts the social disruption associated with war. Masked players terrorize the community for the duration of the festival, but the people know perfectly well that this activity is not really war (98). The cancellation of the performance revealed that "real warfare" might indeed erupt from the festive recreation.

Western festivals, though they may not explicitly reenact warfare, do

often harbor an undercurrent of violence. The violence of festivals threatens to reveal the current organization of the world as contingent, arbitrary, and changeable. It also perhaps makes explicit the violence inherent in any system of order that must repress some people and impulses in order to sustain and satisfy others. The carnival forum, as Bakhtin suggests, has always existed as a dais where the people could voice their grievances, celebrate their values, and even take action against forces of oppression. And yet, as we have seen, historically, the lower classes never seem to gain actual power or permanently alter their situation through such actions. Are festivals and carnivals then merely what they appear to be at first glance, namely violent saturnalian games?

In analyzing the kaiko celebration of the Tsembaga of the Highlands of Papua New Guinea, Richard Schechner describes what he sees as the relationship between real and symbolic behavior in this performance and other forms of Western theater: "The transformation of combat behavior into performance is the theatrical heart of the kaiko. The transformation is identical to the action at the heart of Greek theater, and from the Greeks down through western theater history. Namely, characterization and the presentation of real or possible events—the story, plot, or dramatic action worked out by people, gods, or demons—is a transformation of real behavior into symbolic behavior" (109). The actions of the French peasants of the eighteenth century likewise contained a threat of violence. Their ritualized symbolic displays were a communication of that threat, not a sublimation of it. Although they were perhaps reviving violent tendencies that had already been effectively subdued in the festival itself, nevertheless the threat of real violence resurfaced in their ritualized behavior.

In chapter 1 we saw that clowning can be regarded as an emblem of popular performance at large. Here we have seen that the threat of violence enjoys a similar status. Both elements are central to popular performance traditions. Drewal, for instance, finds a link between violence and clowning in the Nigerian masked Agemo festival: "The action surged back and forth between poles of joking and fighting, so that to get involved in Agemo was indeed to become a trickster . . . In keeping with the trickster deity's personality, participant/observers had to be quick and agile, fickle and flexible, ready to joke one moment and fight the next" (Drewal 113). Violence is as important to the political dimension of festivals as joking and clowning. The oscillation between the two is also what allows festive practices in Western cultures to take on the trickster function of providing a liminal, ritualized space in which genuine transformation can take place. Festivals lie somewhere between theater, ritual, and revolution, moving sometimes toward one, sometimes toward the other. However, the threat of violence is perhaps what imbues festive practices with their distinctive revolutionary edge. It defines the borderline between ritual disruption and unrestrained chaos. Popular forms, nurtured in a festive environment, retain an impetus toward violent social disruption.

In his account of the occupation of the Odéon in 1968, Jean-Louis Barrault draws an explicit comparison with the French Revolution: "For nearly a week the words had been flowing nonstop: $7 \times 24 = 168$ hours of words. 'In '89 they took the Bastille, in '68 they have taken the Floor. . . . In Paris, in four weeks, we had lived through the whole of the French Revolution: from the celebrations of the Fédération in '89 to the Terror, and then to Saint-Just" (Barrault 317, 324). The militants who occupied the Odéon and incited unrest all across France were participants in a movement that regarded itself as a continuation of the Revolution of 1789. For them, the Revolution had been a failure in many ways, most notably in betraying the lower classes by simply trading in one system of social and economic domination for another. The Revolution removed royalty and aristocracy from their positions of power and put the bourgeoisie, and with them middle-class cultural values, in their place.

The lower classes, however, were left economically and politically disadvantaged in both the old and new regimes. They were likewise excluded from all dominant cultural spheres. The artistic academies viewed popular art, music, and theater as vulgar folk forms, unrepresentative and unworthy of "French culture." By 1968, the new would-be revolutionaries regarded the Revolution of 1789 as having robbed the lower classes not only of political and economic power but also of cultural recognition. Elite culture had given way to middle-class culture, which the youth of 1968—of all class backgrounds—found stifling.

In May '68, the countrywide strikes set the tone for the new French revolution then erupting in the political and the cultural spheres. It was one that French theater practitioners would echo in their productions, trying to fulfill the promises of this social transformation. Champagne shows that the liberation in festivity that the protesters sought was already a political reality as well as a goal in the discourse of the New Left: "At the Sorbonne (occupied May 13) a piano was dragged out into the courtyard for free jazz improvisations. On the barricades a euphoric feeling of festivity and unity prevailed, especially on the weekend of May 10–11" (6–7). Festivity meant a lifestyle of freedom and joy in contrast to the oppressive structures of bourgeois life.

The opportunities festive forms offer for moving spectators to action is no doubt part of what appeals to theater practitioners specifically committed to political goals. The Théâtre du Soleil, Armand Gatti, and others of that period felt a deep connection between the political events that inspired their work and the theatrical events they created. They felt that both the politics and the performances were making a contribution to social freedom. For them the choice to use popular forms was an obvious one, drawing on the festive atmosphere of the strikes and the legacy of the Revolution. However, as the political moment of May '68 receded into the past, these artists found themselves in the position of trying to rekindle its spirit rather than supporting a real ongoing political struggle.

The Théâtre du Soleil incorporated the decline of the political moment and the disappointment they took away from that period in their 1970–71 production about the French Revolution, *1789: The Revolution Must Continue to the Perfection of Happiness,* a piece that drew parallels between the Revolution, the strikes of May '68, and popular theater forms. In *1789* the Théâtre du Soleil recounted the story of the Revolution from the point of view of the lower classes, as told by fairground performers just after the events themselves. The performance took place on five separate stages surrounding the audience, with action often occurring on all of them at once. It incorporated a variety of popular forms, including puppetry, clowning, acrobatics, and whiteface pantomime. The production itself became a festival that re-created the atmosphere of Paris in both 1789 and 1968. At one point audience members were even invited to play at carnival games in which they tossed balls at mock-ups of the king. The Théâtre du Soleil's show captured the sense that a carnivalesque atmosphere can unite people in a common cause. However, the piece ended with "a mock performance of the revolution for the amusement of a group of gaudy *nouveaux riches,*" demonstrating that the revolution had been "absorbed and co-opted by the society it opposed" (Champagne 38). The Soleil's expression of disappointment applied as much to the would-be revolution of 1968 as to the

Revolution of 1789 itself, since their audience was also predominantly bourgeois.

The director Armand Gatti[2] was also inspired by the events of May '68. Gatti sought to create a theatrical form that would give ordinary people a chance to express themselves. With this in mind, he went with some of his students to the Brabant Wallon[3] region of France where he collaborated on a theater piece with the entire community. The result, performed in 1974, was a 28-hour spectacle that included nearly everyone in the area. Even some local women who didn't actually perform participated nonetheless by baking tarts for the occasion. The production involved huge puppets and made use of 125 vehicles. The play itself consisted of various short pieces, created from a collective writing process, and was performed at a variety of locations throughout the villages in the area. A procession of actors and audience moved from one location to the next, linking the scenes together. The story told of the journey of "a kind of modern Noah who emerged in the work with the children," and who "wanted to escape from the problems of pollution and highway construction and return to a more natural life" (Champagne 59).

In getting the people of Brabant Wallon to create theater relevant to their own lives, Gatti launched a huge communal festival akin to the mystery cycle presentations of the Middle Ages. Yet even in this case, in which the production was far removed from elite Parisian theatergoers, and in which the local people had the opportunity to voice their own concerns through their own theatrical creation, the performance-festival that ensued did not live up to Gatti's aspirations for political engagement on the part of his participants. Gatti did not find a "passionate need for self-definition and self-expression" among the people of Brabant Wallon equal to his own, and he was disappointed by "the hesitation of young people in the 18 to 26 year old range to participate and the general absence of any significant degree of political consciousness among the population" (Champagne 59). Participation in the event itself was not, by Gatti's standards, sufficient for bringing political consciousness to this provincial population.

The Théâtre du Soleil used festive forms to question the legacy of two revolutions. Armand Gatti used them with the hope of inspiring common people to take political action of their own. In the end, neither seemed to bring about discernibly greater political engagement on the part of their audiences as a result of their methods. The political approach of their productions did not result in concrete political practice. Yet the use of popular forms does not necessarily promise a concrete outcome, only the basis for a movement in that direction.

A theater cannot create a revolutionary movement on its own, of course. Its work must be in sync with the prior political engagement of its audience. Yet popular forms preserve a spirit of festivity and revolution, both the aspects of joking and of violence. At certain periods one aspect may become more prominent than the other, yet both are always present. By keeping these forms alive, theaters are able to harness and preserve the explosive potential of the festive-revolutionary, so that—when the time is right—it can be uncorked.

How did popular festive forms evolve into open-ended, anti-establishment forms? How did they come to be associated with the lower classes of society? How did they develop the specific characteristics that I have called festive-revolutionary?

The historical development of these forms in France is inextricably linked to the successive power struggles in that country's political history. The following is a brief, selective review of the history of French theater that attempts to shed light on the political position of popular forms and to account, at least to some extent, for the development of their characteristic features. We will see that these features come to be associated with popular theater partly as the result of the power struggles being played out in the wider cultural arena. Popular traditions such as the commedia dell'arte, mime, and clowning have flourished in France, often hand in hand with contemporary political events. While the following constitutes a history of theater in France, the lessons it teaches about popular forms developing in response to political oppression is relevant to western European popular theater as a whole in virtue of the similar class divisions that obtained throughout Europe.

Dario Fo speaks equally for the entertainers of France and Italy when he quotes from Muratori, an eighteenth-century Italian scholar who stresses the importance of traveling performers as agents of expression and communication for local communities in Europe: "The theatre was the spoken and dramatized newspaper of the people of that time . . . the *jongleur* was born from the people, and from the people he took their anger in order to be able to give it back to them, mediated via the grotesque, through 'reason,' in order that the people should gain greater awareness of their own condition" (1–2). He goes on to say that it was because of this active involvement in the lives of the people that the *jongleurs* of the Middle Ages were persecuted—often being killed, being flayed alive, or having their tongues cut out. As one of the few forums where one could speak to—or for—an entire community, the theater was a very powerful social force, so that those who controlled the theatrical voice could influence the social and political spheres as well. The situation in France, in which theatrical and political struggles were closely linked, was therefore not unique.

But the antagonism between the church and the theater is where the story of popular forms in France truly begins. Historically the Catholic Church has been hostile to acting and actors. Though there are no actual church laws against performing, actors have traditionally been refused church sacraments such as baptism, marriage, and last rites, as well as the right to be buried on consecrated ground.[4] One reason that the church was, from early on in its history, so antagonistic to actors and the theater has to do with the theater's association with barbaric spectacles such as gladiatorial events, in which Christians were sent to their deaths in the arena with wild beasts (Maugras 29). Another explanation for the church's hostility to theater is philosophical. As the Prince de Conti wrote in 1666, "Between comedies, the aim of which is to arouse passions, and the Christian religion, the aim of which is to silence, calm and destroy them as far as possible in this world, opposition is complete" (Mongrédien 37).[5]

But Gaston Maugras discounts all these excuses and insists that they were secondary to the church's desire to remove all obstacles to the spread of Christianity throughout Europe. Roman theatrical productions were in fact pagan ceremonies, hence antithetical to the church's goals. Since the Roman performances and gladitorial events were "religious ceremonies, real acts of devotion toward the gods" (30),[6] the church had no choice but to condemn them and all who took part in them. The condemnation of "actors," a broad term applying to "clowns, mimes, pantomimes, dancers, musicians, chariot drivers" (Maugras 29),[7] was the result of a religious power struggle in which the church promoted Christianity to the exclusion of every vestige of pagan practice. It consequently banned actors, and indeed theater at large.

Before long, however, the church itself began using theatrical presentations to disseminate its own propaganda. Maugras attributes this to the fact that the theater is such a "precious means of seduction and influence" (47).[8] The church was able to enlist theater for the purpose of promoting Christian doctrine. It was not the morality of the theater per se, then, that the church opposed, but rather the spiritual direction it took. Religious officials were perfectly willing to tolerate theatrical presentations as long as they were all to the glory of the church, for the church's policy has always been to "transform what she could not destroy" (50).[9]

The church also appropriated pagan festivals that had provided the occasion for theatrical performances and transformed them into Christian festivals such as Christmas, Epiphany, Easter, and the Saints' Days, as well as less serious holidays like the Feast of Fools (Maugras 47). These holidays were now occasions for church plays and celebrations, which ironically kept pagan traditions alive. The Feast of Fools, in which acolytes took over the church, performed satirical, profane masses, and otherwise desecrated sacred practices, was essentially a transformation of the Roman Saturnalia.[10] In the Middle Ages there were 175 festival days a year (Maugras 35), nearly half a year of vestigial pagan ceremonies cloaked in Christian garb. This fact lends credence to Bakhtin's claim that popular festive practices constituted a parallel culture to the dominant Renaissance culture and were not simply occasional or trivial occurrences. It also demonstrates a certain opportunism on the part of the church, which was ready and willing to rewrite the popular traditions it could not easily suppress.

In taking over pagan celebrations, the church could not resist adopting other seductive theatrical techniques. The introduction of performance in the service of church teachings grew from simple illustrations of the liturgy. At some point these elaborations evolved from antiphonal parts of the liturgy to pieces acted out by individual performers assuming distinct roles. These reenactments developed further, incorporating more players and additional scenes until eventually they moved outside the walls of the church. A variety of religious performances grew from these modest beginnings, and it is ironic that such an array of theatrical presentations flourished in a church that had been, in theory anyway, opposed to theatrical performance in principle. The festive tradition among the people was evidently too strong for the church simply to ignore or suppress, and instead it reasserted itself in the form of Christian plays and processions.[11]

The medieval dramas that grew out of the Christian church were for the most part religious. However, as texts such as *The Second Shepherds' Play* and *Noah's Flood* demonstrate, there was ample room for less sacred, more comical approaches to religious stories. It is interesting to note in this context the origin of the word "farce." *Farce,* in French, derives from *farcie,* which means stuffed. The word was used to describe church plays in which colloquial language was interpolated, or "stuffed," into the Latin texts.[12] We can already see a split taking place in French theater between the church plays in Latin, controlled by the church fathers, and those that used colloquial language, thereby giving the laity greater access to and control of the performances.

A general picture of the different branches of French theater at this early stage of development thus begins to emerge. On the one hand, a pre-Christian tradition of Greek and Roman farcical plays, mime, and acrobatics already existed and may have been kept alive by actors who became traveling minstrels or *jongleurs* after the fall of Rome.[13] Alongside these were pagan carnivalesque celebrations adapted in the form of Christian festivals. On the other hand, new theatrical traditions emerged from within the church itself. In these early origins of French theater, characterized by a distinction between new church practices and older surviving pagan traditions, lie the seeds of the theatrical battles that would take place between the official theaters and the unofficial fairground theaters in the centuries to come.

In 1402 the Confrèrie de la Passion (the Brotherhood of the Passion) was chartered for the distinct purpose of performing religious plays outside the church. The Confrèrie was made up not of professional actors but of *petits bourgeois* who formed the organization because church plays had become popular enough that people wanted to see them all year round, not just during holidays. In 1518 they were given a monopoly on theatrical performances in Paris. This monopoly made them responsible for producing religious plays and prevented anyone else from performing spoken drama. The monopoly served to control the theater and its religious content. The Confrèrie's productions, however, moved farther and farther away from sacred drama and closer and closer to low farce. In 1548, the church, concerned about the defamation of the scriptures, finally prohibited the Confrèrie from performing plays on religious subjects. Interestingly, the church neither banned their performances nor revoked their privilege. The group was only forbidden to treat biblical subjects in what had become frankly bawdy farces.

The Confrèrie therefore continued to stage plays at their theater, the Hôtel de Bourgogne, and to maintain their monopoly even though, not performing religious plays, they no longer served the function for which they were originally chartered. Indeed, they took advantage of their privileged status. "A tax farmer more than a patron of theater," Frederick Brown has written, "the Brotherhood held fast to its preserve, suing poachers and invariably receiving favorable judgments" (Brown 44). One might surmise that the Confrèrie's control over Parisian theater persisted for the sole purpose of preserving the economic and political interests of the church.

In 1595 the Paris fairgrounds were declared "an island in the city" (Brown 44), hence no longer falling under the Confrèrie's jurisdiction. This was the first coup against the Confrèrie's theatrical monopoly, and it embodied the clash between the church and the state at that time. The fairgrounds were subsequently opened to provincial actors who performed there along with acrobats, jugglers, and troubadours, all of whom provided some competition for the Hôtel de Bourgogne.

A differentiation between established and nonestablished theaters was emerging, if not merely enduring from earlier times. Official Paris theater was performed under the auspices of a single established body with set standards, while the fairground offered a more permissive environment and attracted itinerant performers and the kinds of mixed crowds found at fairs. The fairgrounds also provided a means for nonreligious and non-Parisian actors to perform near the seat of government power.

One can see the fairground entertainers as the inheritors of both pre-Christian farce traditions and pagan festive practices. The Confrèrie's performances were often lewd and farcical, not at all pleasing to the church. In contrast to the fairgrounds, however, they were the inheritors of liturgical drama, at least inasmuch as they provided a privileged, controlled context for theatrical performances sanctioned by the authorities and tied to the legal power structure. The split between the official and the unofficial theaters, and so between the distinct sectors of society they represented, would persist and, by the eighteenth century, would spark a series of legal battles over which companies had the right to perform which kinds of shows.[14]

From the moment medieval religious theater moved outside the church, the locus of theatrical control began to shift from the church to the state.

With Louis XIV the process was complete. The king had total control over the French nobility, and he centralized the government with himself in Paris and Versailles. He was equally expert at gaining control over all theatrical activities. He granted privileges to certain companies and, along with those privileges, monopolies over different areas of artistic production, usually classified by genre. For instance, in 1672 he granted Jean-Baptiste Lulli[15] the privilege to perform opera and, in so doing, canceled the privilege previously held by Pierre Perrin.

In 1658 Molière's troupe returned to Paris from the provinces and performed for the king with such success that the king's brother subsequently became their patron. The legitimation of Molière's troupe initiated a new rivalry between it and the Hôtel de Bourgogne for the privilege of performing spoken drama in French. Mongrédien gives a detailed account of the competition that developed between these two companies and the machinations and intrigues that ensued as they vied for audiences and for the king's favor. The privileges granted should have minimized these rivalries; instead they enhanced them. The competition inspired the groups to improve the quality of their performances, but they were also subject to the king's whim, since his commands could drastically alter their fortunes. At one point the Théâtre du Marais was brought close to ruin when Bellerose, manager of the Hôtel de Bourgogne, was able to convince the king to order the Marais's top actor, Floridor, to leave that theater and join his own. When Floridor left, he took his wife, an actress, and Corneille's new play *Héraclitus* with him (Mongrédin 78–79). Though this was precisely Bellerose's intention, the king alone had the power to bring it to fruition by issuing orders the actors were bound to obey.

After Molière's death, when the Confrèrie had already been defunct for two years, Louis XIV founded the Comédie-Française by combining the Hôtel de Bourgogne with what was left of Molière's troupe. With one remaining privileged theater, the state now had tighter control than ever over theatrical practice in France. Under the king's control, the Comédie-Française inherited a monopoly on the performance of spoken drama in French.[16] Only the Italian Players company in Paris, which worked in the tradition of the commedia dell'arte and was a favorite at court, was exempt from the restrictions and allowed to continue its performances.

Two new rival theaters thus emerged. On the one side was the Comédie-Française, whose work was based on the performance of a repertoire of what would become the great neoclassic tradition of Racine, Corneille, and Molière. On the other side were the Italian Players, who capitalized on the physical comedy of the commedia and who were accepted at court performing their often vulgar plays in Italian. The language barrier forced them to stress the physical aspect of their comedy, so their style may well have resembled the fairground performances even more than Molière's had done. It was perhaps this bawdy style that led them to get away with more than their contemporaries could, which led in turn to their political daring, which led in turn to their exile from Paris, following their preparations for a production called *The False Prude*, allegedly an attack on the king's mistress, Mme. de Maintenon. This theatrical transgression was taken not just as an insult but as an affront to the king's absolute control of the state.

When disfavor in the eyes of the French court forced the Italian Players out of Paris, they found refuge among the fairground entertainers of the Foire Saint Germain. This was perhaps the company that best suited them, as their theatrical style was more in line with fairground revelry than court decorum. The fairground performers had no special privileges and were forbidden to perform spoken drama in French. Instead they offered a variety of entertainments involving acrobatics, rope dancing, singing, and puppet shows. The rivalry between the Italian Players and the only two remaining licensed performance groups in Paris, the Comédie-Française and the Opéra, continued in spite of the change of venue. Eventually the Italian Players were forbidden from speaking on stage at all, even in Italian. This restriction amounted to a literal silencing of their theatrical voice, just as their exile from Paris had silenced them politically and symbolically. Even deprived of speech, however, the Italian Players could not be completely silenced, and in 1697 they were exiled from France altogether.

The proscription against spoken dialogue on stage was only one of a series of restrictions enacted against all fairground performers. These regulations grew in number with the merging of the Hôtel de Bourgogne and Molière's troupe. No longer in competition with each other, these two theaters jealously guarded their singular privilege and turned against the fairground performers with each new violation. Every restriction on the fairground performers was designed to control the nature and content of their shows in order to protect the position and theatrical repertoire of the Comédie-Française. But the fairground performers persistently countered such interventions in creative ways by concocting entertainments that complied with the letter but not the oppressive spirit of the laws.

For instance, when dialogue was forbidden, the fairground performers countered by having a single actor run on stage, make a speech, and then run off just as another ran on to respond. This technique was known facetiously as "*L'Art de parler seul, inventé par la Comédie-Française*" (the art of speaking alone, invented by the Comédie-Française) (*Mémoires de Jean Monnet* 24). Another tactic required one performer to speak and another to reply through pantomime. When all speech was forbidden, the performers resorted either to written signs or to musical monologues.[17] When performers were forbidden to sing their lyrics, they instructed audiences to sing the words displayed on the signs. There were also the so-called *pieces à écriteaux* (poster plays). In these performances the actors' lines were written out in large type on roles of paper that they pulled continuously from their right pockets, showed to the audience, and then stuffed into their left pockets. They also planted actors in the audience and paid them to sing couplets that the audience would repeat in chorus. Audiences loved these innovations and enthusiastically supported the actors who worked around the regulations while persisting in their art. As Champardon says, "Through their applause, they encouraged the fairground actors in the unequal battle they waged against the Comédie-Fraçaise" (*Memoires de Jean Monnet* 25–26).[18]

These performances ridiculed the official theaters, the restrictions against the fairgrounds, and the government that imposed them. Robert Isherwood shows that some of the fairground performers' parodies struck directly at the official theaters and their typical failure to be as entertaining as the fairgrounds. In a 1722 *opéra-comique*, performed with marionettes (puppets were exempt from the restrictions on song and speech), one character tells Morphée, the god of dreams, "to take his boredom to the French theaters" (Isherwood 93) and reign there in his place. In another example, the fairground theaters made fun of the Comédie-Française attempting to do their own version of the fairground's popular *opéra-comique*. In a prologue a Pierrot says:

Ma foi, Messieurs les Corsaires,
Il est bien honteux à vous
Pour rétablir vos affaires
De piller gens comme nous

[My word, Messieurs Pirates,
It is very shameful of you
In order to retrieve your losses
To plunder folks like us.]

(Isherwood 81–82, my translation)

Though the fairground theaters often parodied the productions of the official theaters, it was in fact the Comédie-Française that was stealing its form and repertoire from the fairgrounds. The monopolies held by the licensed theaters prohibited the fairground performers from using the official repertoire, assuming they would if they could. However, nothing prevented the privileged theaters from stealing from their unofficial counterparts. The official theaters could not ignore the creativity and vitality of the fairgrounds, and it is no surprise that theatrical borrowing went on in both directions.

The flexibility and creativity of the popular performers is evident in the variety of alternatives they devised in order to get around the restrictions placed on their performances. No doubt their determination to continue performing, being heard, and earning their living kept them going. In fact, such creativity was instrumental in the innovation of the *opéra-comique* itself, which became the most popular theater form of the day among all classes.

It was in this environment, too, that the art of pantomime developed. Pantomime used gesture in place of words, which had been forbidden. Though a kind of pantomime had existed in England in the Dumb Shows of the Middle Ages, a new form developed in France under the government restrictions and was then imported to England, where it merged with other forms to create the Christmas entertainments that are known today as English Pantomimes.[19]

The commedia character Harlequin was central to the pantomime tradition and evolved along with it. The originally ribald Harlequin triumphed by overcoming the government restrictions on fairground theaters. In the nineteenth century, when he was removed from the fairgrounds and came to entertain bourgeois audiences in private theaters, he took on distinctly sentimental qualities.[20] Pantomime, in its sentimental form, was more palatable and adapted to middle-class values. It no longer preserved the popular theatrical impulse. The disempowerment of popular forms through the sentimentalization of characters and themes is a common trend. However, when forms like pantomime have ceased to reflect the needs of the common people, they are usually succeeded by new forms that revive the vigor and robustness of popular traditions.

Pantomime's strength as a popular form resided in its silence, a silence that represented repressed speech. It is this form of silence—often quite "outspoken"—that Leabhart's term "mime" broadly denotes. As Leabhart says, it is not essential that mime be silent. What is important is what silence and nonverbal physical expression represent in a world of sounds. The mime herself is a symbol of the actor who speaks, though being denied a legal voice. In seventeenth- and eighteenth-century France the mimes' silence represented the silencing of the theatrical voice of the fairground performers.

Isherwood argues that the fairground theaters were as popular with aristocratic audiences as the Opéra and the Comédie-Française, if not more so. Nonetheless, the division between the licensed and the unlicensed theaters reinforced a cultural division between high and low drama. This dichotomy reveals a paradox inherent in many popular traditions. The fairground theater was meant for a specific group, the lower classes, yet it was appreciated by everybody, so much so that even the Comédie-Française borrowed from it. Yet the concurrent development of a French notion of "taste" reinforced the assumption that lower-class and upper-class theater styles were separated by an abyss.

Frederick Brown attributes the French hierarchy of taste to the style-conscious court of Louis XIV. The court established a world of external particulars by which aristocrats could evaluate each other, especially each other's taste. These particulars included clothes, etiquette, and one's use of language. The newly formed Académie Française, responsible for maintaining standards of formal linguistic correctness, also dictated what constituted "good taste" in the use of the French language. Language became an important means of establishing and preserving an entire culture of taste. The language that disseminated through the theater, therefore, had to be controlled.

From at least the seventeenth century, French served as an international lingua franca. As it spread throughout Europe, so too did French standards of taste. But the pristine French spoken by international officials was not common to all French speakers, least of all the working class and those who lived far from Paris or Versailles and spoke local dialects. The language hierarchy, now institutionally preserved by the Académie Française, deepened the gulf that already existed between the upper- and lower-class society. Mirroring this gulf was the division between the Comédie-Française, where performers spoke only the most refined, literary French, and the fairground theaters, where speech was prohibited altogether.

The restrictions imposed on the unlicensed theaters were responsible not only for separating low culture from high culture but also partly for creating and preserving the characteristic features of low cultural forms. For instance, the fairgrounds did not distinguish between musical and spoken drama, as the privileged theaters did. Instead, they used every means at their disposal to counteract and circumvent the restrictions, elaborating their shows with a variety of entertainments, all mixed together, including music, having purchased the privilege from the Opéra during a financial crisis.[21]

Frederick Brown notes that speech itself was sometimes allowed on the unlicensed stages if it was sufficiently vulgar, which is to say, the kind of speech deemed appropriate for the common folk. Fairground performers could speak somewhat, provided their prose made no attempt to rival the academic French of the Comédie-Française. In order to continue performing, then, the fairground theaters developed and persisted in a style as far removed as possible from that of the national theaters. Even if they had been otherwise inclined, the fairground performers had to adapt their productions to preconceived notions of lower-class entertainment. By keeping their shows sufficiently "vulgar," the fairground performers reinforced the linguistic and cultural differences that already divided high and low. By the same token, however, they were able to keep alive a forum in which the popular voice could be heard.

This brief glimpse at the fairground theaters in the seventeenth and eighteenth centuries shows the way in which flexibility and versatility make it possible for popular forms to persist in the face of overt repression. In these instances popular forms were useful not only for their sheer entertainment value but also because they allowed the performers to circumvent restrictions placed on them and on popular culture as a whole. The court culture of seventeenth-century France in effect forced the unprotected theaters to develop and persist in a distinctively popular aesthetic.

The French Revolution of 1789 briefly suspended the great gulf that had developed between the different strata of French society. The theater that had been trapped in the same class divisions as the society at large and was also affected by the brief but sweeping changes. Thomas Leabhart points to an incident that exemplifies how the people's liberation, once brought about through revolution, further liberated the theaters from their oppressive situation: "Perhaps the most absurd restriction was the one that required actors to perform behind a gauze screen; when the actor Plancher-Valcour heard, on 14 July 1789, that the Bastille had been stormed, he broke through the gauze curtain shouting, 'Long live liberty!' " (5). In a reversal of the situation in the 1690s, when the people's voice was both symbolically and then literally silenced in the theater, Plancher-Valcour both really and metaphorically reclaimed the people's theatrical voice on stage.

As I have said, the new sense of freedom and the social and cultural reforms instituted by the Revolution lent a carnival atmosphere to French society in general. This carnival atmosphere paralleled that of the popular theatrical forms of the fairgrounds, making them a fitting emblem of the people's struggle for liberty and democracy.

As they had done with official festivals, the First Republic used the theaters as a forum for educating people about the ideals of the new regime. The *citoyens* added the symbolic control of the theater to their actual hold on power by liberating the theaters and abolishing censorship. But the theater now had to display its true revolutionary colors and even dressed its heroes and heroines themselves in the *tricolore,* the colors of the flag. These symbolic demonstrations of patriotism soon amounted to a reverse censorship. In March of 1794, the *Commune* banned Racine's masterpieces. The theaters, like the republican festivals, were made over in the image of the new Republic. Like the festivals, the theaters now labored under an ideology of closure, one antithetical to the aesthetic of the fairground performances. Even in these times of alleged freedom, control of the theater still symbolized control of the state, and the government began to mimic the monarchy in the restriction it imposed. In 1807, Napoleon, another monarch who wanted to rule the state and dictate "taste," reinstated the old, pre-Revolutionary rules governing performance.

The story of the development of theater in France from the Middle Ages to the nineteenth century shows to what extent political struggles have affected both the position of theater in society and theatrical style. It shows how theater practices associated with pagan festivals developed in opposition to a distinct official theatrical tradition, one protected by the church, then the royal state, then the republican state. The division between these two theatrical traditions is inextricably linked to economic and social-class distinction. Festive-revolutionary theater forms are the products of social and political struggles played out in the wider cultural sphere.

Popular forms are also related in many ways to mass uprisings and the open society a revolution promises. The celebratory atmosphere of festivals and festive forms parallels the frenzy of spontaneous rebellion. Both festivals and revolutions as well as fairground theatrical forms emphasize an aversion to closure. The political potential of popular forms grows out of a mixture of the intrinsic qualities they share with revolutionary ideals and the historical circumstances in which they develop. The specific social conditions obtaining in different European countries, of course, yield different stories of theatrical development.

But while festive and revolutionary practices are intrinsically linked, one does not necessarily lead to the other in actual fact. A revolution cannot simply be imposed on a festival, although festivals have always been contexts ripe for the expression of revolutionary sentiments. Like popular forms in general, festivals are structured or ritualized events within which there is room for improvisation and occasion to respond to the needs of the people at a given historical moment. But the moment is crucial in determining the political nature of a festive event.

Nonetheless, the deeply rooted historical alliance that I have traced between popular theatrical forms and popular uprisings shows those forms to be more than mere metaphors for popular political action. The multifaceted nature of these forms, their emphasis on physical over verbal expression, their endless inventiveness, and their continual incorporation of new material and new techniques have developed in response to real social oppression. Popular forms are bundles of tactics for overturning, ridiculing, and subverting that oppression. Consequently, they always have one foot on the path to revolution. The right historical circumstances are necessary to push them fully in that direction. Gatti and the Théâtre du Soleil were both trying to revive a revolutionary fervor that had already died out. While they could not inspire real political action, they could rekindle the atmosphere of the festive strikes of May 1968, and with it at least the *possibility* of political action.

Of course, this is not to say that these theatrical experiences were wholly negative or fruitless. They provided insightful social critiques and helped encourage a critical attitude and foster political awareness among their audiences. In historical moments characterized by complacency, however, these productions were not a sufficient means of producing the revolutionary activity they acted out on stage. Their revolutionary intent could not be fused with concrete action in the streets, since no such action was about to occur. However, where a revolutionary atmosphere already exists, festive-revolutionary theater can become an important means of expressing and facilitating the desire for genuine social change.

The San Francisco Mime Troupe has encountered the same problems in their use of festive forms for political purposes as the Théâtre du Soleil and Armand Gatti did. Their great popularity and political effectiveness in the 1960s were in large part owing to the fact that they were addressing an already politicized culture. Yet, even though that fervor has long since died down, the Mime Troupe still sticks to popular forms as a means of rekindling the possibility of revolution. As I will argue further in chapter 5 by drawing on the revolutionary potential always latent in popular forms, the Mime Troupe tries to keep that potential alive until the historical moment itself can once again spark real revolutionary action.

The political zeal of popular forms finds direction and meaning in the specific characters, plots, gags, and practices of the popular theatrical traditions that embody it. The following chapter will explore how the specifics of a single popular form are able to capture and translate a general sense of festivity into substantive political theater.

3 From Pulcinella to Punch the Red

On a San Francisco street corner lined with parking meters, a young woman ruffles through her handbag searching for change. "Oh dear, Oh dear," she mutters. Her change purse is empty. She has no coins to feed the meter so that she can park, so that she can go to the Hall of Justice, so that she can pay her parking fines. She is caught in a modern absurdist dilemma, an exasperating catch-22.

Luckily, she is saved. Rescue arrives in the form of a hook-nosed hand puppet that pops out from a brightly colored portable puppet stage. But this wiley Punch does not appear with a handful of change. He is not a simple deus ex machina (or *pupa ex pyxi*) descending on the scene magically to solve the problems of modern urban life. Instead, he offers a different solution, one more in keeping with the corruption of city living. His very character makes him more suited to this role than to that of the gods of ancient Greek tragedy. Punch, after all, is a crass hand puppet who litters his speech with expressions like "as much as a turd in a teapot," who refers to the meter maid as a "gorgeous hunk of brutal femininity, num, num," and who makes off-color jokes about having a man's hand up his skirt (San Francisco Mime Troupe, *Meter Maid* 111). Nonetheless, he has at his disposal two extraordinary weapons that will rescue this woman from the legalistic bind she finds herself in—namely, information and a soda can tabtop.

The information is a weapon against myths perpetrated by the city government concerning the benefits of parking meters, namely, that they keep traffic flowing, that they provide important revenue for the city, and that they increase the turnover for small businesses. With the help of a few "scientific diagrams," Punch the puppet tells the woman, along with the audience of passersby who have gathered to watch, that traffic flow has not in fact improved since the installation of parking meters, that the revenue mostly pays for the upkeep of the meters and the salaries of meter maids, and that small shopkeepers are being run out of business by chain stores that can offer their customers large, free parking lots. This information liberates the woman, an otherwise law-abiding citizen, from her psychological need to pay by dispelling the feelings of guilt this minor violation of the law would otherwise cause her. After all, if the meters are indeed doing more harm than good and are only serving large chain stores, then it is surely one's duty *not* to pay.

The second device the puppet brings her is a handy-dandy soda tabtop (or pop-top), easily obtainable back in late '60s. Punch shows how one can use this tabtop in place of change to get free parking meter time. If the meter maid and the city aren't willing to admit the fallacy of parking meter logic, and since together they have more power than the average citizen, a little cheating should not be out of the question, nor a little sabotage, in case the meter jams. As Punch sees it, using tabtops in this way constitutes "Democratic self-defense, a blow against U.S. Imperialism, and litterbugging" (113).

The woman takes Punch's advice, and his tabtop, and is blessed with an urban dream come true: forty minutes of free parking. However, this dream turns into a nightmare when the meter maid arrives on the scene and tries to arrest her. The woman fights back, armed with the information she now has concerning the truth about parking meters. Unfortunately, she is faced with a bureaucratic power that favors brute force over rational argument. Accused of "hippie backtalk," she is shot by the meter maid. In her final moments, as she falls lifeless, guilty only of wanting forty minutes of free parking, she heroically passes her message on to those who will continue the fight: "Remember folks, tabtop from a 12-ounce can of Lucky Lager, Diet-Pepsi, or Shasta Soda Pop—And if you're not thirsty, there's millions of them lying all over the streets—Ooof—Parking is such sweet sorrow. Drink Beer tonight. Park free tomorrow" (115).[1]

Tabtops may be a thing of the past, but parking meters and the myths surrounding them are not, nor are the ways city governments have of nickeling and diming (and quartering) their constituents to death. Because of the imbalance of power that always exists between large institutions and the individuals they deal with, the need for disruptive characters like Punch is likely to endure. Indeed, this is probably why versions of Punch have thrived for hundreds of years throughout Europe. Punch and his ancestors have a long and glorious history of rabble-rousing.

The Mime Troupe's portrayal of the puppet figure Punch in *Meter Maid* as a lascivious, underhanded, civil saboteur comes as a shock only to those who are unfamiliar with his history and who know him only in his nineteenth-century incarnation as the friendly, drawing-room puppet of children's entertainments. But this current conception of the Punch and Judy puppet show as simply kid stuff does justice neither to the robust, violent, satirical farce it once was nor to the vast popularity it enjoyed throughout western Europe, Russia, and Turkey. In his various incarnations as Pulcinella, Polichinelle, and Petrushka, as well as in the related figures of Guignol, Hanswurst, Kasperl, and Karaghioz, the English Punch appeared onstage time and again as a champion of the oppressed.

As I have said, popular performance traditions typically rely on improvisation, an emphasis on the body of the actor as agent, and a thematic overturning of the status quo. But they also adapt these general features to particular historical circumstances to create unique forms with recognizable characters and standard plots and gags. Popular theatrical traditions keep the spirit of festivity and revolution alive, though of course it is the specific qualities of a form that will determine its continuing relevance and political efficacy. Of course, each of these so-called Punch traditions needs to be regarded as unique and appreciated for its own particularities. Yet the traditions do share a number of common traits that bind them and make them all examples of festive-revolutionary theater.

By examining a single popular form, Punch, its unique features, and its rise and fall in history, I will in this chapter attempt to answer some of the following questions concerning the revolutionary qualities of popular forms at large: How do the specific features of a form determine its political import? What pragmatic constraints do those features impose? How and why do certain traditions grow, spread, and die out? And how can a tradition from one time and place remain relevant in new contexts? Again, the distinguishing feature of popular forms has always been the balance they strike between structure and openness, between established convention and novelty and improvisation, between repetition in form and renewal through reformulation. That balance allows them to keep pace with the often changing political world in which they find themselves, and to continue even as they continually transform.

The Punch tradition is a good subject for this study for several reasons. First, it is a tradition that the Mime Troupe incorporated, not only in the short guerilla skit *Meter Maid* but also in one of their most successful productions, *L'Amant Militaire.* Both shows feature a contemporary American version of the figure of Punch, but *L'Amant Militaire* in particular highlights Punch's fundamentally violent nature. It is important to keep in mind the violence that underlies many popular forms, which raises the question whether violent action is necessary in turning festive production into revolutionary practice. In *L'Amant Militaire* the Mime Troupe set Punch's aggressive character against their own pacifist opposition to the Vietnam War, in part as a kind of self-criticism. Seeing how they managed this conflict and used Punch to their own advantage affords some insight into how companies can appropriate popular traditions for their own social and political purposes.

Although occasionally important in Mime Troupe productions, puppetry admittedly has never formed the backbone of the Troupe's style. It does, however, provide an important area of investigation for a study of popular traditions and may even be said to be iconic of popular theater in general. In the United States puppetry is associated almost exclusively with children's entertainment. It is, therefore, all the more interesting to discover its political potential in the European tradition and in the work of the Mime Troupe. It is the example par excellence of combining seemingly frivolous media with serious intent. Punch and his cohorts reveal the ways in which popular forms can allow performers to engage in political critique. Numerous examples from the Punch tradition, and from related forms, testify to the widespread use of puppets for just that purpose. The childish appearance of the Punch show served as a kind of camouflage for the puppeteer's sometimes daring commentary. The cartoon quality of this hero/villain at once lampooned figures of authority and at the same time prevented them from retaliating, since it would be absurd to take seriously such a ridiculous little prankster. As we shall see, other particulars of the form, including its portability and its crucial reliance on improvisation, also made it an excellent vehicle for political content.

However, while the Punch tradition set itself against figures of authority and forces of oppression, it was also compromised by its reliance on sexist and racist stereotypes. The use of stereotypes and other prejudices is not unique to Punch but is a danger that plagues popular performance traditions generally. Particularly problematic in the case of Punch is the derision he often heaps on blacks, Jews, and women. Punch's prejudices reflect the milieu in which he originated. Other popular traditions will reflect the cultural predispositions of their own backgrounds. How, then, can politically-minded performers sift out or deconstruct the prejudices embodied in a popular form while preserving those aspects of the form that can still serve their own progressive ends? Exploring the prejudices passed down in a specific tradition like Punch tells us something about how a company might do this, and about the continuing relevance and usefulness of such traditions for political theater in general. This discussion is not meant to suggest that popular forms should be sanitized for the purpose of some kind of "political correctness." On the contrary, it is meant to provide an understanding of how prejudices may be associated with a particular form so that theater practitioners using it can maintain control over their own political message.

In view of its history as a thriving street and fairground entertainment throughout Europe, and in the general pattern of transformation it has undergone from a ribald, violent, satirical farce to a harmless yet somewhat unsettling distraction for children, Punch is in many ways a prototype of the festive-revolutionary. A look at Punch's unique history will shed some light on both the advantages and the pitfalls in the use of popular forms for contemporary political theater.

The Punch character that the Mime Troupe adapted for *Meter Maid* and *L'Amant Militaire* comes out of a long tradition of popular puppetry. In this tradition puppet shows were not primarily for children but for a mixed, mostly adult audience. From portable booths on street corners, at local fairs, or in makeshift spaces, puppeteers spoke to the general population. A tradition of festivity and festive celebration was common throughout Europe and created a place for popular entertainment. The fact that such festive practices already existed for Punch wherever he went partially accounts for the ease with which he was able to assimilate into so many different cultures.

Punch's origins are found in Italy in the figure of Pulcinella, which is in turn related to the masked commedia dell'arte character of the same name. There is some disagreement among historians as to whether the puppet or the masked figure was the original.[2] In any case, Pulcinella traveled throughout Europe in puppet form and, in keeping with his often lascivi-

10. Punch, Judy, and their baby. These Punch puppets were created by designer and puppeteer Amy Trompetter. They bear many of the characteristic features of traditional Punch and Judy figures. Photograph by Taylor Carman.

11. Punch and the Policeman, also created by Amy Trompetter. Photograph by Taylor Carman.

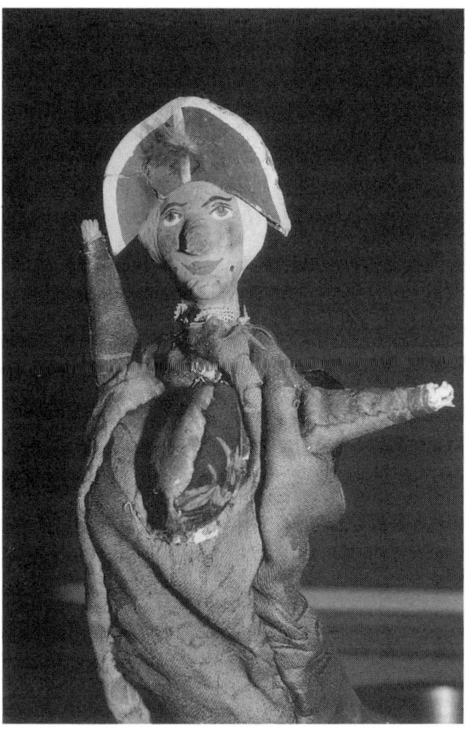

12. A French Polichinelle hand puppet with the character's traditional bulging belly and humpback. Dramatic Museum Collection, Rare Book and Manuscript Library, Columbia University. Photograph by Taylor Carman.

ous character, sired a great progeny.[3] While remaining true to the original in many respects, the Pulcinella figures that appeared throughout Europe took on new qualities in order to adapt to each new setting. They became distinct characters but, nonetheless, maintained some significant features of the original.

George Speaight argues convincingly that, though the historical record clearly indicates an Italian origin for the English Punch, many of the characteristics that distinguish him from other versions of Pulcinella are drawn directly from clowns, jesters, and other puppet traditions or "motions" that already existed in England before Pulcinella arrived. For example, Punch's partnering with Judy and his role as a henpecked husband follow the English Mystery Cycle's depictions of Noah and his shrewish wife.[4] Punch's adaptability and his affinity with the earlier folk traditions of England made him readily acceptable to local audiences, and as a result he integrated easily into English culture. In any case, whether Punch is mostly Italian or mostly English, the English certainly consider him one of their own. They refer to Punch whenever they need to invoke an emblem of the comic. Indeed, the enthusiasm with which Speaight insists that Punch really belongs to England is itself some indication of the degree to which the figure has become embedded in English culture.[5]

Pulcinella also came to France and there became the puppet and masked commedia character, Polichinelle. In the nineteenth century, however, Laurent Mourguet, a silk factory worker from Lyon, transformed Polichinelle, or rather reinvented him, into the even more indigenously French character, Guignol. An economic depression had caused widespread unemployment in Lyon, and Mourguet began performing puppet shows to earn a living. He worked initially with a Polichinelle character, but in 1808 he carved the figure that became Guignol and that was, incidentally, modeled on himself.[6] A popular engraving of the 1920s by Eugène Lefebvre concerning the life of Laurent Mourguet says: "Polichinelle amuses but does not satisfy, for he is not one of us"[7] (Fournel, *L'Histoire* 33). What led Mourguet to create his Guignol was precisely a desire to develop a more familiar character that he and his neighbors could call their own.

Guignol was not only a French counterpart to Polichinelle, he was unique to the region of Lyon. Other regional puppet heroes that developed throughout France included Lafleur in Picardie, Les Cabotans in Amiens, Jacques in Lille, and Barbizier in Besançon (Fournel, *L'Histoire* 32). All of these puppets were, like Guignol, relatives of Pulcinella and Polichinelle, now transformed to fit their new regional homes.[8] Even in Italy, where Pulcinella originated, there emerged a variety of different puppet figures based on or related to Pulcinella, but specific to different regions. Pulcinella himself was from Naples and spoke with a Neapolitan accent. But as Michael Byrom states in his book on the Italian puppet theater, other regional masks like Leporello were just substitutes for Pulcinella, adding local characteristics and speaking the local dialect (92).[9]

In Russia the Italian Pulcinella became Petrushka. Catriona Kelly finds that from 1840 to the 1870s the two names "Pulcinella" and "Petrushka" were just alternative designations for the same puppet figure. By the 1880s, however, "the hero's name had become fixed in the Russian version, 'Petrushka.' " Though the adoption of the name "Petrushka" occurred as late as 1870, Petrushka fits so well in Russian folk tradition that scholars have sometimes tried to assign him a much earlier origin. Kelly refers to a long tradition in Russia of attempts to date Petrushka earlier than its true nineteenth-century beginnings (49). Nevertheless, there is evidence that some puppet entertainments existed in Russia before Petrushka. So again, as in England, though the specific conventions of the Petrushka puppet show may be comparatively recent, the new puppet no doubt adapted to and absorbed familiar local traditions already in place. More important, however, as in England and France, the strong link between this new hybrid puppet and long-standing folk traditions partially accounts for the readiness with which Russians embraced Petrushka as one of their own.

Other countries have traditional puppet figures similar in character to Pulcinella, though it is not clear whether they are directly related. In Germany, Pulcinella's counterpart was the puppet Hanswurst, who was later replaced by Kasperl. These puppet figures emerged from a Germanic folk tradition but were comparable to Pulcinella in many ways. They were possibly more like cousins than direct descendants of the Italian figure, perhaps indicating a wider popular tradition throughout Europe. An even more distant relative was the puppet clown Karaghioz. He originated in the Ottoman Empire and was a shadow puppet rather than a hand puppet or marionette. Though Karaghioz may seem far removed from Pulcinella, Bil Baird notes that he is often thought to be an ancestor of Punch (he precedes Punch by several hundred years) and that he has very similar qualities: "Like Punch, he is a roisterer and a rogue. He is a libertine, impetuous, vain, violent, with no respect for authority and determined to have his own way" (78).

The many incarnations of Punch testify to the adaptability of popular forms. However, while Punch continually transformed to fit new surroundings, he was also readily accepted because he was in many ways already familiar to the new communities he entered, and to their folk practices. Frank Proschan points out that while puppetry works best when "both performer and audience members partake together of a community of interest and a community of expectation," it is also true that "folk theater forms, and especially folk puppetry, flourish as well in areas of cultural contact and are often performed by itinerant performers. Indeed, sometimes even the language of performance is different from that spoken by the auditors" (39). The same elements that help popular theater flourish in one setting—a familiarity with the local culture, a reliance on "in jokes" and topical allusions—also threaten to render them unintelligible in foreign contexts. Yet, as we have seen with Pulcinella, and as Proschan points out, popular forms are highly adaptable and are often well received beyond the confines of their original homes. They are often quite successful as itinerant performances and frequently take root in their new host countries.

One reason for the success of popular traditions like Pulcinella in new venues has to do with their reliance on physical humor. Physical action transcends language barriers, making performances comprehensible to foreign audiences. Pulcinella's success also has to do with the general adaptability of popular forms. They are malleable structures that can easily incorporate new material into their performances and thereby adjust quickly to new situations.

But Pulcinella's wide acceptance also owes a great deal to the fact that a common lower-class culture existed in Europe during the period of his renown. While the French language and aristocratic artistic forms helped spread and unify an elite culture across Europe, Pulcinella and other popular entertainments helped spread and reaffirm a common lower-class culture with the international language of physical gesture and the beating stick. The working class of France, for instance, especially those who came from rural villages where inhabitants spoke a variety of local dialects, may have felt closer to the working class of Italy through their familiarity with Pulcinella and other popular forms than they did to the French elite. Divisions between high and low culture were not as strict as they might appear, as the Comédie-Française's pillaging from the fairground theaters attests. Nevertheless, throughout Europe a lower-class culture stood in contrast and opposition to the elite, and popular entertainments served not only as a forum for the people's voice within a community but also as unofficial ambassadors between communities.[10]

The European festive tradition originated in pre-Christian, pagan practices. It was not ingrained in American culture, however, which since colonial times had been firmly rooted in Puritan values. Puritan values account in part for Punch's lukewarm reception in America, for though he did eventually travel to the United States in the nineteenth century, he did not fare as well there as he had in Europe. It was not just Punch that was missing from the streets of American cities, however, but a whole world of carnivalesque, fairground entertainments. As Speaight observes, the absence of street performers was keenly felt by European visitors:

> When Mrs. Trollope wrote her *Domestic Manners of the Americans* in 1832 she lamented that: "I never saw a population so totally divested of gaiety . . . they have no fêtes, no fairs, no merrymakings, no music in the streets, no Punch, no puppet shows." Similarly, when Charles Dickens visited the United States in 1842 he lamented the quietness of the streets of New York: "Are there not itinerant bands; no wind or stringed instruments? No, not one. By day, are there no Punches, Fantoccini, Dancing-dogs, Jugglers, Conjurors, Orchestrinas, or even Barrel-organs? No, not one." (*Punch and Judy* 128)

These observations offer a glimpse into just how many festive street entertainments did exist in merry old England. The lack of a tradition of festive practice in the United States not only accounts for Punch's absence from this country it also complicates the Mime Troupe's attempt to adopt such forms for American audiences.

However, as *Meter Maid* shows, the Mime Troupe was able to find an American voice for Punch. In their hands he became "Punch the Red." This "professional agitator" and "armed revolutionary socialist" certainly found like-minded audiences in the counterculture of the 1960s (*Meter Maid* 113–14). Yet snappy language of the Troupe's Punch may be indebted to a distinctly American idiom, for instance the gangster film (consider his reference to the woman in *Meter Maid* as "Toots"). Here Punch is still a popular rabble-rouser, but with an American accent. If resurrected today, perhaps his lingo would have to change yet again (the woman probably wouldn't let him get away with calling her "Toots"). Maybe we would even find a feminist version of Punch. In any case, a recognizable, up-to-date Punch is certainly not out of the question.

What qualities, then, identify Pulcinella throughout his various manifestations in so many different parts of the world? In whatever form he takes, he is primarily recognizable by his unique character, drawn from the lower-class culture common throughout Europe. Pulcinella was originally an imitation of Neapolitan peasants, and many of the characteristics he acquired at that time still comprise his most readily identifiable qualities.[11] According to Speaight, "in spirit he was always a primeval peasant, a slow-witted country booby, but with the cunning and guile of his race. With the years he developed other more farcical characteristics; he was gross of speech, indecent in gesture, and a braggart man who ran away at the sight of danger" (*Punch and Judy* 13). Pulcinella displays his trickster quality by defying all categories that would confine him to any single aspect of his personality. Different countries therefore emphasize different aspects of their respective Pulcinellas. It must be stressed again that each country where a Pulcinella-type figure flourished had antecedent traditions that helped to shape the character that developed there, and that each of these puppet traditions reflects its unique cultural environment. Yet there is no doubt that all Pulcinellas are of the people, the lower classes, whether peasant farmers or urban laborers, and that they invariably set themselves against structures of authority. These few salient features are at the very heart of every Pulcinella. Sometimes they defy authority through the beatings they administers with a stick, sometimes through their wit and trickery. In all cases Pulcinella is a rogue who gleefully foils those around him. He is thus a figure that represents the lower classes in triumph over oppression. Even in the hands of the Mime Troupe, as a self-proclaimed "professional agitator," this hand puppet retains Pulcinella's most essential traits.

Antonio Pasquelino adds a mythical dimension to our understanding of Pulcinella. According to Pasquelino, Pulcinella is not merely a representative of the oppressed rising up against oppression. His defiance of the social order links him to the natural order, endowing him with seemingly superhuman powers: "Finally he is like some kind of supernatural being representing life or death. This third identification is suggested by the following facts—he resuscitates himself, he is dressed in white, color of death, he is sexually ambiguous, and his beak nose and peculiar voice make him resemble a bird, the word bird (*ucello*) being used to refer to the male sexual organ" (20). Pulcinella covers the spectrum from secular to sacred clowns. In his supernatural aspects he resembles the sacred clown-puppet Semar of the West Javanese tradition discussed by Foley. Yet as a representative of an older, pagan form of the sacred, he remains unhampered by and defiant of church rules. He is a prototype of Caputi's *buffo*: born from a pagan tradition, he carries an optimistic message of social renewal into the present day. Pulcinella also carries on the *buffo* tradition of attacking the authority of the church. When he, the most devilish of characters, is brought to the hangman for his flouting of authority, he emerges as a new martyr and a champion of the people. His virtues are not those of Jesus—love, compassion, and mercy—but boldness, defiance, cleverness, and a desire for freedom. Pulcinella maintains a link to the supernatural while being firmly rooted in the natural, bodily world of the present.

ılcinella tradition developed in the marketplaces and fairgrounds of old Europe, which Bakhtin describes. Its specific characteristics reflect these origins and are ideally suited to entertaining at crowded, outdoor venues. The same features that accommodated these practical aspects of performance also turned the show into a forum for defying authority and voicing the people's concerns. There is a strong connection between the form and the function of the Pulcinella tradition. Understanding the formal qualities that allow Pulcinella to function as an agent of political subversion will help us understand how this form might still be used in political theater today. The politically salient features of the form include the individual puppeteer's control over the production and ownership of the means of production; the portability of the performance; the relatively nonfigurative aspect of hand puppets in comparison with marionettes and human performers; the childish appearance of the show, which allows the performers to speak politically while avoiding censorship; the encouragement of audience participation; and finally the use of improvisation. Each of these factors contributes to the usefulness of hand puppets, especially those coming out of the Pulcinella/Punch tradition, for voicing popular concerns in the face of possible censorship and in defiance of authority.

As I have said, the live performer is the heart of popular theater. And the puppet theater is the live performer's art par excellence, for even though the performer himself is hidden, he alone is responsible for the actions of all the different characters.

The Punch and Judy tradition in England puts the burden of an entire performance in the hands (literally) of a single performer. While the "Punchmen," as they are called, usually work with one other person, called a "bottler," it is the Punchman alone who operates the puppets. Although the bottler sometimes gets into the act by translating Punch's high squeaky and often incomprehensible voice,[12] his main job is purely practical: he helps rally an audience, keeps people from peeking behind the Punchman's curtain, and—most important—passes the hat at the end of the show. But it is up to the Punchman to manipulate the ensemble of puppets and to create the voices of all the characters. The Punchman must also master the use of a small instrument held in the mouth known as a "swazzle," which produces the piercing tones of Punch's unique squeaky voice. A puppeteer must have a keen understanding of how to manipulate these few elements in order to create many characters and tell an entire story. Baird points out that, even outside of the moment of performance, the Punchman is the impresario of his own theater, for he is "the author and designer, and the singers and actors of his entire repertoire of plays" (101).[13]

The mastery that puppeteers must display testifies not only to the performer's technical skill but also to the wide range of physical and expressive potential of the human body. Puppeteers, as Dina and Joel Sherzer point out, must be able to represent "the sociolinguistic repertoire of an entire society, community, or region, and even beyond," and must also master a variety of sound effects including "shouts, screams, whistles, cries, whispers, weeps, laughs, nose blows, snores, yawns, coughs, sneezes, groans, grunts, burps, and farts" (48).[14] Despite their simple appearance, puppet shows require a great deal of skilled artistry. They are often very crude in scenographic craftsmanship yet highly advanced in terms of personal technique, creativity, and ingenuity. The burden of the performance lies with the performer and is not dependent on expensive, elaborate, or controlled elements outside of the show itself. Solo performance can therefore be a liberating aspect of popular forms since it puts control of every aspect of the production in the hands of a single autonomous agent.

The fact that outdoor Punch and Judy shows like those in England are typically solo performances allows the physical apparatus of the production to remain small and easily transportable. The puppet booths themselves are easy to make, set up, and move to new locations. Portability gives a puppeteer freedom with respect to his venues and audiences. The puppeteer can easily move, if audiences are sparse or unreceptive, and can revisit places where the show is guaranteed greater success.[15] Ghetanaccio, a nineteenth-century puppeteer, took advantage of his stage's portability and performed directly underneath the windows of the actual people he was satirizing in his plays (Byrom 35). The mobility of his production allowed him both to select strategic spots for his performances and to move quickly from those spots if the police were called in to silence him. Moving quickly was thus a distinct advantage for avoiding censorship or arrest. Baird adds that in the German tradition mobility definitely helped the puppeteers. They could move quickly and easily between Germany's more than three hundred principalities and successfully avoid censorship. By the time the censors arrived, the puppeteers had already left town (74).

Freedom of movement and solo performance have the liberating effect of putting the performer in charge of both means of production and artistic expression. A single puppeteer in effect becomes the sole owner and operator of an independent business. It is rare in the field of performing arts for a player of modest financial means to produce her work and to have complete control over both its form and its content. Puppet theater, however, makes this possible. By remaining independent agents, not beholden to anyone but their audiences, puppeteers retain the freedom to voice their opinion. As a result, they can address controversial issues where others might not.

The Mime Troupe's *Meter Maid* was a very portable show, requiring only one actor, one puppeteer, a light puppet stage and—of course—a tabtop. Almost all the Mime Troupe plays are portable to some degree, though current productions require several hours setup time. In the manifesto "Guerilla Theatre: 1965," R. G. (Ron) Davis instructs prospective performers to "set up a portable stage, twelve by fifteen feet, made into eight sections with a backdrop hung on a pole strung along a goal post supporter. All equipment must be portable and carried in a *borrowed* three-quarter-ton truck" (152). The Mime Troupe still uses a large truck and a stage somewhat like this for their shows, although today's sets are usually more elaborate. Of course, such a stage cannot quite rival the portability of a puppet box and the easy means of escape it allows a truly provocative performance. But it lets the Troupe move about easily and take their shows to the people they most want to reach. The Mime Troupe's equipment also has the advantage of transforming an open, public space and claiming it, temporarily, as a site for community expression. In this way they take charge of their own urban planning and fit the shared social space to their own ends. They re-present the world's flexibility once again, this time by transforming a park into a theater, and light outdoor entertainment into an occasion for serious political discourse.

Another aspect of the Pulcinella tradition that makes it useful for political purposes is its use of hand puppets. The Italian theater shows us that Pulcinella-type characters have been performed with both hand puppets and marionettes. Yet it was the hand puppet version that spread throughout Europe and Russia, especially in the public sphere.

The hand puppet is a medium well-adapted to outdoor marketplace venues, for a performer must be bold and conspicuous to compete for the attention of a shifting crowd with the noise of the street, vendors, and other performers. The wooden-headed hand puppet's hard-hitting style and general roughness are well suited to the hubbub of the marketplace. Marionettes, by contrast, and the care that the manipulation of their many strings requires, are better suited to indoor venues and are often more appropriate for drawing-room entertainment. In order to accommodate the control of the puppets from above, marionette theaters are generally larger than hand puppet theaters, hence less portable. The marionettes themselves often require several people to operate them, which also complicates the production considerably.

Hand puppets, as the term implies, are worn on the hand, and this lends them a uniquely organic character that informs the political purposes to which they are so often put. The distinctive shape and movement of the hand within the puppet is palpable. The centrality of the performer's body and physical skill that is so important to popular forms is maintained here. Not only do we see the physicality of the performer's hand, but the puppets themselves, especially Punch, take on very robust, earthy—often caricatured—features. Hand puppets on the whole are concrete and rough-hewn, and their appearance is not quite human.

Marionettes, by contrast, are often made up to have more realistic, more refined human qualities. Yet, being manipulated from above, their actions do not embody the performer's presence nearly as concretely. Marionettes tend more toward the world of illusion, at times magically gliding across the stage. Their realistic features, however, link them to the world of human actors.

The general proximity of the marionette to the human actor, as opposed to the hand puppet's ambiguous position between character and object, has important consequences for the role of Punch and his cultural counterparts as outspoken critics. Marionettes frequently emulate human beings and are generally appreciated for their capacity to mimic real human movements. Hand puppets, on the other hand, are in general not to be mistaken for human figures.[16] They are extensions of the human body, yet they transform the body by disguising it. They remain objects and perform absurd, inhuman actions, even as they continually try to gain recognition as real human characters. They are bound to a narrow range of movement but are not confined by real social norms in the way marionettes are. Precisely because they are not human, puppets can in general take greater liberties than live human actors. As a result, hand puppets make possible more radical social commentary than marionettes (Kelly 106).

Pasquelino reports that the distinction between the hand puppet and the marionette is evident in the different fates of the masked Pulcinella figure as it developed in the *guaratelli* (hand puppet shows) and the *opera dei pupi* (marionette shows). In the marionette theater Pulcinella and similar figures from other regions became "well behaved symbols of urban working class respectability." The hand puppet versions of the same characters remained "rebellious peasants, with disquieting traces of their descent from the demons of the agrarian fertility rites" (9). The marionettes also generally conformed to the social roles of the human beings they depicted, while the hand puppets did not.

As I mentioned, there is also a masked commedia character named Pulcinella. The difference between the masked commedia characters as played by humans and their puppet counterparts mirrors the distinction between hand puppets and marionettes. For example, the human mask of the character Accerra is "submissive, cowardly, greedy, and lazy, but good humoured." His counterpart in the puppet tradition, however, is "ready to quarrel and brave in a fight." A. G. Bragaglia draws this distinction: "The human buffoon is a great receiver. The glove-puppet is a rebel" (Byrom 124). The marionette, imitating the human actor, thus retains the submissive qualities of the masked character.

Pulcinella belongs to the tradition of clown figures that Towsen describes, covering the spectrum from the sacred to the profane. Within the area of profane clowning, however, there is also a wide range of character types, from the buffoon clown to the rebellious clown. Human Pulcinellas are buffoons. Puppet Pulcinellas, however, can be more violent and aggressive than the human characters and still remain comic. The hand puppet Pulcinella, the least anthropomorphic, is at once the most rebellious. Consequently, as a hand puppet Pulcinella posed a greater threat to authority onstage and off than either the commedia character or the marionette figure of the same name.

Again, the hand puppet lends itself to fast-paced action, brash, unsubtle movements, and a lot of knockabout play. Pulcinella's medium has shaped his character, and this is why his chief action is simply hitting. Beating and being beaten constitute the main action of the Pulcinella play and amount to a concrete physical representation of the relation between oppressor and oppressed. The power center of the puppet world is fluid as the locus of power changes depending on who is doing the beating. Pulcinella, a lowly peasant, who in real life would have no status at all, elevates himself in these shows simply by taking a stick and beating the other puppets. Through the beatings he administers to others, Pulcinella is able to reverse hierarchies and dominate other characters in the play.

The use of a hand puppet certainly works to the Mime Troupe's advantage in *Meter Maid* and *L'Amant Militaire.* In both shows the puppet is set in contrast to live actors. In both instances the puppet is allowed to push the limits of the antiestablishment activity that the piece can condone. In the former he merely advocates undermining the parking meter system. In the latter, as we shall see, he goes farther by advocating blowing up weapons depots as a means of protesting the Vietnam War. In each case he takes up a more radical stance than his human counterparts, more radical even than the masked commedia figures in *L'Amant Militaire.* His status as a hand puppet with a slightly grotesque face allows him to make quips and to foreground his own unreality as a mere puppet, while emphasizing his very vibrant, lively character. As an object rather than an agent, he is less accountable for his actions than a live actor must be. As a performing object, he does not elicit the same expectations a human figure would and is not held up to the same moral standards as his human counterparts. By transgressing our own conventional boundaries, he shows us what possibilities lie beyond them.

Performing objects range from marionettes to hand puppets to masked performers to other more abstract animated objects. The usefulness of such objects for popular political theater work also varies considerably. Those that are physically more organic-looking and grotesque are at once more ribald and outspoken in character. Those that are physically more refined are also more staid, less potentially aggressive or radical.

The colorful puppets, their small stature, the silly antics of the show, and Punch's own clownish nature all create an atmosphere of childish fun around these festive puppet plays. This childish appearance is partially responsible for our recent acceptance of Punch as an entertainment for children. But Punch was not originally intended for children. The sense of fun in the play surely accounts for its popularity among adults, but Punch's childish facade also served another purpose. The silliness of the puppet show became a kind of camouflage behind which performers could risk putting forward more serious messages.

The Punch play's childish qualities often served as a strategy that made it seem insignificant, and so protected it from censorship. In England, for instance, censorship of theater was widespread, especially after the Civil War of 1647, when the Puritans came to power. By new laws imposed at that time, any players discovered performing would be flogged, and spectators would be fined five shillings apiece. Punch was unique among theatrical events in seeming too insignificant to be suppressed. As Speaight reports: "The puppet plays, too lowly for legal interdiction, continued unhindered" (*Punch and Judy* 37). When more radical messages were discerned behind the puppets' innocent visages, officials were often at pains to figure out how to control their speech without looking foolish. One can imagine, for instance, how ridiculous Italian officials must have felt on at least one occasion that Byrom mentions when "the offending puppet itself was arrested and presented in court as material evidence for the prosecution with a card attached to it inscribed, '*corpus delicti*' " (95).

Punch's foolish character and comic cleverness often saved him and his puppeteer from arrest. His remarks were meant to excite laughter, not recrimination, and this often amounted to an effective tactic of dissimulation. One example of how such subversion worked is from Naples, where officials went to great lengths trying to censor Pulcinella: "The puppet theatre was attended by a uniformed Commissary of Police who sat in a private box near the stage on a high-backed chair adorned with faded crimson velvet; behind his back, two large wax candles and the royal arms of the Two Sicilies painted on a board" (Byrom 92). However, even this intimidating presence could not silence Pulcinella, whose comic antics got the better of those who were sent to keep an eye on him. As one British observer remarked, "not all this official splendour could repress the hilarity or stifle the roguish impromptus of friend Punch; and we have at times seen the starch-visaged commissary, after some vain attempts to maintain his dignity, hold both sides and join in the universal roar of laughter: and this too even when Signor Polcinella had gone beyond bounds and handled matters strictly tabooed" (Byrom 92).[17]

Those who tried to censor these puppets took the risk not only of looking foolish but of becoming the targets of satire themselves (if they were not already). In England, during Puritan rule, the Lord Mayor of London tried to banish puppet shows from Bartholomew fair. However, "he died the next year and the shows returned, irreverent as ever, with the Lord Mayor reappearing as a puppet. The Devil probably carried him off" (Baird 71). Punchmen could therefore retaliate against their oppressors in the real world, just as Punch did in the puppet world.

The Mime Troupe has also used this cover to their advantage in other ways. In 1966, members dressed up as characters from Hieronymous Bosch and Bruegel paintings and went caroling at Christmas, singing songs against consumerism. They collected money and blocked traffic and were soon arrested for begging. An actor wearing a bear head was the one who actually held the cup, but the jury could not convict any of the actors since no one could verify which one of them had been dressed as the bear. In this case, a disguise literally saved an actor from being identified by the authorities and made the entire case seem ridiculous (Davis 71).

Various forms of camouflage or disguise have often enabled popular traditions to endure and maintain themselves as forums for radical commentary. They deflect repression with humor and the appearance of mere fun and foolishness. Popular forms revert to an innocent, playful demeanor just when their most radical tendencies begin to emerge. But such frivolity has led to the contemporary misconception that these forms, especially puppet shows, are really no more than trifling entertainments for children.[18] People have come to mistake the appearance for the reality, obscuring the true nature and value of popular forms generally.

Audience participation is also an essential part of Punch shows. It fosters interaction and a give-and-take between audience and performer, and it requires the performer to be in touch with the feelings, ideas, and concerns of the audience moment by moment. The art of prompting audience participation, however, still grants performers great freedom and allows them to shape the message of the show.

Frank Proschan's article on a contemporary Punch and Judy show performed for an audience made up primarily of children offers some insight into how such a puppet show could have been an empowering, revolutionary presence for an adult, working-class audience. Proschan first shows that audience participation can empower the spectators by in effect granting them a kind of authority over the performance itself. The puppeteer in the show Proschan studies get the children involved by asking them "to report on events or to ratify an interpretation of events." In this way the children are "given the opportunity to demonstrate their observational skills and to control understanding." Audience participation also has the power to unify an audience into an active, cohesive group. In Proschan's example, "The children, witnesses together to the events, can speak with one voice, and can speak the truth" and thereby "create a consensus and shape meaning, and have that meaning accepted by others as the basis for action" (43).

In truth, encouraging audience participation involves manipulating and guiding the spectators as much as giving them freedom and control. The children in Proschan's example feel that they are in control of understanding, but they are in fact being taught how to conform to social norms. "In the Punch show, children can freely indulge their conformist or authoritarian inclinations and can serve as the voice of society, condemning Punch's wife-beating, Joey's sausage-theft, Jack Catch's gullibility, and the repeated lies of one or another character" (43). Effective audience participation requires a puppeteer who knows what to expect from an audience and who can gear a show toward eliciting just that response. Proschan's audience of contemporary children has been taught to condemn "antisocial" behavior. Yet an audience of working-class adults in the sixteenth or seventeenth century might have been ready to condone those same actions. An audience already resentful of some form of repression and imposed order might just as easily side with Punch and applaud his audacity. In such a context, a Punch show could rally the spectators in support of Punch and in defiance of the status quo.

A puppet's antiestablishment potential is determined by the audience's reception. In the case of the children who admonish Punch, the puppeteer caters to their predisposition to condemn antisocial behavior. Yet even here Punch somewhat defies the puppeteer by getting away with all his crimes and retaining his impudent character. Even the children who boo him clearly delight in his recalcitrance. At the closing of Proschan's show, Punch is punished but not reformed. So, although the radical potential of a puppet play is constrained by the contingencies of performance and audience reception, Punch and the form that nurtured him continue to exhibit an undeniable revolutionary aspect even in a politically conservative environment.

The puppeteer's ingenuity extends beyond the physical manipulation of puppets to the creative process of on-the-spot scripting, that is to say, improvisation, one of the most important aspects of puppet performances. The performer's quickness and wit are central to the show, and the performer's skill is gauged by the amount of money people leave in the hat. Improvisation, however, demonstrates not only the depth of a performer's skill but also the scope of his freedom. It allows puppeteers to voice their opinions on any subject, relevant or irrelevant to the play, and to throw in topical, often political asides on the spur of the moment. The improvisational aspect of the puppet theater has therefore often made it the target of censorship.

Improvisation made up a major part of the Guignol shows in France. Paul Fournel finds that the sketchy plots of Guignol plays served as pretexts for the puppeteer's improvisations, which constituted the core of the show's appeal and included reports and commentary on local events.[19] Guignol, for example, functioned as a kind of local gazette for the people of Lyon, keeping abreast of local gossip and passing it on in performance (*L'Histoire* 34).

The Guignol shows consequently came under attack by the French government in the Second Empire for disseminating information to the common folk, for as Fournel remarks, "To spread news is to take sides and to make those take sides who do not enjoy the right of looking on at the march of the world" (*L'Histoire* 35).[20] The government tried to censor the shows by demanding that written texts be presented to the police for their prior approval. This created a number of problems for puppeteers. Until then there had been no written texts for Guignol shows at all. "Scripts" were passed on in an oral tradition by people who memorized the scenarios and then improvised on them. Performers now had to compose a text, indeed one that would satisfy the officials. But since they were often illiterate, Guignol performers had to hire people to write the texts down for them, and these scribes often took it upon themselves to omit elements that they thought would meet with the displeasure of the police. The texts were thus manipulated not only by the censors but also by the performers trying to meet with police approval and by the scribes who made the actual written records. In live performance, however, improvisation still took precedence over the written word.[21]

The fact of this censorship, coupled with the improvisational nature of the shows in performance, puts scholars in an awkward position. Most extant records of Guignol performances are the censored scripts given to police, together with their official comments. These scripts are therefore in no way representative of the performances themselves. Thus there are few, if any, reliable records of the dialogue of actual Guignol shows.[22] For the texts we have were not composed with the intention of conveying a true sense of what the performances would be like, nor to establish a historical legacy for Guignol. On the contrary, they were written, at least in part, to obfuscate and mislead. The personal styles and improvisation skills of the puppeteers were still the most important highlights of the performance. When the written texts were adopted as the basis for new Guignol shows, they lacked the very elements that accounted for the success of the live performances. This happened to all the Pulcinella-type puppet shows. As a result, revivals are often flat and sterile.[23]

Improvisation occupies an important place in the Italian Pulcinella tradition as well. The puppet Pulcinella, like the commedia mask and like Guignol, appeared as a player in a variety of different stories and scenarios. In hand puppet or *guaratelli* performances Pulcinella was usually the main character in the play, while in the marionette or *opera dei pupi* shows he appeared merely as comic relief. In the hand puppet shows there was on the whole much more room for improvisation since the shows themselves were less elaborate. Yet Pasquelino tells us that even in the *opera dei pupi* Pulcinella and related characters retain their street performer qualities and are interpreted through improvisation.[24] The comic scenes of the *opera dei pupi* were entirely improvised or performed from memory and could be introduced into any plot at any time. They were not subsequently written down, so it was up to the performers to invent or reinvent them afresh with each new performance. Even in the marionette theater, then, Pulcinella retained the privilege of free speech.

In contrast to the myriad plays that incorporate the characters Pulcinella and Guignol, in England the Punch and Judy show coalesced into one fairly recognizable text.[25] *The Tragical Comedy and Comical Tragedy of Punch and Judy,* before being written down in the last century, was little more than a sketchy scenario. Part of the Punchmen's job was to embellish the sketches with their own jokes and topical references. Nevertheless, some basic elements remained the same each time the play was performed. The main "plot" consisted of Punch tricking and beating a variety of characters, including Judy, their child, the Policeman, the Hangman, and the Devil, but all the performers imbued the show with their own style and added their own jokes and allusions (Speaight, *Punch and Judy* 83). Punchmen also included contemporary characters. The principal characters tended to remain the same, but additional characters drawn from public life could range "from Nelson to Winston Churchill, from Paul Pry to Hitler" (Speaight, *Punch and Judy* 91).

Robert Leach gives an example of a 1910 Punch and Judy show in which current events are given a prominent place. Since there is generally little record of what was actually said in Punch and Judy shows, this provocative sample offers a rare glimpse into what may have been standard practice in popular European puppet plays from the sixteenth to the twentieth century. It shows how a puppeteer was able to bring a political perspective to bear on the standard format of a Punch and Judy show to create a popular performance with genuinely radical import. Leach's own remarks contextualize the event and explain some of the show's implications, so it is worth quoting him together with the description of the scene itself. Leach refers to

> the detailed description of a show pitching near His Majesty's Theater in the winter of 1910–11, when England was dangerously near revolution again, with Irish republicanism, syndicalist trade unionism and the suffragette campaign all threatening the government. This show capitalized both on Sir Herbert Beerbohm Tree's notorious production of Henry VIII at the adjacent theater and the rising suffragette agitation. A bell signaled the start of this performance in a "booth that stood toweringly high," at ten o'clock in the morning. The curtain rose and Punch appeared, made some "bold personal comments" about the spectators, and vanished again. He reappeared as Henry XXVIII:
>
> It was all right, he told us, for the ordinary run of fatheads to sit through a long-winded play by tiresome William, but he had entirely rewritten Shakespeare, brought him down to date, cut out some superfluous wheezy twaddle and verbiage, and now we were going to get it, hot off the griddle: the "Merry Monarch" held a beauty show, and his eight wives were duly marshaled out and told in turn that they could vote if they wished. Seven shrewdly rejected the ballot, but the last one held out, eager to grasp it. It was poor Anne Boleyn, who longed for liberty. To the consternation of the assembled royal familey, Henry decided that the seven shrewd ones, being worthy English wives, could continue to live, but that Anne . . . must be beheaded. The executioner appeared, and was about to cut off Anne's head, when the axe slipped and striking the "Merry Monarch" in the face, decapitated him instead. (108–9)

Here one of the traditional endings of the Punch and Judy show, that in which the Hangman attempts to hang Punch but is hanged himself instead, is reversed. This time Punch is hanged instead of his suffragette wife. In this scenario, Punch becomes the authority figure and his rebellious wife represents the spirit of freedom. The text of Punch and Judy as it is generally found in written form does not and cannot represent the kind of creative reinvention of the play displayed here. It is likely that before a written version of the text existed and was widely available, this kind of personal revision of the show and its meaning was common.

The advantage that popular performances have always had over the powers they oppose lies in their ability to adapt and change on the spur of the moment. This flexibility keeps them up-to-date and relevant. It also means that they can substitute innocuous play for radical or controversial material whenever they are in danger of being shut up or shut down. Popular traditions preserve their liberty by freeing themselves from the confines of the written word. The written text preserves for posterity; the uninscribed play is ephemeral and lives only in each new moment of performance. Transforming an oral tradition into a written text is one means of controlling it, rendering it static, and ultimately silencing it as an engaged response to the world and events of the day.

The written transcription of the Punch plays marked the demise of the form's radical potential. By the late nineteenth century the violent Pulcinella figures had in effect been tamed. In England, laws regulating street vendors moved the puppet shows indoors, and Punch and Judy evolved into a parlor entertainment primarily for children. Punch had been domesticated. From now on, puppeteers underplayed his violent tendencies and inclined toward a more sentimental rendering of the characters. Leach makes clear just how drastic this change was: "the transformation of this once highly affronting, violent outdoor show was done to such an extent that in 1885 a children's book written by F. E. Weatherly, entitled *Punch and Judy and Some of Their Friends* could start with the opening sentence: 'In spite of what many people say, and in spite of what many more believe, Punch and Judy lived a very happy and peaceable life' " (87). This is an astonishing claim, considering that the plot of the plays, even then, typically included Punch throwing his baby out the window, killing his wife and a number of other people, being caught by the police and hauled off to jail, facing execution by hanging, hanging the hangman instead, and finally escaping the clutches of the devil himself. In the course of this sentimentalization, the show became more and more geared to the entertainment of children.

Speaight claims that there is evidence for this gradual change in the print record of Punch and Judy shows themselves. In early prints of street performances it seems that "his audience is composed of adults, mainly laboring class, with a few children" while in nineteenth-century prints "children outnumbered the adults and by the end of the century they practically composed the entire audience" (*Punch and Judy* 125). A predominance of children in the audience was, however, characteristic of even eighteenth-century marionette entertainment.

The demise of Guignol, too, began with the imposition of censorship, which led to the reliance on written texts, and like Punch, Guignol survived as a simple park entertainment for children. In this century, Guignol also found new life in marionette extravaganzas that emphasized special effects and mythic themes. These themes catered more to the tastes of middle-class audiences and fundamentally altered the qualities that had made it a popular entertainment in the first place. The audience therefore shifted not only from adults to children but from workers to the middle class.

Petrushka also lived on as a show for children.[26] Along with other popular entertainments, it was pushed from its home in the fairgrounds by the proliferation of technological attractions, including exhibitions of the camera obscura, "electronic roundabouts," and "vagodromes" for cars and bikes. The puppet shows also found a rival in new, extravagant, large-cast shows that sometimes involved as many as a hundred people and thirty horses in elaborate spectacles (Kelly 55).[27] In the puppet theater the individual performer was the locus of all action. The puppeteer's individual talent, ingenuity, and creativity shaped the event and carried the show. He interacted with the audience on a personal level, sharing a common experience and creating a communal bond. The technological attractions that replaced the puppets, by contrast, removed the human agent from the fairground. The only human creator was now the unseen inventor who was responsible for the wonders on display. The entertainment consisted in people interacting with machines, not with other people. Individuals lost the immediate sense of agency inherent in live performance and gave it over to machines. Of course, large-cast shows were themselves live performances, but the performers forfeited direct control over their work and personal interaction with the audience owing to the grand scale of the productions. This transformation in popular performance marked the beginning of the technological entertainments that we know today and the decline of festive-revolutionary traditions of old.

The evolution of vital popular traditions into sentimental nursery-room fare is a common pattern for these forms. Something similar happened to the character Pierrot. Once the buffoon of the French fairgrounds, he became the sorrowful, white-faced clown now pictured on greeting cards. Such changes effectively normalize popular forms, rendering them less violent, less responsive to political realities, and in the end less critical. Moreover, they cease to grow, so that the energy and vitality of the form diminishes.

But although such a state of decline might look like a direct transition from life to death, popular forms have a way of remaining true to their own inner nature by progressing cyclically from life to death—to rebirth. As with clowns, the emblematic popular figures, death for popular forms is only a pratfall from which they can always recover with renewed vigor. With Falstaff, who is after all one of their own, such popular forms can boast: "Counterfeit? I lie, I am no counterfeit: To die is to be a counterfeit, for he is but the counterfeit of a man who hath not the life of a man; but to counterfeit dying, when a man thereby liveth, is to be no counterfeit, but the true and perfect image of life indeed. The better part of valour is discretion; in the which better part I have sav'd my life" (*The First Part of Henry the Fourth* 5.4.114–21). On the one hand, the Punch/Pulcinella/Petrushka/Guignol figures have survived only in counterfeit form. On the other hand, their present incarnation as sentimentalized children's fare may make them no more a counterfeit than Falstaff himself, for they retain the mark of their origins in living popular tradition.

Early on the Mime Troupe introduced what they called the "Gutter Puppets" in a series of children's shows, including Christmas specials in which the Troupe killed off Santa Claus as part of a Marxist attack on holiday consumerism. They found they had great difficulty figuring out each year how to kill Santa without upsetting the children in the audience. Another Mime Troupe puppet project involved a show about a bookworm—literally, a worm who likes to eat books. The show played in cooperation with bookmobiles that frequented minority neighborhoods. According to Ron Davis, however, the children at the bookmobiles were apparently more interested in getting "into the action" than watching the show. "Not being able to develop a cohesive theory of community action," he reports, "we let the bookmobile go it alone after ten shows" (Davis 111).

Both projects are reminders of how the radical potential of puppets can easily be lost on children. As Scott Shershow makes clear in *Puppets and "Popular" Culture,* it is primarily in virtue of their diminutive stature that puppets have so often been associated with children. Moreover, children are quite receptive to the nineteenth-century drawing room Punch, and of course they enjoy the rowdy antics of hand puppets in general. What makes radical puppetry work, however, is the way it subverts our expectations and challenges conventional values. A genuine appreciation of radical puppetry therefore demands some prior understanding of those values and expectations, as well as an openness to criticism. And indeed, as we have seen in the case of Punch, the advent of puppetry as a children's form is a late development coinciding with the subduing of its radical potential. The Mime Troupe relearned this lesson in trying to create politically-minded puppet shows for kids. They enjoyed more success in their use of puppets in the shows they produced for adults, the audience for whom such forms were originally intended. In using puppets to address adult audiences the Mime Troupe took advantage of all the elements the tradition offers that make it advantageous to doing political theater.

But even taking Punch and airing him out, moving him back onto the city streets as the Mime Troupe did, demands that one take a closer look at the prejudices that have attached themselves to the character. The popular voice, though often speaking out against oppression, is not always the most tolerant or universal. For even a collective voice typically expresses particular interests and appeals to a particular audience.

As Catriona Kelly points out, "the fairground genres did not undermine the idea of hierarchy, they set another up in its place. It is no great political change to have a fool as king if that fool-king comports himself as despotically as the authority he has replaced" (12). The new inverted culture that emerged at carnival time thus presented a hierarchy of its own. It placed those who had power in the real world, along with the values they represented, on the bottom, and the fool-king and foolishness on top.

But Punch's stick did not just land blows on people with power. In addition to the Hangman,[28] the Policeman, and the Devil, another traditional character of the Punch and Judy play was a black character, sometimes a slave, sometimes a foreigner. As a foreigner, the character could only say "Shallaballa," probably meant to be a parody of some African language. Punch would beat him mercilessly as well. After the American minstrel shows came to England, this character took on the clownish features of the black minstrel and also became known as Jim Crow (Speaight, *Punch and Judy* 87). The treatment of blacks in the Punch and Judy show therefore played into already prevalent prejudices against blacks.

Jews also became the victims of Pulcinella. In many ways popular culture set itself against the authority of the church, but religious ritual also became an occasion for popular celebration. Jews were excluded from this sphere of popular culture as well as from the elite culture associated with the church. Prejudice against the Jews was thus a common element at all levels of society. Michael Byrom tells us that "the Jews were given a hard time by the Italians, having been enclosed in ghettos following the papal bull of 1555." Jews suffered at the hands of the people and the church: "At carnival time in Rome, they were rolled in barrels, forced to run races naked, and subjected to other unspeakable indignities. The many Jew farces (*giudate*), which very often include Pulcinella, were the least bad things that could happen to them" (15). Speaight shows that the same anti-Semitism existed in the English puppet theater. Not only did Jewish characters figure as Punch's victims but the Punchmen even bragged that no Jews had ever been in the business (*Punch and Judy* 113). A Jewish character was also a traditional victim in the Petrushka plays (Kelly 75, 100, 124).

Needless to say, the representation of women in Punch and Judy is problematic for contemporary feminists. Punch's wife is depicted as a shrew. Punch beats and kills her. Judy does get to fight back, but she is not generally meant to enjoy our sympathy. She acts as an agent of oppression who threatens Punch's freedom. Other women also occasionally appear in the show as objects of Punch's lust. This same representation of women is also found in the Pulcinella and Petrushka plays. Such prejudices against women, blacks, and Jews are certainly a cause for concern.

In one of the traditional scenes in the English Punch and Judy play, Punch tosses his own child out the window. This blatantly immoral behavior could be disturbing. Even contemporary audiences who might be sympathetic to Punch's radical anarchist message would hardly condone wife beating or child abuse. This is not to say that audiences would take these events in utter seriousness. Yet the images of women in these puppet shows, like those of blacks and Jews, could be said to perpetuate rather than combat their oppression.[29] In the past, Punch represented the lowly peasant battling against power and authority. As a white European male character, however, he can no longer easily claim to represent today's underprivileged or disempowered groups. We must ask, then, whether Punch can still be used as a model of liberation today as he has been in the past.

Perhaps the greatest cause for concern is the general tendency of a form like Punch simply to reinforce prejudice. If there are great advantages in allowing a marginalized voice to be heard in a context of oppression, there is also a danger in simply reasserting antagonisms and promoting prejudice. Punch's violence can in principle be turned in almost any direction, so it is crucial to understand who he is in order to know how to use him well.

It is not only Punch's prejudices that theater practitioners need to analyze when updating him but also his taste for violent retaliation against his enemies. Punch's anarchic nature once again brings to the fore the disturbing tendencies that underlie a number of popular forms and that owe much to the festive-revolutionary tradition from which they descend. The beatings in Pulcinella plays confront us as concrete images of oppression, but the often mindless violence of the show remains problematic. On the one hand, violence enhances the revolutionary potential of the form. Violence puts the puppets on the border between play and serious action. In recent decades, however, social activists have turned more and more to nonviolence as a vehicle of social change. This is especially true of the Mime Troupe itself. The idea of passive resistance and the belief that in a democratic society revolutionary change can take place within existing social structures both call into question the justification and efficacy of violence in political action. From these perspectives, violence appears to be more of a source of social problems than a means to their solution. The debate concerning both the morality and the strategic usefulness of violence preoccupied such leaders as Martin Luther King Jr. and Malcolm X and continues in radical circles today. Whatever side of the debate one takes, using Punch in political theater requires that we confront his violent nature and somehow deal with it explicitly.

James Twitchell suggests that violent entertainments have evolved primarily to appeal to male adolescents. Technological popular culture, or "junk" culture, as he calls it, is for him a contemporary version of violent entertainments like Punch and Judy that have always existed to cater to the fantasy life of adolescents.[30] Interestingly, Kelly reports that the audiences at Petrushka shows were predominantly male and that at the fairgrounds "gender division, rather than regional or educational differences" figured prominently (39).

The Punch tradition could be problematic for contemporary feminists, minority activists, pacifists, and indeed anyone who sees how Punch's characteristic features can turn in anarchic, reactionary, or even fascist directions. One would not want to lose the true impact of Punch by sanitizing him and asking him to live up to some pristine moral code, as the nineteenth-century drawing room version did. Indeed, Punch is useful and exciting to us precisely for his anarchic, antisocial tendencies. However, theater practitioners who want to be in control of the social or political message they put forth should be aware of the prejudicial attitudes embedded in the theatrical forms they take up so that they can shape them to their own advantage.

So the question remains whether theater groups today can use the Punch tradition to voice a progressive cause, and if so how. Leach's example of the 1910 spoof on *Henry VIII* shows that the Punch play itself can be turned around. The Punchman here sides with the suffragettes. He uses the same metaphors of violence and oppression, the same Punch character, and the same basic elements of the Punch show, yet he makes the suffragette the victor and Punch the vanquished. Although the Punch tradition can be a powerful tool in speaking out against oppression, theater practitioners need to be aware of the pitfalls the form holds in terms of its depiction of race and gender and its use of violence. Personal creativity can then transform the powerful metaphors at work in the play to address contemporary political concerns.

When the San Francisco Mime Troupe used Punch in *L'Amant Militaire* their 1967 adaptation of a commedia piece by Goldoni, they exploited Punch's anarchic tendencies to convey their own radical message. They did not confront Punch's racism or sexism but instead used his violent tendencies to call into question the viability of pacifism. Here, as in *Meter Maid,* the Troupe used Punch in conjunction with live actors. The contrast between the human figure and the puppet allowed Punch to be more radical than ever.

The Troupe used *L'Amant Militaire* as a means of voicing their opposition to the Vietnam War. The plot of the play centers on a war between Italy and Spain that the military and big business have perpetrated together for their own gains. Pantalone, an Italian businessman, wants to keep the war going because he is profiting off arms sales and other forms of trade that support the military. Garcia, a Spanish general, is preoccupied with the prospects of glory and victory. These characters and others in the play are based on traditional commedia characters. Pantalone is the miserly old man, while Garcia fits the type of Capitano, the braggart soldier. The cast also includes Rosalinda, Pantalone's daughter, who is in love with the Spanish soldier, Alonso; Corallina, Rosalinda's maid; and Arlecchino, Corallina's lover.

The stage is thus set for a traditional commedia, fueled by love and intrigue and full of deceptions and comic turns. The Mime Troupe, however, chose to emphasize the war issues rather than the love plot. They used topical allusions to reinforce the associations with the war in Vietnam. But the play moves beyond a simple antiwar message "to expose a pacifist's impotence" (Davis 86). When Rosalinda finds out that her lover is going off to war and may be killed, she decides that the war is wrong and becomes a pacifist. Her plan of action consists in "Words! Speeches, books, articles, leaflets, petitions! We will speak to them, we will speak to them, Corallina, and the sweet voice of reason will silence the thunder of battle" (Davis 185).

Simply speaking out, however, turns out to be of no help in stopping the war. The General is not convinced by Rosalinda's pleas and turns all her declamations against her. When she argues that "it's especially unjust for a large and powerful country to impose its will on a country that is small and defenseless," Garcia agrees and replies, "That is why the countries that my country takes over are usually small and defenseless ones" (189). Garcia reveals the futility of Rosalinda's entire approach when he says: "Freedom of speech is our most valued principle—nay, our most vital domestic policy. Whenever foreign leaders ask me how our country avoids revolution, I tell them that we have—freedom of speech!" (188). Not only is just "speaking out" futile in the face of brute force, it can even keep people from taking more direct and radical action. Those in power can easily ignore mere speech. Speaking freely gives one a feeling of having taken a stand, but in fact it may do little by way of changing events, or even opinions. Rosalinda is dealing with a cynical general who is not afraid of force and violence and who is unmoved by her words.

Corallina prefers a more radical approach than her mistress. She suggests luring the General into the house, and then—"I chop him up in little pieces, and I kill him!" (185). Corallina's plan is violent, but it is also buffoonish. Punch brings a more serious radical perspective to the play. In his own puppet booth at the side of the stage, apart from the action, Punch provides commentary on the play. His function is, as Ron Davis says, to "give the audience direct actional information, i.e., come out and precisely say what the stage action only implied" (Davis 82). Punch's penchant for violence gets to the heart of the matter: "You know the war is just a little bit tougher than this clown show. Why, if we really wanted to do something about it we might drive on over to our local gun shop . . . pick up a mortar . . . drive on over to Port Chicago . . . set up the mortar in the backyard of a nice little house, barbecue a few ribs, open a couple of beers, lob a mortar over into a napalm depot and BLO-O-O-M—*enlightened democracy.* Bye-bye. I'm leaving for some country with a good puppet government. [*exit*]" (190). The violence Punch proposes is directed not at fictional characters in the play but at real targets out in the real world. He suggests actually sabotaging the American war effort by destroying its capacity to wage war. In stating his views, Punch confronts the pacifist tactics to which antiwar protesters customarily turn. His words are couched in comic dialogue, yet his intentions are serious. The words "mortar" and "napalm" introduce a realism into the play that "chop him up into little bits" does not. Corallina's violence comes off as comic; Punch's comes off as threatening and dangerous.

L'Amant Militaire highlights the contrast between the moral limitations imposed on actors and the freedom afforded puppets. Punch is set in juxtaposition not only to Corallina but also to Arlecchino, another clownish character. A subplot of the play revolves around Arlecchino's being tricked into joining the army. He is told that by doing army service he will become rich. When he realizes that he might also get killed, he decides to leave the army, but it is too late for that. He ends up running away, dressed as a woman, and is hunted down by the recruiting officers.

This subplot offers a comic perspective on army recruiting, and in the

13. The final scene of *L'Amant Militaire* (1967). Corallina (Sandra Archer) as Da Pope sets everything straight. *Left to right, in the foreground:* Corporal Espada (Kent Minault), Generale Garcia (R. G. Davis), and Sergeant Brighella (Jason Marc-Alexander). Photograph by Gerhard E. Gscheidle.

process it instructs audiences in the grim realities of war. Punch, however, only laughs at Arlecchino's plight: "Dig it: the system forcing that poor slob into the army—hah! What a cop out—hey who puts this show on, the communist party? Listen—nobody *has* to go into the army. There are lots of ways to get out. You blow up the draft boards, commit a crime, go to jail, pour blood on the records, stay in school for twenty-seven years—or you can psych out" (184). Punch takes the deceptions of the army for granted and prefers to educate people about how to take action against them. Although Punch does not use any actual physical violence in the play, the tactics he suggests are aggressive and straightforward. Arlecchino's tactics for evading the army, by contrast, are deceptive and comical.

At the end of the play it is Corallina, the maid, who finally takes decisive action against the war. Dressed as the pope, she declares peace. She also decrees that Rosalinda and Alonso will be married, thereby resolving all the romantic conflicts in the plot. Her final statement encapsulates the play's message: "Listen, my friends—you want something done? Well, then, do it yourselves!" (193) The point is that people should get involved and take action to change the world. The play questions the efficacy of nonviolence, yet does not simply advocate violence; indeed the Mime Troupe's own tactics are more like Rosalinda's than Punch's. The Troupe attempts to educate people and force them to question their assumptions. Punch occupies a unique position in being outside both the world of the play and the real world. He is not bound by the constraints of society and can therefore suggest what might be unthinkable for others. His suggestions, while not necessarily providing a viable solution, articulate the radical stance of the show itself. Punch's violent nature thus became essential to his presence in the production. Making Punch himself a pacifist would have reduced him to the sentimental counterfeit of the nineteenth-century drawing room. But his violence is useful, given the needs of the show, bringing an outside perspective to bear on the action of the play and providing an interesting counterpoint to, and indeed critique of, the Mime Troupe's own political standpoint.

But the Mime Troupe has also used other hand puppets besides Punch to convey their revolutionary message. In a short, radical puppet show called *Little Black Panther,* for example, the lead character is just about to be hit by a policeman when he is saved by a bigger panther. The big panther advises the little one that although violence can be a useful form of protest, it must be organized in order to be effective. Once again, the Troupe exploits the violent propensities of the hand puppet, which become the central focus of the play. While a traditional Punch may be racist, sexist, and anti-Semitic, other puppets have taken on his qualities to represent the struggle for civil rights.

Both *Little Black Panther* and *L'Amant Militaire* replace the random violence characteristic of the traditional Punch with the idea of organized resistance. The old Punch had no specific plan or goal. He simply lashed out against his oppressors as they came along. The black panther puppet points up the need for organization and reasoned strategy in achieving specific objectives. The Mime Troupe has updated and reshaped these puppets. Their actions are guided by a self-conscious political agenda. Hand puppets have always spoken for the people, but in the Mime Troupe shows they become the voice of a unified and organized people, articulating a plan of action with definite ends. While their intentions remain essentially the same, namely to battle oppression, their political consciousness is more highly developed. The Mime Troupe takes up the general spirit of the popular puppet heroes and harnesses it to concrete causes. In so doing, they keep the vitality of the popular tradition alive while at once carving out a political position of immediate contemporary relevance.

The Mime Troupe thus turned Punch's violent nature from a potential handicap into a political asset. They did not, however, deal with the racism and sexism inherent in the form. In the next chapter I will explore some instances in which the Troupe has used racist and sexist stereotypes embedded in popular forms precisely for the purpose of exploring issues of race and gender. In these instances the forms they drew on derived from American popular traditions more immediately relevant to contemporary political life than the European forms they had used in the past.

Minstrel Shows and the Play of Stereotypes

The audience members in San Francisco's cavernous Herbst Theater rustle and whisper, waiting for the show to begin. This afternoon performance, however, commences not with the usual dimming of lights and raising of curtains but with some sort of backstage argument that the audience can't help but overhear. The noise of angry voices rises until three black actors dressed in nineteenth-century costumes enter, dragging behind them a white woman in a large hoop skirt. They try to get her to sit down in the chair at the center of the otherwise bare stage.

Harriet: What am I accused of?
George: Shut up and we'll read the charges. Sit down!
Eliza: Don't hurt her.
Topsy: Missy is accused of creatin' stereotypes—
Harriet: I did no such—

The white woman pleads her innocence in vain as the accusations mount against her:

George: We've been stuck with these stupid bug-eyed images you made up for us a hundred and fifty years!
Harriet: I did my research . . . I visited plantations. I met dozens of girls like Topsy. I did not make you up!
Topsy: But all I did was dance in your novel!
Harriet: Dancing is wonderful, especially the way you dance. If I could dance like you, Topsy, I would dance all the time.

The dispute between Harriet, failing to comprehend the anger she has aroused, and the characters who accuse her, seems unresolvable. This ad hoc court is clearly on its way to convicting Harriet when sounds from the back of the auditorium seize the audience's attention.

A tall, stooped black man in ratty jacket and pants has just entered. He shuffles slowly toward the stage, excusing himself as he moves through the audience. A big, silly grin on his face, he makes kindly remarks to individual audience members and occasionally dusts their theater seats with his handkerchief. He punctuates his ad-libbed lines generously with hearty "yes-suhs." The audience laughs. They clearly enjoy being included in the show, and they are grateful for the comic relief his presence brings, temporarily drawing attention away from the argument on stage.

The shuffling figure finally makes his way onto the stage, mopping his sweaty brow with his colorful handkerchief. The peaceful interlude comes to an end as he now becomes the target of anger and accusations:

George: Get him out of here Harriet!

. . . .

Eliza: Nobody wants to see you. We're just trying to get on with our new lives. George is an executive now—with Clorox!

Harriet, by contrast, greets the new arrival warmly, confident that he has come to help her plead her case:

Harriet: There seems to be some confusion as to who's on trial here. I'm glad you've come back, Uncle Tom. I know you'll defend me. Tell them how my book helped emancipate your race.

But instead of chiming in with his support, Uncle Tom undergoes an unexpected transformation. First, he slowly uncurves his spine; his servile demeanor drops away as he stands up straight and tall. From his full height, powerful and imposing, he looks Harriet directly in the eye. In a voice surprisingly deep and full of self-confidence, he says, "Let's get a few things straight, Ms. Stowe. First of all, I ain't yo' uncle!" (Alexander 7–8).

In this defining moment from *I Ain't Yo' Uncle: A New Jack Revisionist Uncle Tom's Cabin,* the actor playing Uncle Tom first enacts and then shatters the safe, familiar image of Harriet Beecher Stowe's Uncle Tom, the character his audience will have known since childhood. In so doing, he at once replaces that familiar type with a new, forceful, self-determining figure. The transformation of Uncle Tom is just one of the many dismantlings of Stowe's well-worn characters that takes place in this play written by Robert Alexander and originally coproduced by the San Francisco Mime Troupe and San Francisco's Lorraine Hansberry Theatre with a

14. The cast of *Uncle Tom's Cabin,* an early version of *I Ain't Yo' Uncle. Left to right:* Uncle Tom (Lonnie Ford), Simon Legree (Jim Griffiths), George (Richard Harder), Topsy (Edris Cooper), and, in front, Harriet Beecher Stowe (Andrea Snow).

Mime Troupe director, dramaturg, and many Mime Troupe members in its cast. Eventually, at Tom's instigation, the other characters resolve the argument that commenced the show by agreeing to act out the story of *Uncle Tom's Cabin* only on the condition that they be allowed to change their characters, actions, and fates whenever they deem appropriate. As they see it, Stowe's text, which rose to prominence in the antebellum period—indeed galvanizing the abolitionists—and which has since become an American literary classic, did not tell their characters' true story, but instead promoted stereotypes and related their history from a white outsider's point of view.

The perpetuation of stereotypes has undoubtedly heightened the racial tension that has marked America since the days of slavery. It is fitting, then, for a socially and politically engaged theater group to take on the task of deconstructing stereotypes within their productions as a way of thematizing racism and racial division. But the construction and dissemination of stereotypes within a theatrical context also raises pressing questions for the consideration of the social and political import of popular forms.

All popular forms rely heavily on easily recognizable, stock characters appearing over and over again in different contexts. These characters make shows easily accessible to large, diverse audiences. They embody simplified emotional and psychological traits and perform very clear actions, often outdoors, before audiences who may choose to come and go during the course of the performance. In their very simplicity, however, these characters also appeal to popular prejudices. The stereotypes prevalent in popular forms are almost always comic caricatures. As the case of Punch shows, comic caricatures can in some circumstances serve as empowering models: Punch, a silly country bumpkin, is also an irrepressible rogue. He offers an empowering image of a lower-class protagonist combating figures of authority. Different versions of this character resonated with a variety of audiences for many years in a number of different countries. Of course, the stereotypes of blacks, Jews, and women that were also typical of the Punch plays were anything but empowering for those groups and seemed instead to perpetuate prejudice. The characters in *I Ain't Yo' Uncle* are themselves making the same point about their own depiction in Stowe's original text.

Considering the danger and the hurtfulness of such negative stereotypes, what possible political advantages could they offer to theaters committed to positive social change? Can such negative images be enlisted for the purposes of genuinely progressive political theater? What is the difference between the positive and the negative deployment and reception of stereotyped images such as those in *Uncle Tom's Cabin* or the Punch plays? In short, how can progressive, popular theaters balance the distinct advantages of easily recognizable types on the one hand with the danger of merely perpetuating prejudices on the other? How can politically-minded companies avoid undermining the progressive message such forms are meant to serve?

The San Francisco Mime Troupe plays with stereotyped characters in nearly all their work. The actors typically perform their characters in an exaggerated, comic style that makes the stereotype itself laughable, even

15. Tami (Sigrid Wurschmidt) says, "This definitely is your picture" to David Goldberg (Michael Sullivan), an American Jew who is mistaken for Salim, an American of Palestinian descent (played by the same actor), in *Seeing Double* (1989), a Middle Eastern Comedy of Errors. Ami (Ed Holmes) looks on gleefully. Photograph by Cristina Taccone.

when the character is drawn sympathetically. In most of their productions every actor will play a number of different roles, each defined and made recognizable for the audience by an appropriate wig or costume and highly stylized movement. No actor fully identifies with any single character. In fact, in *Seeing Double,* a play that dealt with the Israeli-Palestinian conflict, the Mime Troupe availed itself of an old theatrical device perfected by Goldoni and his performers and had a single actor playing two identical-looking characters who, through a series of mishaps, get mistaken for each other.[1] This play set the cultural and political divisions between the Israelis and the Palestinians in sharp contrast to the conspicuous similarity of the Jewish-American and Palestinian-American characters played by one and the same actor. At the end of the play, the two nearly indistinguishable characters are both victims of an accidental Israeli bombing of a Palestinian home. One is killed, the other wounded. (The explosion scene is played with two large, Bunraku-style puppets.) The intertwined fates of the two characters highlight the common ground of humanity that unites the two groups on either side of the larger conflict.

Seeing Double reveals the differences between the Israelis and the Palestinians through the costumes, the beards, and the wigs they wear. These outfits represent the stereotypical ways in which such cultural groups identify themselves and each other. They are also theatrical devices that signal their respective allegiances. Such highly stylized costumes draw attention to the constructed nature of identity and prejudice. Yet the actor's own identity is never fully obliterated within the production. The play of identity and difference in *Seeing Double* relies on the fact that the audience knows throughout the piece that one actor is playing both roles. The piece continually highlights the actor's skill in portraying two distinct, though to the eyes of the others on stage nearly indistinguishable, characters. One of the most memorable scenes from the 1989 production of *Seeing Double* involves a chase. Michael Sullivan, the African-American actor who plays both Salim Razali and David Goldberg, emerges from behind the backdrop curtain, first as one character. He then runs behind the drop and, followed by the character chasing him, emerges again, almost instantaneously, as the other character. This quick-change feat continues over and over, picking up momentum with each go-round. The bit reaches a climax of sustained action and the audience cheers the display of theatrical virtuosity.

The actor's own identity comes into play even more overtly in productions that deal in depth with issues of race. In such productions, an actor who puts on a theatrical mask that refers to a specific racial group, whether her own or not, is already engaging in a political and social dialogue on race and representation. Of course, whether comically or in an exaggerated or stylized way, assuming the appearance of any distinct ethnic or social group is at heart a dangerous practice that risks offending someone. In many cases, as in the portrayal of an unsympathetic political figure, the attack is fully intended.[2] However, when lampoon is not the desired effect, the use of stereotyping or exaggeration of portrayal may undermine a work's other political aims—that is, unless the piece also addresses the construction of the racial images it presents.

In 1964 the Mime Troupe's production of *The Minstrel Show, or Civil Rights in a Cracker Barrel* made use of blackface minstrelsy as a way of dealing with the issues of segregation, institutionalized racism, and racial injustice, which the civil rights movement was then bringing to national attention. The choice was a bold one and not only influenced the costuming of the performers but also defined the entire production and how it presented and questioned racial identity in America.

Racial stereotypes were central to the old-time minstrel shows, in which white men dressed up in blackface and fright wigs and performed clownish interpretations of blacks. In their *Minstrel Show* the Troupe made no attempt to deny or downplay the negative racial images featured in traditional minstrel shows. Instead, they turned to the form as a means of confronting contemporary problems in race relations. An understanding of the way the Mime Troupe transformed this theatrical tradition can shed light on how otherwise negative stereotypes can work in the service of theater devoted to positive social change, that is, in the case of a theater that maintains a popular aesthetic. This example can be considered in contrast to other more postmodern attempts at deconstructing stereotypes, like that of the Wooster Group.

Much is to be gained by examining the role of racial stereotypes in the historical minstrel show, nineteenth-century America's most popular theater form. The minstrel show form confirms the fact that while class issues most often fueled the popular theater traditions of Europe, in antebellum America race (literally) took center stage. The problems inherent in the use of racial stereotypes are even greater when the designated racial group has undergone the kind of oppression Africans and African Americans suffered under the institution of slavery. Looking at the use of stereotypes in such a highly charged context, then, gives us insight into the advantages and dangers of using stereotypes in general.

Gaining an understanding of the possibilities of resilience and resistance in the face of oppression is an important first step in appreciating the value the black minstrel clown image may have had for black performers in the period in which it originated. The success of any struggle against oppression requires countless social and economic forces to conspire in the empowerment of those who lack power. In spite of extreme social injustice and the desire for freedom it inspires, true resistance to oppression in the form of revolution or rebellion is, more often than not, nearly impossible. In such circumstances, oppressed groups, like the black slaves and former slaves in nineteenth-century America, may adopt various strategies that allow them to cope with their situation and not be completely consumed by it. In a context in which they are systematically denied all means of self-expression and self-definition, they may yet find ways of carving out an identity for themselves. In so doing, they maintain a sense of control over themselves and their destinies.

As we shall see, the stereotype of the minstrel clown may have emerged out of such a strategy. Interacting with their white masters in the institutional context of slavery, blacks were perhaps as much responsible for creating the image, adopting it as a means of resistance, as whites were in subsequently re-presenting it to white audiences. Strategies of resilience rather than direct confrontation are often the only reasonable options open to oppressed groups. They are also often just the first steps in setting the stage for genuine resistance in the future.

It may be impossible to determine who is in control of the presentation and reception of a given stereotype in any given moment of performance. However, the question is crucial for coming to a deeper understanding of the appropriation of stereotypes for political theater. The notion that a performance (perhaps one with a "message") comes directly from the actors on stage to the audience receiving it beyond the footlights is simplistic at best. It fails to take into account the multivalent nature of performance. Performance events are multifaceted interactions that involve continually changing dialogues, interpretations, and negotiations among a whole host of people: creative artists, producers, and audience members, to name just a few. The "message" a theater artist may wish to convey to an audience is shaped by many factors, including the time frame of the performance, the venue and time of day of the presentation, the advertising techniques employed to publicize the show, the desires or whims of the producers, directors, actors, and designers, and both the cultural background and the immediate environment of the audience that comes to the show. It is therefore almost impossible to single out any one group that could be said to be in control of the interpretation at any given moment. Yet the multifaceted nature of interpretation within performance can allow for the re-formation of preconceived ideas. It can also provide an opportunity for acts of resistance on the part of ordinarily disempowered groups in institutional settings structured by otherwise well-defined power relations.

In a theatrical context someone playing a role, or watching or organizing a performance, can directly determine the positive or negative meaning a given stereotype takes on. In the late nineteenth and early twentieth centuries the minstrel clown character performed both by whites and by blacks became a site of struggle for control over the representation of blacks, both in America and abroad. Who was in control of the minstrel stereotype at a given moment could determine whether it had an empowering or a vilifying force. Though prior to the civil rights movement of the 1950s and '60s blacks in America were systematically denied equal legal status in society, racist institutions themselves internalized a dialectical relationship between blacks and whites that defined and affected the meaning of black stereotypes. While, of course, control lay mostly in the hands of whites, blacks could at times take control of the stereotype and speak through it.

The black minstrel character has qualities similar to many of the other clown characters discussed in chapter 1, such as circus clowns and commedia *zanni.* These clowns all wear comic, exaggerated clothes and makeup (or masks.) They are simpletons, yet they are full of verbal wit and playful cleverness. However, the limitations that the minstrel role imposed on both the theatrical and nontheatrical lives of black entertainers points up a deep difference between the minstrel clown and these other clown figures. For the minstrel clown designated a group that was not only politically, socially, and economically oppressed, but one that was racially defined in a society constructed by racism, and in which race and class were (and are) inextricably linked.

The differences in social context within which such clowns performed also distinguishes the black minstrel clown from earlier European clowns. European clowns were supported by a large popular audience who identified with them and their alternative popular culture, a culture that not only persisted in the face of oppression but may well have existed prior to the elite culture that sought to dominate it. In the social context of the minstrel show, however, the minstrel clown represented a minority population that did not necessarily support or even attend minstrel performances. The minstrel show was indeed "popular" entertainment, but its audience was mostly white, and consequently not on the same social footing as the black minstrels themselves. European popular forms offered lower-class performers a means of lampooning and criticizing the elite culture that dominated them. American popular forms, by contrast, offered common Americans a way of doing the same not only to Europeans, who they regarded as elitist, but also to blacks, who occupied a socially inferior position. While it is certain that, like other clown characters, the minstrel clown could be used to subvert the status quo, the historical context of its development put strict limits on how effective that subversion could be.

The targeting of a racially specific and disadvantaged group is what makes the minstrel clown so insidious and dangerous. For, more than other clown figures, the minstrel clown is attached to a whole community of people outside of the theatrical arena. White audiences associated the image of blacks onstage with the entire population of blacks offstage. The conflation of the images of blacks onstage and off clearly served to confine them in the wider social arena by manipulating their image in the theatrical arena. One can surmise, then, that the subversion of the image onstage might have profound consequences for the realities offstage. The possibility that such a subversion could take place only became apparent when blacks took over the minstrel roles and began playing the stereotype themselves. That appropriation of the roles was therefore an important step in the eventual destruction of the stereotypes. By taking control of the stereotypes themselves, blacks could not only begin to subvert those images, they could begin to redefine them.

From its beginnings in the 1840s, the minstrel show drew on and helped to fashion a stereotype of blacks that would infiltrate all aspects of American culture. This stereotype persisted in the minds of Americans at least until the civil rights movement of the 1950s and '60s. While minstrel shows addressed a variety of subjects, the minstrels' predecessors, the "Ethiopian Delineators," claimed to be portraying blacks "as they truly are," and this remained the central focus of the show. The exhibition of black stereotypes was more than just a vehicle for jokes and variety acts; it was, to some extent, the show's driving purpose.

Of course, the minstrel clown was not the only black stereotype that thrived in the United States. Donald Bogle distinguishes a variety of character types that America's theatrical world imposed on blacks: "After the tom's debut, there appeared a variety of black presences bearing the fanciful names of the coon, the tragic mulatto, the mammy, and the brutal buck. All were character types used for the same effect: to entertain by stressing Negro inferiority. Fun was poked at the American Negro by presenting him as either a nitwit or childlike lackey" (4). The stereotype of African Americans specific to the minstrel show is what Joseph Boskin simply calls "Sambo." This particular type represented blacks as clowns. White minstrel performers blackened their faces with cork and exaggerated their lips and eyes with white makeup to create a comic mask that caricatured black features. The clownish figure was filled out with wild fright wigs and tattered, mismatched, or excessively dandyish clothes. The minstrel's speech was also comic, with an exaggerated black dialect and incorporating an endless barrage of puns and malapropisms.

The standard minstrel show was divided into three parts, each featuring a different form of entertainment, each promoting a different aspect of the black stereotype. The first part of the minstrel show consisted of rapid-fire jokes. These exchanges took place either between two of the endmen[3] or between one of the endmen and the Interlocutor, who would sit between them, wearing whiteface or no makeup at all. He played the straight man to the minstrels' comic characters and represented the voice of reason in the midst of foolishness. Here is a typical example of the kind of rapid-fire exchange between the Interlocutor and one of the endmen, here called "Gimme":

Gimme: I done live with de Indians up there for a long time.
Interlocutor: I have heard from various sources that some of the Indians up there consider dog meat a delicacy. Did you ever taste any dog-feast stew?
Gimme: Twice, Mr. Interlocutor, twice. Once when it went down, and once when it come up. Last time I went huntin' up there I shot mah dog.
Interlocutor: You shot your dog? Was it mad?
Gimme: Well, he weren't 'zactly mad, but he weren't 'zactly pleased either.
Interlocutor: What did you hunt mostly up there?
Gimme: My way back to camp.
Interlocutor: I mean, did you ever go on a deer hunt?
Gimme: I never went on one dat was cheap. (Kaser 42–43)

The Interlocutor also corrected and restated the minstrel's comic responses. For example:

Gimme: I sho' got a wonderful job now.
Interlocutor: And what is this wonderful job you have?
Gimme: I's runnin' a inflamation brewery.
Interlocutor: Now what in the world is a inflamation brewery?

Gimme: You know, somebody wants to know somethin,' an' I tells 'em.
Interlocutor: Oh, you mean an information bureau! (38)

The first part of the minstrel show cast the blackface minstrels as clowns alongside the whiteface Interlocutor who acted as straight man and the voice of authority. This arrangement enforced a hierarchy in which black features, comic foolishness, and inferiority stood in opposition to white features, high status, and reason. The hierarchy reflects the relative status and power of blacks and whites in society at large.

And yet the comic setup works to the advantage of the clown, who gets all the best lines and all the laughs. The role of straight man, by contrast, is and has always been a fairly thankless one. Though the clown character is of low social status, carnivalesque reversals place him at the top of the comic hierarchy. The comic situation gives foolishness and irrationality a claim to wisdom and common sense. Conversely, though the clowns' jokes often would get the better of the Interlocutor, the Interlocutor, acting as master of ceremonies, remained the linchpin of the show, maintaining order and representing reason. From the very beginning, the black stereotype occupied an ambiguous position, winning favor through comic irreverence on the one hand, yet becoming the butt of the joke as a deviant or a simpleton on the other.

The second part of the minstrel show, the "olio" section, consisted of songs and novelty acts including dances, acrobatics, and the playing of water glasses. This portion of the show reinforced other aspects of the stereotype by portraying blacks as natural singers, dancers, and entertainers. Yet this image, too, turned out to be a double-edged sword. The songs and dances featured in minstrel shows were meant to represent something unique to black culture. White performers stressed the exotic and the grotesque in their acts, always depicting blacks as "other." The culture that Africans had brought with them to America was thus reduced to an exotic entertainment, rendering it less threatening to whites. The audience response to the minstrel shows consisted in both a praise for white performers along with an objectification of black culture. At the same time, blacks who performed in these shows, though they won great acclaim for their talents, were at once objectified by the prejudiced notion that singing and dancing were somehow innate capacities rather than acquired skills.

The stereotype of blacks as natural entertainers may have been appealing to whites because it seemed to replicate the social hierarchy. The relationship between audience and entertainer in some ways mimics that between master and slave: the entertainer is in a subordinate position, is at the audience's disposal, and is there to satisfy them. Black entertainment for white audiences therefore fit neatly into the social structures already in place.

The final section of the minstrel show was a one-act skit with a loose storyline that usually served as an excuse to make jokes about current events and to parody popular plays. These skits were often set on a plantation and, like many of the jokes and songs of the minstrel shows, painted a nostalgic picture of plantation life, depicting slaves as happy children in the family of a magnanimous master. Stephen Foster's "Old Folks at Home" (1851), for example, which was often used in minstrel shows, embodied this image. A minstrel, presumably playing an ex-slave, sings:

All up and down de whole creation, Sadly I roam
Still longing for de old plantation, And for de old folks at home.
Refrain: All de world is sad and dreary, Ev'rywhere I roam
Oh! darkies, how my heart grows weary, Far from de Old Folks at Home.
(Hardey 92)

In another Foster classic, "My Old Kentucky Home" (1853), a minstrel sings:

The sun shines bright in the old Kentucky home, 'Tis summer, the darkies are gay;
The corn tops ripe and the meadow's in the bloom, While the birds make music all the day.
(93)

In this song plantation life is bucolic, the slaves are "gay," and everything is in bloom. It mentions "hard times" that come only when "the darkies have to part." The depiction of plantation life as joyful and peaceful rounded out the black stereotype with the implication that blacks were simple people, suited to plantation life and happy in their lot as slaves. Another common theme of jokes and skits in minstrel shows, almost a corollary of the first, further reinforced this idea. This one described blacks in the big cities of the North, on their own and out of place once confronted with their own freedom and with the industrial hustle of urban life, implying that they were more suited to plantation life than they were to life in the city.[4]

The minstrel show is a complex phenomenon. Beginning as a comic portrayal of blacks by white Americans, it became the first indigenous American theater form and one of the most popular forms of entertainment of its day.[5] Robert C. Toll attributes much of the success of the minstrel show to the way it helped alleviate the fears and anxieties whites faced both in regard to the institution of slavery and concerning their own identity as Americans:

> Whites wanted this great distinction between blacks and whites clearly drawn, so minstrels consistently emphasized the "oddities, peculiarities, eccentricities, and comicalities of that Sable Genius of Humanity." Everything about minstrel caricatures of Negroes—their grotesque looks, their silly dialects, their strange behavior, their incredible stupidity, and their unusual music and dance—made blacks something to feel superior to and to laugh at. The minstrel show offered no heroic white characters as popular plays and books did, but its stereotyped blacks provided even more certain assurances of white common people's status and identity. (*On with the Show* 99)

Before the Civil War, white Americans needed to be reassured about the moral correctness of slavery. They also needed to be reassured about an American identity that was so vulnerable to doubt and ridicule when set in contrast to the centuries-old cultural traditions of Europe. The early minstrel shows helped white Americans find and articulate that identity. The minstrel shows served in this capacity for northerners even more so than for southerners, for northerners on the whole had much less contact with blacks and the minstrel show helped calm their more abstract fears of blacks and assured them that plantation life, much less familiar to them, was indeed congenial to slaves. In the idyllic image of happy slaves, whites projected their own romantic longing for a return to nature as territorial expansion and industrialization swept over them and changed the face of the country.

According to Joseph Boskin, however, all this tells only half the story of where the minstrel show stereotype came from and why it persisted. Boskin suggests that the origins of the different facets of the "Sambo" stereotype developed not solely in the minds of whites but through a dialectical process between blacks and whites relating to each other through the institution of slavery. Boskin's compelling argument stresses that the stereotype developed partly as a coping strategy, a response by blacks to their oppressive situation as they tried both to retain some control over that situation and to conform to the expectations whites had of them: "Whites were in the dominant position of setting the parameters of the exchanges, but blacks were able to develop a repertoire of retaliatory humor to partially offset their situation. Thus, humor lessened the chance of further violence in a system already determined by violence" (58). In accounting for the rise and persistence of the image of blacks as clowns, Boskin cites many examples of how the humor slaves found in acting foolishly or stupidly would often save them from beatings, win them favor, or even benefit them materially. A submissive rather than an aggressive stance often worked to the slave's advantage in defusing tension and anger directed at them. This was an attitude welcomed by the white slave owners, who preferred to think of their slaves as docile children. The foolish character became a useful mask that allowed slaves to take liberties and protect themselves from harm. In this case the strategy of using clowning as a form of resistance in the face of oppression parallels practices of European clowning. Here I have focused primarily on clowns as they appear in obviously theatrical contexts, but clowning is also a forceful strategy in nontheatrical contexts where some form of "masking" is necessary to distance people from immediate and often harsh realities.

Boskin's theory also accounts for the stereotyped representation of blacks as natural entertainers. As he explains, white plantation owners were fascinated by black styles of singing and dancing that were so unlike their own. While slaves were subject to the voyeurism of their owners, who would watch them sing and dance, the assumption of stereotypes gave them the opportunity to preserve part of their African heritage and develop new forms of music and dance. Songs often functioned as codes to comment on the masters or to communicate other information. For example, the song "Swing Low, Sweet Chariot" served as a code to indicate that the underground railroad was open on a given night. Here, too, assuming an identity they had not constructed for themselves ironically provided slaves new opportunities for self-definition.

The songs and dances showcased in the minstrel shows exaggerated the more exotic features of black culture. According to Boskin, though, it may be that elements of these songs and dances derived from those performed by slaves whose masters demanded entertainment. He suggests that to some extent performers may have played into the stereotype that whites had created, so that the audience got what it expected. Slaves may have even been parodying their masters' comic renditions of these dances. Again, a dialectical process between whites and blacks accounted for the song and dance motifs that would later appear in minstrel shows.

As we have seen, many minstrel-show ballads lamenting the passing of plantation life reinforced the image of the happy slave. The shows attributed a nostalgia to the minstrels portraying slaves who had left the South to find freedom in the North, suggesting that the slaves preferred the life they had left behind to their new freedom. Boskin suggests, however, that slaves could also gain advantages by appealing to this same idyllic image of the plantation, as they often did in order to deflect suspicion or anger. Playing into the image of the happy slave could reassure whites in the wake of aggression and conflict. It was an alternative tactic that slaves could marshal in conjunction with other more confrontational and defiant ways of coping with their condition.

The comic Sambo character and the minstrel entertainments grew out of an exchange between whites and blacks in the context of the institution of slavery. The stereotypes therefore reflect the slaves' own attempts to take advantage of the few liberties they were allowed. Playing into the stereotype could represent a kind of resilience in the face of oppression, and resilience is often the first step toward full-fledged resistance.[6] In working with stereotypes, slaves were perhaps able to retain their strength and their dignity and make possible more direct forms of resistance in a situation that offered few other options.

The first minstrel show performers were white men who put on blackface, but during the Civil War blacks began to perform in their own minstrel companies. Ironically, these performers themselves often put burnt cork on their faces in order to match the minstrel type already current. By "corking up," black performers at once conformed to the stereotype and at the same time rendered it problematic precisely by showing that it was necessary even for blacks to put on makeup in order to represent the images that were meant to represent them. The black minstrel makeup worn by black performers thereby underlined the artifice of the minstrel character itself—that it was theatrically constructed, not natural. In fact, black performers who went without the makeup had trouble and could not, in spite of their clowning, elicit the same positive response from their audiences. In one way, then, the blackface mask restricted and defined the black performer, while in other ways it liberated him.

In minstrel shows and in other forms of entertainment that embraced the black stereotype, black performers faced a dilemma. Notwithstanding the claustrophobic limitations imposed by the image of the minstrel clown, performers could also take control of the stereotype and subvert it and the racial prejudices it embodied. Boskin sums up the trap inherent in the situation in this way: "That four black men could engage in a prolonged conversation about a current and complex subject indicated that the Sambo image was not rigid. At the same time, it was not open-ended, either. Rather, as the minstrels would later demonstrate, it suggests that Sambo could talk on relevant matters, from politics to religion, so long as he remained within the limits of the image" (73). The mask of the minstrel clown by no means gave black performers complete freedom of expression, yet it was a kind of safe haven that allowed for greater expression than was otherwise possible. Stowe and Grimsted argue that, behind a mask of blackface, actors were able to express a broad range of feelings and discuss extremely touchy subjects:

> Certainly minstrelsy played on and influenced the social stereotype of Blacks. Just as certainly, however, black-face, corked or real, seemed to audiences a mask which allowed deep expressions of emotions of loss and longing, as well as ridicule of social and intellectual platitudes and the discrepancies between American dreams and American realities. The black mask, like the sentimental or farcical format, distanced things enough so that truths could be expressed which would have been profoundly troubling or socially dangerous if presented or taken in serious form. (82–83)

Stowe and Grimsted's further claim is that the minstrel show in fact afforded black performers a wider theatrical range than many of the other ethnic or regional stereotypes portrayed on the American stage during the same period. That range included "wit and buffoonery, music sentimental and comic, dancing stately and grotesque, pretension and simplicity, pathos and farce, all were stressed and held together by a consistently shrewd simplicity and naturalness" (82).

There were other, more concrete ways in which blacks may have profited by their appropriation of the black stereotype. The notion that blacks were somehow natural-born performers may well have convinced white Americans to accept them in the field of entertainment, while at the same time fighting to keep them out of so many other spheres of public life. Not that black performers had any real control over the minstrel show itself or the terms of their own participation in the entertainment industry at large. Still, the minstrel circuit did provide a way for blacks to earn a living and often brought them great popularity and recognition as performers.

Bogle argues that many twentieth-century black actors who worked in movies, in spite of being offered only roles of servants and maids, were able to move beyond these stereotypes to create not only great theatrical performances but also images of black dignity and power: "Indeed the thesis of my book is that all black actors—from Stepin Fetchit to Rex Ingram to Lena Horne to Sidney Poitier and Jim Brown—have played stereotyped roles. But the essence of black film history is not in the stereotyped role but in what certain talented actors have done with the stereotype . . . Later, when real black actors played the roles and found themselves wedged into these categories, the history became one of actors battling against the types to create rich, stimulating, diverse characters" (x, 4). Bogle cites as an example Hattie McDaniel, who had many roles in film, often playing servants, and who won an Academy Award for her performance of Mammy in *Gone with the Wind.* Rather than succumbing to the inferior position that her role as Mammy seemed to dictate, Bogle sees McDaniel as giving Mammy "a self-righteous grandeur that glows" (89).

What goes for actors in movies goes even more so for entertainers in the live theater who have more direct control over their work, especially in the moment of performance itself. In comic forms like the minstrel show, it was even more likely improvisation created the possibility of undermining stereotypes even as they were being portrayed.[7]

Of course, the acceptance of blacks onstage, and the relative freedom allowed them there, was no remedy for the ongoing prejudice and discrimination offstage. Prior to the civil rights movement, segregation prevented even the most famous performers from staying at the same hotels and eating at the same restaurants as their white counterparts. Black entertainers might talk politics on the stage, but they had little if any political power in daily life. The entertainment industry provided only a very limited arena in which African Americans could gain recognition and respect in a culture in which they were otherwise systematically marginalized.

White minstrel shows had always advertised themselves as genuine presentations of the songs, the dances, and even the character of blacks. Black companies therefore had the advantage of being able to claim a greater authenticity than their white counterparts, while still playing into the stereotype created and made popular by white performers. Consequently, although the black companies soon became more popular than their white counterparts, the myth that minstrels were portraying blacks "as they truly are" was so strong that some audiences actually thought the blacks were not "performing" at all but simply being themselves, so little could they distinguish the stereotype from the reality. Seeing the stereotype acted out before them even tended to reinforce it and legitimate it in their minds.

By the middle of the nineteenth century, audiences had embraced the minstrel show as the first indigenous American theater form. Its popularity in the United States led to its being exported to other countries and resulted in the ever wider promotion of stereotyped images of African Americans abroad. Ironically, then, the most oppressed segment of the population came to represent America as a whole throughout the world. By stressing racial division, the minstrel show also painted a fairly accurate portrait of American society itself.

The life of Bert Williams, a renowned black performer in the early part of the twentieth century, is an excellent case study illustrating the alienation that many black performers felt in America prior to the civil rights movement. Williams's experiences reveal the minstrel stereotype to have been a double-edged sword. Born in the West Indies, Williams came to the United States in 1885. After attending Stanford University for several quarters, he turned to a career in show business. He was at first unfamiliar with the minstrel stereotype but soon had to learn to play the role, to talk and act like a clown, in order to gain the favor of white audiences. Williams learned to do this brilliantly and became very successful, teaming up to perform with George Walker. Toll quotes Williams himself in arguing that the black comic mask actually helped him to open up as an actor:

> "Then I began to find myself," he recalled of the first time he blacked up. "It was not until I was able to see myself as another person that my sense of humor developed." As "clown white" did for some performers, the black mask allowed Williams to act differently than he otherwise could have. But Williams was not just another clown. He was a black man wearing a black mask, a mask that had come to symbolize the stereotyped, simpleminded black fool, a symbol of racial

inferiority in race-conscious America. The mask liberated Williams as an entertainer, but it stifled him as a man. (123)

Walker and Williams's original show *In Dahomey* went to Broadway in 1903, and Williams performed on Broadway many times after that. But although Williams was a highly acclaimed comic and entertainer, he was also a victim of discrimination, for in spite of his widespread popularity and appeal, he never had top billing in the United States. Still, throughout his career he continued to believe that white society would judge him according to his talent and reputation and would eventually accept him both onstage and off.

Both the minstrel stereotype and discrimination, in show business and at large, put strict limits on Williams's career, the characters he could develop, and the fame he could achieve. The connection between his acceptance as a performer and his rejection as a human being was brought home to him when he performed in England. There he enjoyed the kind of acclaim he could never enjoy in America, and his popularity onstage brought with it social acceptance outside the theater, including an invitation to become a member of a racially integrated masonic lodge. So, although the minstrel character is similar to other clown characters in affording the performer a measure of creative freedom through the use of a mask, the performative and political constraints that the role imposed on black entertainers like Williams distinguish it crucially from other clowning traditions.

In 1964 the San Francisco Mime Troupe decided to use the format of an old-time minstrel show and the stereotype of the blackface clown to address contemporary racial politics. Here the black stereotype was in the control of a racially integrated but mostly white, leftist theater group, sympathetic to the struggle for civil rights and welcoming the end of segregation.

It should be noted of course that the Mime Troupe was not the only theatrical company at this time using the stage and racial stereotypes to address volatile social issues. LeRoi Jones/Amiri Baraka's powerful play *Dutchman* opened that same year, and starting in 1965 Luis Valdez (trained in the Mime Troupe) and his Teatro Campesino created "actos" like *Los Vendidos* that used Chicano stereotypes to explore issues relevant to the

Chicano community. Luis Valdez's use of stereotypes in performance is, understandably, close to that of the Mime Troupe. An exploration of his work would engender similar arguments about the careful manipulation and exposition of stereotypes necessitated in this kind of theatre. Baraka's project was quite different, as he did not draw from popular theatrical traditions. However, the abundance of examples from these artists and others underlines the importance dealing with racial stereotypes on stage took on at this period. Though this may have been a mark of the times in the 1960s, the problem of how to address racial stereotypes in theatrical work remains a live issue today. Popular forms bring up this dilemma more directly than other forms of theatre as they rely on stereotypes to bring across their message. The minstrel show, resting exclusively on a series of derogatory black images, brings out the problems of popular forms and stereotypes in its most forceful aspect.

The Mime Troupe availed itself of stereotypes, virtually static social images, for progressive ends, namely representing the past and present condition of African Americans as a fixed point from which genuine social change might proceed. The Troupe's minstrel show challenged such images, broke them down, and finally replaced them with new images, new stereotypes, more radical and militant than the old ones, as models for political action. The Mime Troupe's strategy has been to use stereotypes and inflate them to huge proportions so that neither the audience nor the actors can avoid confronting them directly. By rendering these often inconspicuous images highly visible, the company can then more easily parody them, question them, and tear them apart. Because of their control both of the images themselves and of the context of their production, the Mime Troupe was able to move the stereotypes from an attitude of resilience in the face of oppression to one of genuine resistance.

The Mime Troupe followed the traditional minstrel show format and in each section presented and then undermined the stereotypes at play. Instead of using an all-white or all-black cast, the director, Ron Davis, cast *The Minstrel Show* with three black men and three white men all playing minstrels in blackface and fright wigs. This mixed casting was meant to frustrate the audience in their attempts to distinguish the black actors from the white actors. As Davis explained, "The process would unnerve them and fuck up their prejudices" (50). The combination of both blacks and whites in blackface also emphasized the fact that the stereotype was essen-

16. The cast of *A Minstrel Show, or Civil Rights in a Cracker Barrel* (1965) in blackface. Photograph by Erik Weber.

17. Two minstrels with the Interlocutor in *A Minstrel Show, or Civil Rights in a Cracker Barrel* (1965). *Left to right:* Willie Hart, R. G. Davis (as the Interlocutor), and John Broderick. Photograph by Erik Weber.

tially a mask that anyone could wear. The casting and costuming therefore helped disassociate the image from the people it was originally meant to represent.

As in the original shows, the role of the Interlocutor was played by a white man without makeup. The setup at the beginning of the show once again put the foolish blackface minstrels in opposition to the strong, stable figure of white authority. The Interlocutor's traditional role as master of ceremonies, introducing acts and participating in rapid-fire jokes, once again took on great social and political significance in virtue of his racial status. As in the original shows, he acted as a rational and benevolent peacekeeper. But if the figure of the Interlocutor had originally been present to maintain order and enforce the racial hierarchy, the Mime Troupe asked what would happen if someone violated that hierarchy. They answered this question by pushing the situation to an extreme.

One of the best examples of this way of challenging the power structures inherent in the minstrel form occurred in a short sketch called "Negro History Week." In this sketch the minstrels act out a series of scenes illustrating the lives of famous blacks throughout history. As the figures become more contemporary, they also become more militant, until the scene ends with the minstrels banging on chairs and yelling, "Black power" and "Blood in the streets" (Davis 57). The Interlocutor is then sent in to calm the minstrels down, distract them with jokes, and coax them back into their "Sambo" characters. He thus performs his role as controller, keeping the minstrels in their clownish roles and preserving the purely "theatrical" character of the show. However, the minstrels have already revealed their true selves to the audience, thus emphasizing the artificiality of the comic mask the Interlocutor forces them to reassume.

In this scene the clowns break out of the images that confine them and take up more direct and aggressive tactics. The scene shows the limitations of the minstrel character in contrast to the more militant figures that could emerge from it. In so doing, it exposes the power structures underlying the minstrel show and, in the minstrel clowns' revolt, constructs new models for political action. In maintaining order within the show, the Interlocutor represents white authority struggling to maintain social power and racial privilege over blacks. The show revealed the important role stereotyped representations play in curtailing the freedom of African Americans.

At the time of the production, 1964, real social uprising was occurring with the civil rights movement and the outbreak of racial riots in the streets of American cities. Beyond these riots, a more extensive social movement for reform supported black liberation and black power. The Mime Troupe's work was a self-conscious echo of the social conditions of the day and was perhaps possible only in virtue of the real events taking place outside the theater. The Troupe measured the violence in the streets against the stereotype that the violence was bent on destroying, thus rendering both more intelligible. In this instance their production made use of restrictive stereotypes of the sort that abound in the popular theater as measures of popular opinion. The production set these old models alongside newer ones so that the audience could see the possibility of real social change made manifest before their eyes.

The Mime Troupe's *Minstrel Show* also included an olio section. In this section the Troupe sought to deconstruct the black stereotype embodied in the olio section of the original minstrel shows. In this part of the show the Mime Troupe's minstrels sing a traditional sentimental song, "Old Black Joe," then bow their heads as the Interlocutors recites. One minstrel, however, does not bow his head completely and begins to masturbate (simulated in graphically mimed gestures) during the dramatic recital. As Davis explains, "There was the complete opposition of elements working toward hysteria. The tone and presentation of 'Old Black Joe' by Bob Slattery was superb, something like Laurence Olivier or Paul Robeson, and directly behind him this blue-coated crazy whippin' it off. The cops could barely write it all down fast enough, the heavy ideologues winced or winked at the childishness, but thousands got hysterical" (56). The scene led to the arrest of some Mime Troupe members on obscenity charges, and on several occasions the show was closed down by the authorities. But there was more to the scene politically than the simply shock value of its explicit depiction of sexual behavior. The violation of sexual taboos undercuts the sentimentality of the song, indeed the sentimental image of the Old South itself, always a dominant theme in the old minstrel shows. More than this, though, the scene radically challenges the stereotype that kept blacks in a subordinate position by picturing them as natural entertainers. If an entertainer is supposed to be subservient in trying to please his audience, then a performer who simply, provocatively gives himself pleasure onstage is guilty of the ultimate transgression of his assigned role. The sexual gesture exposes the tacit power relationship between actor and audience and thereby violates social and political hierarchies as well as codes of obscenity.

In the final section of the show the Mime Troupe performed several short skits. These skits substituted representations of black life in contemporary society for the old minstrel show's bucolic images of the plantation, and in so doing intimated that the power struggle between blacks and whites inherited from slavery persisted to the present day. One scene known as the "Chick-Stud" scene portrays a white woman and a black man having sex. The woman is played by a blackface minstrel wearing a white mask and a blond wig. Their conversation after making love reveals that they are both manipulating the relationship in a kind of a racial power game:

Stud: Woman! Ain't no body tole you baby? You ain't nothin but a white Chick. You're status and satisfaction and revenge. You're pussy and pale skin and you know no white man can satisfy you like I can. Now me, I'm different; I'm all NEGRO, with the smell of Negro, and the hair of Negro, and all the goddam passion of Africa and wild animals. I haven't got the same hang-ups, have I?
Chick: I felt sorry that so many bad things have happened to you. I really want to love you, because you need love.
Stud: You're a whore.
Chick: Don't say that!
Stud: You're a whore. you're trying to sell me something. You want me to buy what you've got. You've got guilt and you're selling it to me under a different label. You love Negroes, but I'm a man, and you can't love me if you love Negroes. (60)

Black Stud and White Chick are reified racial stereotypes. The woman is reduced to abstract attributes and associations ("status," "pussy," "pale skin"), and the man describes himself in the same way ("smell of Negro," "hair of Negro," and "Africa and wild animals"). The relationship being acted out is so stereotyped that the confrontation is really taking place between two images, not two human beings. Again, the Troupe uses stereotypes as a way of revealing the deeper issues of racism and manipulation that lie behind the development of such images. And yet in spite of this intention it is difficult to dissociate the attributes from the images to which they refer, and the images from the people represented in them.

At the end of the scene the man strangles the woman: "Mimetic reaction: She takes off mask and skirt, holds them before her, moves tenderly, pleadingly toward stud, offering herself. He becomes cool, frightened. Mask and skirt continue toward him, swinging and coming on. Angry, Stud lunges for the imaginary neck of the mask and skirt figure. He strangles the image as the other minstrels lower the image to the floor. Stud discovers that the skirt is not filled, is empty, kicks it. First minstrel still has mask on hands, begins to laugh, as other minstrels laugh and scream, he pursues black stud off stage with threatening pink mask. Blackout" (60). The elements that stereotype the female character—the blond wig, the pink mask, the skirt—become detached from the actor and remain emblems of the character. The character herself has vanished. By the end of the scene the stereotypes are peeled away from the characters embodying them, prompting one to examine them and reflect on their meaning in abstraction from the real people to which they are attached.

The image of the black man here is taken straight from the stereotype that Bogle calls the "brutal black buck." The brute and the buck, two aspects of one figure, are both types whose aggressiveness is linked to their sexuality. Bogle describes these types, popularized by filmmaker D. W. Griffith, as projections of white anxiety:

> The black brute was a barbaric black out to raise havoc. Audiences could assume that his physical violence served as an outlet for a man who was sexually repressed. In *Birth of a Nation,* the black brutes, subhuman and feral, are the nameless characters setting out on a rampage full of black rage . . . Bucks are always big, baaddd niggers, oversexed and savage violent and frenzied as they lust for white flesh . . . Among other things, these two characters revealed the tie between sex and racism in America. Griffith played on the myth of the Negro's high-powered sexuality, then articulated the great white fear that every black man longs for a white woman . . . But in covering the attraction of black to white, Griffith failed to reveal the political implications. Traditionally, certain black males have been drawn to white women because these women are power symbols, an ideal of the oppressor. But Griffith attributed the attraction to an animalism innate in the Negro male . . . Griffith played hard on the bestiality of his black villainous bucks and used it to arouse hatred. (13–14)

In the Mime Troupe production, by contrast, the figures reveal the social constructs that determine their relationships. They enact familiar social and psychological patterns. This paradigmatic relation between a black man and a white woman blends issues of race, class, and gender. While mimicking the D. W. Griffith scenario, the Mime Troupe at once tries to deconstruct the situation and thematize its distinct elements.

And yet the violence perpetrated against the female figure, her dissolution at the end of the scene as well as her evident simple-mindedness, remains disturbing and does not speak well to a feminist perspective. The purpose of the production as a whole was to transform the image of blacks from a position of subjugation to one of power. However, throughout the play, all the black figures are male. The piece never addresses the problem of women as an underclass in both the white and black communities. The Chick-Stud scene is the only one in the play that represents a woman, and incidentally even she is played by a man. She is white and so represents the oppressor. The piece in no way addresses her own vulnerable position in white society. The violence she suffers is not unique to white woman black man relationships. The situation reflects broader trends within both black and white communities. In this instance, the Mime Troupe, not unlike D. W. Griffith, falls into the trap of accepting and using common images rather than exploring and questioning the social realities underlying them.

The Minstrel Show sets out to question and refigure images of black men in American society. In so doing, however, it neglects other variables in the social equation, effectively ignoring black women and taking up an image of white women that calls for the same kind of deconstruction. The piece begins with the image of black men defined by the minstrel mask and moves beyond that type to show the variety of possible transformations it can undergo. However, it fails to explore stereotypes of women as deeply or as critically as it does those of men. One image of a woman appears in the show, but we never see the ways in which it, too, might be challenged and transformed. The only other time the show even addresses women is during intermission when the minstrels move into the audience and pick out white women to dance with them. The real women from the audience, paired with their blackface dance partners, reenact the multiracial pairing that had just been played out earlier in the Chick-Stud scene. The show thereby forces these female audience members themselves into a prescribed role that they have not defined and that grants them little autonomy.[8]

Now of course the focus of *The Minstrel Show* was on race and not gender, and of course in 1964 the Mime Troupe could not have been expected to predict or comprehend the feminist movement that would erupt in the seventies and radically transform women's positions in American society. I do not mean to suggest here that they had any obligation to accomplish this impossible feat, or to deny the extremely powerful production the Troupe created. Nonetheless, from today's perspective one should at least acknowledge this blind spot in the Troupe's early and otherwise extremely progressive work. To point out this lack of a feminist point of view shows just how careful one needs to be when appropriating popular traditions in creating theater committed to positive social change. The Mime Troupe made stereotypes the subject of the show even as they made use of them within it. Though they dealt shrewdly with a number of such stereotypes, they availed themselves of others without fully questioning or undermining them in the same way. This example also points out just how much our acceptance of stereotypes changes over time. Theater practitioners must continually reassess the stereotypes they appropriate from older theatrical traditions and question how those images are serving the social and political message they would like to convey. The question of women's roles within a production like this would not be so crucial to this discussion if it were not also the case that it is difficult to find women characters in traditional forms who are anything more than sexual objects or shrews. The feisty and clever female servants of the commedia dell'arte tradition are perhaps the most positive female stereotypes, but the role of the female performer within popular forms is an important one that needs to be addressed.

The final sketch of *The Minstrel Show* begins as a comic scene between three characters called simply Nigger, White, and Negro, all vying to use a public restroom. As their names indicate, these characters are also two-dimensional stereotypes used to illustrate the situation in broad terms rather than explore their personal psychologies. White and Negro defer to each other when Nigger bursts in and pushes his way up front. He is a character who appeals to basic practicality and the call of nature. He ridicules the other two men, who have managed to turn going to the bathroom into a major event, and in so doing he exposes what is really going on as a kind of race-relations game. White is a middle-class liberal, deferring to Negro to ease his own guilty conscience. Negro, on the other hand, is cast as an "Uncle Tom" who is simply pandering to whites and thereby effectively turning his back on his own cultural heritage. The scene is critical of the compromises he makes and of his "type" in general. The scene ends with Nigger pulling out a razor and saying, "One of you is goin' to get it, and maybe both. All I gotta do is figure out which one of you I hates the most" (63). All the characters are stereotypes, but it is Nigger who becomes a model for direct action, since he proposes to change the status quo by killing off the other stereotypes.

Nigger's move towards militancy marks a dramatic change in the black stereotype. The aggressiveness of this figure identifies him with Bogle's "brutal buck." Yet Nigger is comic as well as militant, whereas the brutal buck was a thoroughly humorless figure. Significantly, the scene represents Nigger's aggression not as linked to his sexuality but rather as a sign of deep frustration in the face of the political inertia of the social system he encounters. It is this militant call to action that the Mime Troupe proposes to counteract both the minstrel clown and the brutal buck. This new figure represents a new form of resistance and a repudiation of all former stereotypes.

The Mime Troupe's *Minstrel Show* was able to turn the old minstrel show on its head because control of the racial stereotypes was now firmly in the hands of performers identifying, or at least sympathizing, with the people objectified by them. The civil rights movement itself is of course what made possible the construction of a new militant image of blacks that the production put forward in place of the minstrel clown. By confronting the stereotypes head-on and taking control of them, the Troupe was able in effect to subvert their meaning. In their hands the minstrel show became a format from which an empowering vision of black power could emerge, rather than merely a derogatory one.

In spite of important changes in the condition of many African Americans since the sixties, and the attempt to deconstruct and subvert black stereotypes, the work of dismantling deep-seated racial prejudice remains to be done. This became obvious, if it was not already, when riots broke out in Los Angeles in 1992 in the wake of the acquittal of the four police officers accused of beating Rodney King. A short sketch in the Mime Troupe's *Minstrel Show* illustrates a 1964 incident in which a white policeman shot a black boy in Harlem. That incident sparked riots too, and the Troupe represented Harlem as the slave plantation of the twentieth century, a black ghetto where white policemen were still masters. The parallels between these two incidents underline the continued relevance of a sketch the Mime Troupe performed over thirty years ago.

Old racial stereotypes persist, and there is still a need to challenge and transform such images. This continuing need has not been lost on the Mime Troupe, whose work consistently addresses issues of current social concern. It is no accident, then, that the Troupe's 1991–92 show once again turned to race relations as its central theme. This time the Troupe used nineteenth-century American melodrama as a basis for their production and sought to deconstruct the sentimental depiction of blacks so prevalent in that form.

The Troupe's 1991–92 production, *I Ain't Yo' Uncle*—or *Uncle Tom's Cabin,* as it was called in its first run—is based on George Aiken's stage adaptation of Harriet Beecher Stowe's famous novel. The choice of this work as a starting point is interesting for several reasons. *Uncle Tom's Cabin* was famous in its day not only as a novel but also in a wide variety of stage adaptations—both pro- and antiabolitionist—and was often parodied in the final sections of minstrel shows. Its sentimental depiction of Uncle Tom, an honest, hardworking slave, victimized by the evil slave owner Simon Legree, played a significant role in turning the tide of American opinion against slavery. While Stowe portrayed Tom as a kind of modern-day Christian martyr, "Uncle Tom" has in the meantime become a derogatory term for blacks perceived to be undermining the dignity of African Americans at large by kowtowing to whites and the racist establishment. The sentimentality of *Uncle Tom's Cabin,* which pictured Tom as a victim, has led to a subsequent disdain of the image by generations of more socially self-conscious African Americans. *Uncle Tom's Cabin* was a white northern woman's perception of the injustice of slavery and was intended to inspire a sense of Christian charity among whites who might then be able to put an end to it. It was a revolutionary work in that it called on people to challenge and transform the status quo. Yet it did this by appealing to those already occupying positions of power, rather than by empowering the victims of oppression themselves.

The Mime Troupe's production turns this situation on its head. From the very first moment of the play, the audience knows that they will not be seeing a traditional version of *Uncle Tom's Cabin.* As we have seen, the play begins with Harriet Beecher Stowe being dragged onstage by the black characters she created. An argument gets under way as the characters complain about the roles into which they have been cast, the negative images to which they are forced to conform, and the fates to which they must succumb. They confront Stowe and the audience with the all the psychological and political barriers her text has constructed around their lives. In the end, as we saw, they agree to continue the play only if they can change their characters, actions, and fates.

This device frames the play in a decidedly unsentimental perspective external to the original narrative. It finishes not only by altering the entire course of the play in the second half of the show but also by providing much of the action with a running commentary that continually contrasts the way the play was "supposed" to go with the new events unfolding onstage. The show thereby highlights the traditional depiction of the characters and sets it in opposition to new images, new stereotypes, new ideals. It thus simultaneously historicizes the original text, the contemporary text, and the context of performance.

Uncle Tom himself confronts Stowe when he says, "First of all, I ain't yo uncle!" This sums up the entire course of events that is to follow: the discarding of old, weak self-images in favor of new, stronger ones. Throughout the play black characters take charge of their lives, in spite of the oppressive circumstances in which they find themselves.

One character who changes his destiny, and with it the course of the play, is George Harris, Eliza's husband. He is a bright, creative man whose cruel master takes him away from a job in which he has found much success. George's master also threatens to end George's marriage to Eliza and marry him off to someone else. George can no longer tolerate his terrible circumstances and, as in the original script, he runs off to find freedom in Canada. Yet the Mime Troupe's George is not satisfied just to find his own freedom; instead he decides to return to the South to help free other slaves. In the original George goes back to the South only to buy and free Uncle Tom. Unfortunately he arrives too late to save him. The old George cannot see the possibility of changing the system but only of helping his friend. The new George's decision shifts the focus of the play from the plight of the individual to that of society at large. In addition to deciding to return to the South, he also decides to empower slaves by bringing them guns and inciting rebellion. The possibility of violent retaliation is thus introduced into the idyllic Old South of Stowe's novel.

At the end of the new play, two slave women shoot and kill Simon Legree, the play's arch villain, with one of George's guns.[9] Rebellion, revenge, and violence are all new elements brought into the play by George's changes to the original script. The new plot additions help overturn the image of the obsequious slave that Stowe promoted and replace it with a more powerful, more threatening character type.

Yet, just as *L'Amant Militaire* also voiced the Mime Troupe's pacifist position, *I Ain't Yo' Uncle* does not simply advocate violent resistance. The gun the slave women use to kill Legree is one that George originally gave to Uncle Tom. However, Tom's response to the gun is:

> **Tom:** (*picks up the gun*). What I'm gonna do with this? White people got to learn to be civilized—how they gonna learn unless we teach 'em? Real change comes from people's hearts not from guns. But don't we got a right to defend ourselves? (*Hides it carefully.*) (58)

Tom does take the gun, but he condones violence only for self-defense, not as a means for genuine social transformation.

Topsy, a rambunctious, uneducated girl slave, is another character who chooses to change her fate. At the end of the Mime Troupe's play she is transformed through the education that the white Miss Ophelia has given her. Yet instead of staying and remaining loyal to Miss Ophelia, as Stowe's Topsy does, she chooses to take her freedom and move to New York. In the final moments of the show she returns in a contemporary outfit, carrying a large boom box playing rap music. Stowe wanted to show that through education even a wild slave like Topsy could become a sweet, civilized young woman. The Mime Troupe's Topsy shows that, far from simply exhibiting a lack of education, Topsy's wild nature was always an angry protest against the oppression and devaluation she felt as a black woman. (The Mime Troupe's Topsy insists that she wants to be white, does voodoo on Little Eva, and sings a rap song about herself.) In her contemporary persona, Topsy has become a strong-willed and rebellious woman, identifying wholeheartedly with contemporary black culture. The Mime Troupe asks of this new Topsy what Stowe asked of the old Topsy: "Do you think she just growed?" The Mime Troupe version of the play presents Topsy not as a wild child in need of education but as the product and consequence of the institution of slavery. Even as a contemporary character she is part of the legacy of that institution and its inheritance of racial hatred and violence.

The Mime Troupe brings a contemporary perspective into the play in other ways as well. Slide projections flash on and off across the back of the stage throughout the performance, usually depicting old engravings of large, idyllic plantation houses from the nineteenth century. However, after Uncle Tom has received his first terrible beating by Simon Legree, he stumbles onstage and the slide projected behind him shows an image more familiar to contemporary audiences: a still shot from the video of Rodney King being beaten by a group of Los Angeles policemen. The congruence of the figure onstage and the projected image links the racial divisions institutionalized in slavery to the abiding racial hierarchy in contemporary American society. Both images represent political power in the form of overt violence.

Just as important as the changes the characters choose to make, however, are the changes they choose not to make. At one point in the play Simon Legree comes onstage and claims that he will not be changing his character. He says that he loves his character as it was written and that he will never die out.[10] He is a stereotype representing the recalcitrance of white racism. He makes it clear that there is no chance of his undergoing a religious or sentimental conversion, as Stowe's original character nearly does.[11] The Mime Troupe's Legree makes it clear that he is a more difficult character with which to contend. His renunciation of Christian salvation shows that religious conversion is not the means for social transformation. He thereby forces us to look to other models of action for putting an end to racial prejudice.

At the end of the play, Uncle Tom also makes a decision not to change his character. As in the original play, Tom is beaten to death by Legree. In the Mime Troupe show, however, the other characters run onstage and plead with Tom to change his action, his fate, his story, and not to allow himself to die a martyr. Yet Tom refuses, saying that had he not died, no one would have remembered him; had he not stayed behind, others would not have been able to move forward. The Mime Troupe's Tom thus redeems the resilient character of all so-called "Uncle Toms." His death as a martyr is his own form of resistance, one that allows him to remain true to his pacifist and religious beliefs while spurring others on to more radical forms of protest. Tom's death is not just one individual death but a cultural symbol that marks and motivates a transition from resilience to resistance.

Though produced almost thirty years apart, both *The Minstrel Show* and *I Ain't Yo' Uncle* illustrate how the Mime Troupe has used stereotypes embedded in America's cultural history as a starting point from which to address racial division and injustice in American society. Both plays begin with familiar cultural forms and stereotypes and then transform them so that empowering new images can emerge from crippling old prejudices. These productions demonstrate the ways in which appropriating a stereotype can be an important step toward eventually taking control of an image and ultimately subverting and transforming its meaning.

While this way of playing with stereotypes has remained constant over the Mime Troupe's nearly forty-year history, other aspects of their work have changed. The following chapter will explore the changes that the Troupe and their work have undergone throughout that history, the ways in which they have remained responsive to the changing political world, and whether the revolutionary potential of their work has suffered.

5 The San Francisco Mime Troupe in Changing Times

Since 1962 when the Mime Troupe created their first outdoor public performance of *The Dowry,* a commedia dell'arte-style piece, the Troupe has maintained a commitment to addressing political issues on stage through popular theatrical forms. However, the political climate surrounding the Troupe's productions has, in that time, changed drastically from the growth of leftist political activism during the Vietnam War and the rise of the feminist movement to the backlash of right-wing conservatism during the Reagan period and after. The Mime Troupe has persevered in looking for ways of adapting their productions to these new realities while remaining true to their own political perspective and theatrical style. In so doing they have, in their best productions, demonstrated the continued relevance of popular theater for questioning the status quo. Their most successful shows propose revolutionary strategies for social transformation.

It is not merely by virtue of using the popular traditions that are the basis of the Mime Troupe's work, however, that a production will be able to evoke the radical potential of festive-revolutionary forms. As previously mentioned, a critical analysis of theatrical strategies, such as the role stereotypes play within a piece, must precede and inform their use. Likewise, the attitudes of the audience with respect to the subject of the play will affect the reception of a show, as will the extent to which the piece itself adopts or fails to adopt a self-critical perspective.

In the examples I have already investigated it becomes apparent that there is a reciprocal relationship between popular forms and the ever-shifting parameters of the historical context of performance. This relationship helps to determine the political potential of a popular form at any given historical moment. Popular forms appear in each generation in new guises but with similar characteristics that reveal a latent potential for motivating revolutionary change. The historical context, however, limits or extends the possibilities for bringing these dormant aspects to light and translating them into concrete political action.

Moreover, if popular traditions rely on trickster-like tactics to reveal the contingent nature of the status quo and thereby promote the possibility for social change and renewal, then whatever political alternatives a production presents cannot themselves afford to be rigid and dogmatic. The new social possibilities that the Mime Troupe stages must be flexible, and the means they present to achieve them must, like a trickster, take us by surprise. It is for this reason that productions that lapse into leftist clichés, smugness, or safe material are not successful and strike observers as mere preaching to the converted. When the ideas presented in a piece appear old and worn out, too tired and familiar, they lose their power to inspire. While a leftist agenda itself is not inherently out-of-date, it must nonetheless continually address the changing political world in a fresh way. Popular forms can be effective in accomplishing this task precisely because they thrive on novelty, surprise, and cleverness—not in order to shock, turning people away, but to delight, amaze, and draw them in. Such forms present a world continually out of balance and in flux, a place where new ideas can take root and grow.

The San Francisco Mime Troupe has often been studied in the context of the alternative theater experiments of the 1960s and '70s. The purpose here, however, has been to place the Mime Troupe's work in the context of a long historical tradition of theaters that use popular forms for political purposes. In the process I have attempted to evaluate both the role popular theater forms can play in supporting social change and their effectiveness in doing so. In this chapter I will review a selection of productions from the now nearly forty years of San Francisco Mime Troupe plays and evaluate how effective they have been in marrying popular forms to political subjects and presenting vital productions that reinspire audiences politically. I will look at the plays in relation to the changing historical context the Mime Troupe has had to address and how the productions have responded to these changes.

From its birth in 1959, influenced by Decroux's corporeal mime technique, to its flowering in works like *L'Amant Militaire,* the Mime Troupe experimented with different versions of physical performance. Through these physical explorations the Troupe finally found their footing in a theatrical style that almost inadvertently launched them into their subsequent political affiliations. The first works of the R. G. Davis Mime Troupe—as the Troupe was originally called—reflected the background of its founder, Ron Davis, who had trained in modern dance and then in mime with Paul Curtis of the American Mime Theater and Étienne Decroux in Paris. The company offered a chance for Davis, his fellow actors, and his students to explore Decroux's innovations in abstract mime. The Troupe's early work is thus akin to that of many of the mime performers that Leabhart mentions who, also influenced by Decroux, are interested in the metaphysical dimensions of the expressive body in performance.

Combining the physical performance interests of Decroux and modern dance with the improvisational techniques developed by Viola Spolin, the Troupe created a series of pieces presented as *The 11th Hour Mime Show*. The show was scheduled at 11:00 P.M. on Sundays at the Encore Theater in San Francisco when the stage was left empty between changes of the theater's regular rotating repertory. In his book about the Mime Troupe's first ten years, Davis describes the work of this period: "We tried new impressions, un-completed images, ideas and intuitive notions when the creative spirit was locked into a conventional form and content. Thus by exploring half-realized ideas, we opened the form to investigation without worrying about the content purpose or message. The audience was a guinea-pig and, hopefully, helped us re-align whatever we did to mean something or at least to understand our process" (21). From this description one can guess that this early work not only steered clear of traditional forms rather than drawing on them for inspiration but was also unconcerned with conveying any meaning, let alone a specific political perspective. It was far removed from the festive-revolutionary theatrical style for which the Troupe would become known. It used the physical expressivity of the body to create a theater of abstraction and disorientation in which conventional form and content were fractured and fragmented rather than transfigured in the service of social transformation.

The Troupe's 1961 production of Beckett's mime play *Act Without Words II* gave a more linear, narrative scenario than the *11th Hour Mime Show* presentations. Beckett's characters in *Act Without Words II* may have been influenced by clowns and vaudeville entertainers as the two tramps in *Waiting for Godot* were, but in spite of any such influence, the picture

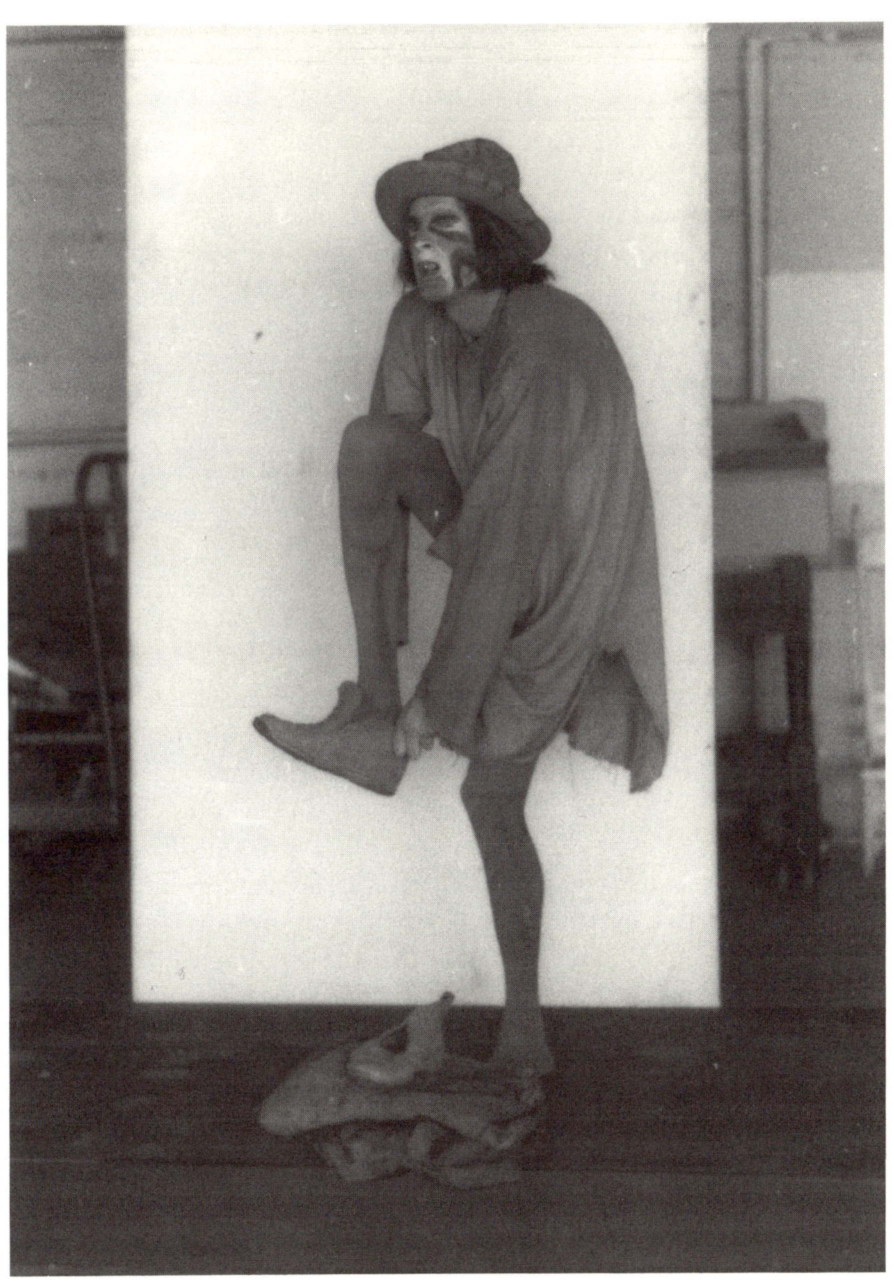

18. Jerry Jump in Beckett's *Act Without Words II* (1961). Photograph by Erik Weber.

that unfolds in this short mime piece is one of anonymous characters trapped in monotonous, pointless, daily routines. It is not one of either festive celebration or political subversion.

Lying in sacks on the stage, two characters identified only as A and B, are prodded each in turn from outside by a goad. Each, when sufficiently goaded, gets up out of the sack and goes through a series of banal daily activities, including getting dressed and undressed. Each eventually returns to his sack. The actions are presented as if they might go on indefinitely. The characters in the piece perform their tasks with no external perspective on them and no apparent prospect of breaking the oppression of this stifling routine. They seem to be at the mercy of the goad, an anonymous outside force, and are evidently unable to envision or attempt any change at all. In this piece the physical expression of the performer is used mimetically to imitate daily activities. These activities create a kind of cage of action for the characters whose lives are defined by their attention to physical needs. Physical action here is an expression of imprisonment, regularity, and routinization, not of freedom, surprise, or transformation as is the case in festive-revolutionary performance.

In 1962, however, the Troupe discovered the commedia dell'arte, the style that would set the tone for most of their future work and open them up to the festive-revolutionary horizons of popular theater. For their first outdoor production, *The Dowry,* the Troupe wove together bits of old commedia scenarios to create their own story, and added songs, jokes, and spontaneous remarks to the audience during the performance. The broad physical style of the commedia put the mime techniques the Troupe had already been working with to new use and transformed them. Davis tells of a moment at the Troupe's first outdoor performance when the purpose underlying the commedia's form became viscerally evident to the performers. An actress who had had trouble grasping her role, came off stage exuberant having suddenly realized that "the reason for the large movements and gestures is because they performed outside" (35). Although the cast had read about commedia, the experience of live performance at an outdoor venue gave them an understanding of the tradition that books could not. The Troupe gained experiential knowledge of how popular forms address themselves to a popular audience. As Davis puts it, "Once outside, theory and reality crashed together into a screaming joyous perception" (35). The use of physical expression in the outdoor commedia performances was concrete rather than abstract and corresponded to the need to communicate with a large, diverse audience whose members could come and go as they pleased. The use of this type of theatrical physicality along with the added jokes, songs, and improvisations set the Troupe's work squarely in the category of popular theater.

Performing outdoors not only gave a festive quality to the Mime Troupe's work, it also fostered the revolutionary dimension of their festive-revolutionary theater, for in trying to secure the right to perform in outdoor venues the Troupe became involved in their first real political struggle. In order to perform outdoors in the Bay Area the Troupe had to have their performance sites approved by the San Francisco Park and Recreation Commission. True to the commedia tradition, the Troupe took the liberty of being both bawdy and politically outspoken. The park commission responded not only by reviewing the Troupe's performance venues but also by suggesting changes in the shows and limiting the availability of performance sites when they thought the plays were too bold. In the summer of 1965 the Troupe staged a protest to fight for their right to free speech against this censorship, and this protest marked the first strong union of the Troupe's political and theatrical ideals.

The Troupe's 1965 outdoor summer production was an adaptation of Giordano Bruno's play *Il Candelaio.*[1] Davis had two civil liberties lawyers review the show before the Troupe brought the play to the streets. The lawyers' assessment was that the piece was "a little brutal but not obscene" (66). The Troupe received an authorization from the park commission for forty-eight performances on the condition that the show meet with their approval. However, the park commission revoked the Troupe's permit after only three performances. When the commission turned a deaf ear to Davis and his lawyer's claims that the Troupe's right to free speech was being violated, Davis left their office promising, "We will see you in the parks and in the courts" (66).

The Troupe held to Davis's promise and continued performing in spite of the park commission's ban. Knowing that the commission would try to stop them, the Troupe turned their subsequent performance into a political event. A large crowd of supporters as well as policemen gathered in Lafayette Park in San Francisco on August 7, 1965, the day set for the Troupe's show. Davis began the performance with Brighella's introductory monologue and, changing it slightly, introduced the show with:

Signor, Signora, Signorini
Madame, Monsieur, Mademoiselle,
Ladieeeees and Gentlemen,
Il Troupo di Mimo di San Francisco
Presents for your enjoyment this afternoon . . .
AN ARREST!!! (67)

On cue, the police came in and arrested Davis. Some other cast members and supporters were also arrested while both performers and spectators helped to keep the show going, for a little while anyway, in defiance of the authorities.

In this memorable performance the Mime Troupe's theatrical and political engagement became one: in performing despite the commission's censorship the Troupe made a political statement about the right to free speech, and Davis's subsequent arrest itself became a theatrical moment.

This theatrical-political event embodied the link the Troupe found between popular forms and radical politics. Outdoor venues and a broad and "impure" physical acting style, both important aspects of popular theater, revealed this relationship. Though these elements of popular theater may not be essential to any single popular performance, they help create the festive atmosphere, the sense of freedom from convention, and consequently the impetus toward revolution, all of which are characteristic of popular forms. In bringing their shows outside, the Troupe invoked the festive aspect of the popular. In so doing the Troupe had inadvertently, or perhaps not so inadvertently, invoked its revolutionary aspect as well. Since *The 11th Hour Mime Show* the Troupe had been exploring alternative theatrical forms and venues. The early pieces reflected R. G. Davis's interest in using theatrical expression as a means of stirring up social complacency if not actually provoking social transformation. Popular theatrical genres allowed the Troupe to do this in a more direct and politically outspoken manner. The revolutionary use of popular theater gradually became the driving force behind the Mime Troupe's work.

It is important to note, however, that what made the theatrical event of August 7 politically significant was not merely the arrests that took place but the presence of a crowd of supporters, including notables like Lawrence Ferlinghetti, who came to cheer the Troupe on and help them fight for their right to perform. The Troupe knew that they were not fighting an isolated battle but one whose relevance extended to a community beyond themselves. In staging a series of benefit concerts to raise money to pay their legal fees the Troupe saw evidence of the support they could count on by the crowds that showed up for these concerts. Davis describes those who turned up at the second benefit concert as "painters, musicians, politicos, theater people, old friends, unknown long-hairs, straights, all mixing, having given two bucks for a worthy fight" (69). What Davis saw, in other words, was the counterculture of the 1960s already burgeoning. This counterculture shaped the Mime Troupe's theatrical work and political philosophy and provided them with the large audience of supporters for whom they played.

A feeling of community existed among college students on many campuses across the United States in the late sixties as students became united through shared antiestablishment political ideas and antiwar sentiment. When the Mime Troupe played on these campuses their message was reaching not merely a radical fringe but a powerful and growing movement, and their work was already intertwined with the concerns of that movement. The Troupe's performances, for the most part, found communities of supporters already present and waiting to hear their message. As Davis says, Troupe members were seen as "lefty stars" (89). They did not have the responsibility of winning over a new community of supportive spectators each time they performed. Their shows became, like the Renaissance carnivals of old Europe that Bakhtin describes, rallying points around which members of already existing communities could come together and reaffirm their identity and their goals. The Troupe shared with their audience a communal language of critique that only needed to be invoked in order to reaffirm its message. Davis has said of that period of their work: "Like good outside agitators, we were most often only additions to already volatile circumstances. We, too, had no network that fed us information or directed our attention to develop action where there was none. We happened to be on the spot when the college kids were moving" (89).

It was in this atmosphere that the Mime Troupe performed *The Minstrel Show* and *L'Amant Militaire,* tapping into the civil rights movement and the anti-Vietnam War protests at the height of their national impact. A true popular theater, their shows echoed the feelings and ideas around them, interpreting them in a theatrical forum.

In the sixties the Troupe gained the reputation of being a radical leftist theater company, challenging and questioning the social, political, and economic status quo at all levels. Taking up this radical stance, however, was perhaps made possible only by the Troupe's confidence in enjoying broad support on college campuses and within the counterculture. The Troupe was as much led by as leading the revolutionary fervor of the times.

In the 1970s the political climate that had nurtured the Mime Troupe began to change. As the United States slowly pulled its forces out of Vietnam, protests against the war died down, cooling the fervor for imminent revolution. The radical community within which the Troupe and their work had found a home began to disperse. However, a new radical movement emerged in feminism. Women who had fought alongside men in civil rights and antiwar protests began to notice their own oppressed positions in both those movements and in society at large. Feminism critiqued not only the establishment but also the counterculture and the sexism that underlay many of its ideals.

Feminism first came to the Mime Troupe when the women in the company began to notice their general subordinate status in decision making[2] and a lack of concern about women's issues in the Troupe's political agenda. In trying to address feminist issues the Troupe had to confront the ubiquitous sexist images of women in popular traditions and find a way to reinterpret them for a contemporary context, just as they had done with characters like Punch and the minstrel clown. One of the Troupe's first attempts to deal with feminist themes took the form of "The Women's Drill Team," a short sketch meant to be performed at demonstrations. The sketch consisted of a group of women directed through a series of traditional drill team exercises by a man. At the end of the exercises the women attacked their male leader. This sketch conveyed a feminist message by showing women taking power and resisting male oppression.

According to Davis, however, the Troupe felt that the Women's Drill Team was not as successful as the Gorilla Marching Band, an earlier Mime Troupe invention also meant to be performed at demonstrations. The Gorilla Marching Band spoofed the tradition of parade marching bands while providing an antiestablishment message. Band members wore "mountains of rags and imitation Mummers' outfits" (98), played glockenspiels, bugles, and drums, and marched out of step. The band came to protest marches and even appeared once in the Macy's Thanksgiving Day Parade in New York. They played the national anthem "made into something of an anti-American tune" and then flipped over signs that read "GET OUT OF VIETNAM" (98).

Davis himself suggests one possible reason for the drill team's lack of success in contrast to that of the Gorilla Marching Band, namely that the drill team's exercises may have been too close to those of a real drill team to be interesting. This problem, he says, was one that the Gorilla Marching Band had at first but moved beyond as the band developed. However, rifts in the company during the period of the Women's Drill Team did not create an atmosphere in which people were willing to experiment, and the project was ultimately dropped.

Perhaps the metaphorical image of the women overtaking their oppressor at the end of the drill could have had as much if not more of a political impact than the political message the Gorilla Marching Band had written on signs, had the Troupe been willing to spend the time required to develop the project, as Davis suggests. However, the Women's Drill Team differed from the Gorilla Marching Band in a number of significant ways. First, what the drill team sketch lacked was a trickster sensibility. The drill team fought oppression in an act of sheer aggression rather than through comic subversion and parody as the Gorilla Band had done. The drill team also took military routines as their model, a model that had no roots in popular traditions. Even the Gorilla Band had associated itself with mumming rituals in choice of dress and musical accompaniment.

Another important difference between the two sketches lies in the nature of the reception and acceptance that each could receive. The Gorilla Band and their antiwar message was already supported by a large number of the people for whom they played. The women's message was still new at this point and critiqued not only the establishment but the counterculture itself. It may have been ahead of what people, even politically liberal and activist people, were willing to accept in January 1968. In spite of the progressive appearance given by the drill team work, the Mime Troupe was itself struggling with feminist issues. The women in the company were fighting not just to see women's perspectives represented on stage but for the company to embody feminist ideals by allowing the women greater input into both organizational and artistic decision making. During this period, in fact, Davis's domineering control of the company as a whole was being questioned. The representational actions of the Women's Drill Team may have concretely represented the struggles taking place within the company itself, making Davis's perspective on it and its demise suspect. Troupe members Sandy Archer and Joan Holden wrote a defense of the Women's Drill Team that emphasized the problems activist women faced even within their own politically progressive circles. It stated:

> On the face of the left we see and hear powerful liberating gestures, but if we inspect the private lives, we find a great deal of left-over bourgeois repressive thinking, forcing their personal lives to undergo a confused period of struggle and separation. Some leaders have broken with their "left" wives and children and moved toward specific ties . . . The serious effect of their confusion lies on the women they leave behind or move toward. In a society of such technological development, in a movement of such grand scope, the problem of infidelity seems incongruous; but it is a psychological problem that most movement people cannot solve easily (we are not dealing with hippies here but with FSM pre-flower days.) At most, we find a dangerously cautious "coping."
>
> The Women's Drill Team was formed to bring information and direction to women in and out of the movement. Women in the movement speak of the need for unity and collective actions that will affect the power structure . . . We have developed a Women's Drill Team to push militantly into lives and communities to give impetus and information on such issues as programs to free women from traditional roles. (Davis 112–13)

Like the blacks and Jews of the Punch and Judy plays, women represented an oppressed group within a counterculture. In the drill team women were portrayed as strong and revolutionary, not just in ridiculing power but in taking it over. The Women's Drill Team was obviously problematic not only for spectators but for the company as well. Its critique threatened all sides of the status quo, that of the company and the counterculture as well as that of society at large, without rallying people to its cause. Thus the Women's Drill Team had two problems to contend with: first, a presentation that used militancy rather than subversive clowning as a tactic, and second, the absence of a sympathetic constituency to whom to appeal.

The infusion of feminist rebellion along with other ideological and artistic differences led to a breakup and reorganization of the Mime Troupe in 1970. One of the other dividing ideological factors was a difference in Marxist ideology. As Theodore Shank tells it, "The conscious Marxists believed that they should focus on playing to the working class.[3] Davis, however, was convinced that they should aim their work at pre-revolutionary young middle-class intellectuals" (61–62). Davis was also firmly committed to retaining complete and sole artistic and administrative control of the company while others wanted the group to become a collective and have the company's decision making become a collective process. The result of these differences was

> Davis and most of the most militant of the Marxists leaving the company. Those who remained felt leaderless. Partly for this reason and partly on principle they formed a theater collective. The structure of the organization came to reflect the ideals presented in their plays as they made the shift from intellectuals commenting on political issues to political activists; from artists who had a proprietary attitude about their individual contributions to art workers with a common objective of bringing about social change. (T. Shank, *American Alternative Theater,* 61–62)

A dispute over artistic style, intricately related to the ideological split Shank describes, was another factor that led to the company's breakup. The Troupe's last production before the reorganization was an outdoor version of Brecht's *Turandot, or The Congress of Whitewashers.* The production brought to light the fact that the Troupe's outdoor festive-revolutionary style, while ideologically close to Brecht's vision of the theater, did not fit Brecht's theories, nor did it allow for the distanced, thoughtful attitude that Brecht tried to foster in his audience. Davis wanted the Troupe to explore Brecht's theories and theatrical work further, while other members of the company wanted to stick to the popular style the Troupe had already developed and for which they had become known. When Davis left the company, he pursued his goals by forming two different groups, one to study Brecht's theories and one to work on Brecht's plays. Those left in the group remained committed to using popular forms for creating political theater.[4]

So political and artistic concerns once again came together as they had in *Il Candelaio,* this time in defining the direction of the new Mime Troupe collective. The new Troupe's first production after the reorganization was an original piece called *The Independent Female, or A Man Has His Pride* directed by Denny Partridge. This piece, based on nineteenth-century melodrama, addressed a variety of feminist issues. Again the Troupe had to figure out how to realign the female stereotypes of a popular form so as not to undermine their own feminist message. In the case of *The Independent Female* the popular form the Troupe chose was melodrama, one of the few whose mode of discourse is not one of subversion and clowning but of sentimentality. If the Troupe chose to use the sentimental discourse of melodrama without subverting it, they would fall into the trap of giving up the many useful strategies that festive-revolutionary forms provide.

The Independent Female is the story of Gloria Pennybank, engaged to be married to John Heartright. Both she and her betrothed work for the same company, Amalgamated Corporate Life. The play begins with Gloria distraught over the fact that John wants her to give up her job after they are married. Sarah Bullitt is the character that takes on the role of villain. A feminist lesbian, she convinces Gloria to fight for her own liberation. Gloria, under Sarah's direction, leads all the women in the company on a strike for women's rights. At the end of the play Sarah is killed by Gloria's fiancé, who is hostile to the women protesters. After her death, John tries to win Gloria back to his side, but she decides instead to continue Sarah's fight. The play concludes with a series of "soap operatic" questions posed by the Barker: "Will headstrong youth's impetuous course be halted? Will mankind recover its pride? Will responsible leadership withstand this assault? Or does the implacable, rebellious spirit of independent females—portend this society's ultimate collapse?" (San Francisco Mime Troupe, *By Popular Demand* 193). The Troupe leaves the possibility for action with the audience as the Barker concludes the play, saying: "Young ladies and gentleman, the future lies in your hands" (193).

The "new" Mime Troupe's first attempt at popular political theater was problematic. By casting the most radical feminist character of the play in the role of villain the Troupe undermined their own attempt to take up a truly feminist perspective. Another problem with the play was that the show's demand for a "happy ending" originally had Gloria giving up her fight for equality to be reunited with her husband. The Troupe showed this original version of their work-in-progress to a group of feminist activists, who pointed out the flaws. The Troupe went through a process of deliberation when they realized the changes that were needed in order for the show to work as a feminist statement: "At first the group resisted the changes because inherent in the melodrama form was the requirement of sharp contrasts of good and evil, and of course the happy ending was considered important. However, during the course of the discussions the members of the Mime Troupe gained awareness about the women's struggle that they had not had previously. They came to feel that the conflict between the form and what they wanted to say had to be resolved on the side of their political intent" (T. Shank, "Political Theater as Popular Entertainment" 114).

By too closely following the form of melodrama, the Mime Troupe ended up playing into stereotypes rather than transforming them. However, their openness to dialogue about their work allowed them in the end to turn their production into one that did justice to their true political intentions. In the final version Gloria redefines our understanding of a "happy ending." In a new kind of positive theatrical denouement she resolves to keep fighting for justice in spite of the possibility of losing her husband.[5]

Melodrama as a form relies much more on sentimentality to gain the sympathy of its audience than on the comic, carnivalesque perspective characteristic of festive-revolutionary theater. It is notably a popular form adapted for indoor rather than outdoor presentation and, in contrast with the other popular forms I have discussed, in the nineteenth century it used large, extravagant sets and theatrical special effects to attract its audience. In these ways it is very unlike festive-revolutionary forms. The Mime Troupe found that in order for *The Independent Female* to work as a positive feminist statement they needed to turn it into a parody of melodrama rather than adhere to a faithful rendition of the form. With this new perspective Sarah's death at the end of the play becomes a comic exaggeration rather than merely a tragic event or a working-out of fate (she is the villain, after all). The audience is then freed to move beyond Sarah's individual troubles in order to heed Gloria and the Barker's call to political action. The element of parody that is characteristic of festive-revolutionary theater lets the audience distance itself from the plights of the individuals portrayed in the show and allows them to become more aware of the social and economic realities situating the action.

In *The Independent Female* the Troupe made a conscious choice to put their political agenda ahead of the specific requirements of the theatrical form with which they were working. By turning their melodrama into a parody of melodrama, the Troupe imposed a carnivalesque reversal on the play itself, moving it closer to the true spirit of the popular, in a festive-revolutionary sense. Popular forms live through constant adaptation and reinterpretation. They are containers meant to be shaped and changed by the immediate requirements of each new historical context. By taking the liberty of speaking through the form rather than feeling bound to its apparent limitations, the Troupe again awakened the festive-revolutionary aspect of the popular. In so doing, they re-embraced the type of theatrical work for which they had previously been known.

In *The Independent Female* the Troupe liberated themselves from a strict adherence to the formal requirements of the popular traditions they used. After this show they began to expand their grab bag of popular conventions to include elements from comic books, films, and television shows. The new pieces that followed no longer drew solely on a single specific form, as *The Minstrel Show, L'Amant Militaire,* and *The Independent Female* had done. Instead, the Troupe mixed together a wide variety of popular traditions within a single production. The *Dragon Lady's Revenge,* the Troupe's 1971 production, reflected this new eclecticism. It used elements from "the old melodrama, from commedia, from the adventure movie of foreign intrigue, and even from comic strips such as 'Terry and the Pirates' " (T. Shank, "Political Theater as Popular Entertainment" 114). The Troupe was able to stay true to the spirit of the popular while expanding both their repertoire of forms and the types of political issues they could address.

While blending together different traditions, the Troupe continued to use popular themes, structures, and comic "bits" to illustrate political issues. The Troupe's plays rely on an ability to capture the essence of a political situation in a theatrical metaphor. In spite of the change in political climate in the 1970s and the changed tenor of their audiences, the Troupe could still use festive-revolutionary forms effectively in tackling discrete issues that were less socially comprehensive than race relations, war, and women's rights. They could use them to help audiences reflect on specific government policies and illustrate how those policies would influence their lives and the lives of those around them. Popular forms could be extremely useful in explaining, simply and comprehensibly, the complex jargon in which politicians couched their actions. Their 1972 play, *Frozen Wages,*[6] provides one of the simplest and best instances of the working out of this basic formula. It is a good example of the Mime Troupe addressing a specific, discrete political event rather than issues that are part of a larger social movement.

Frozen Wages illustrates how a wage freeze instituted by the Nixon administration in 1972 would affect workers and industry. The Troupe represented the archetypal factory and its production line by a string of six actors juggling six pins back and forth between them. The play begins with the New Economic Policy Angel arriving at this factory and announcing that a freeze on wages and on "some prices" has been instituted to curb inflation because, as she claims, "High wages are the cause of inflation". The wage freeze obviously makes the workers unhappy. The boss, Mr. Beaver, is also displeased because, as he and the NEP Angel reason: "If prices are frozen, where are profits going to come from?" (San Francisco Mime Troupe, *By Popular Demand* 236). The NEP Angel tells him that he need not worry. He can still increase his profits by paying fewer wages, in other words, by firing some of his employees.

One by one the factory workers are fired. The first to go is Gonzales, who is sent off with the NEP Angel's blessing: "Rejoice, modest minority member, for unto you it is given to go first down the road to your industry's salvation" (236). The next to go is Mrs. Finkelstein, a Jewish employee. The factory of jugglers now has fewer people juggling the same number of pins as before. The task has evidently become more difficult. The remaining workers decide to practice a work slowdown in protest. Their juggling slows down. In response, the NEP Angel grants a wage increase to the employees, telling the boss: "Honey, this is an election year, and we've gotta give something—TO THE ONES THAT ARE LEFT" (239).

In order to keep his profits up in spite of this new wage increase, the boss fires two more workers. This time it is the only women left in the factory who are let go. They protest: "MYRTLE: Why us? You only pay us half a wage anyway." The boss's answer is a punch line: "BEAVER: That's why I have to fire both of you" (239).

There are now only two employees left from the original six, still juggling the same six clubs. The final blow falls when the boss announces, "We've got to step up production or close down" (240). He gives the two workers an extra club. There are now only two workers trying to juggle seven clubs. They are forced to juggle faster than before. The combination of the constant decrease in the number of factory workers (jugglers) as well as the increase in speed soon results in disaster. The workers are overburdened. They drop their pins and the factory-works are seen to break down. The boss then fires his last two workers, hoping to give their jobs to the employees he has already fired at greatly reduced wages. The ex-employees, however, resist the boss's last attempt to exploit them. They unite and strike against the factory. At the end of the play the boss and the

Angel are trapped amidst juggling pins as the protesting workers surround them. Now the workers wield their pins as weapons.

In a note in their collection of plays, *By Popular Demand,* the Troupe remarks that "this was the Mime Troupe's only successful attempt to find a dramatic use for juggling" (232). The principle of using popular forms, tropes, and stunts to create theatrical metaphors for political situations, however, is a consistent part of their work. In this play juggling becomes a useful means of illustrating the relationship between the availability of employment and Nixon's economic policies. The main plot, subplots, jokes, and asides all weave through the central image of the line of jugglers. The juggling metaphor is easily accessible, concrete, and entertaining. Its entertainment value, however, is not merely a "sugarcoating" that makes the political lesson more palatable. The easy flow of juggling pins through an assembly line represents the smooth functioning of the economy. The failed juggling trick (two men and seven pins), the result of the employee cutbacks, represents the breakdown of that stability. At the end of the play the juggling pins are transformed from objects that oppress the workers into weapons they use to fight against the forces driving economic policy. This last moment extends the metaphor that the Troupe has established to give spectators an empowering model for political action.

The successful use of popular forms in *Frozen Wages* to reveal the effects of political policy on ordinary individuals contrasts with that of the Troupe's 1993 summer production *Off-Shore. Off-Shore* was an attempt to illustrate the interrelationships between U.S. economic policy and America's interaction with Asian countries. The acting style of several of the characters in the piece who came from Asian countries incorporated stylistic elements from the Kabuki and the Chinese Opera. Instead of truly serving to elucidate the political allegory that the Troupe was telling, however, the Asian techniques were used purely ornamentally and served to confuse the issues rather than elucidate them. Moreover, the Asian movement vocabulary was unfamiliar to most of their audiences. While the audiences may have enjoyed the play and its use of Asian theatrical forms, the forms themselves did not truly serve to explicate the political situation. When the intrinsic link between the style and the content of the plays is missing, the plays are less successful.

In the 1980s the political climate in America continued its move away from the revolutionary atmosphere of the 1960s. A backlash against the changes of that earlier period had developed. Under the Reagan administration, increasingly powerful conservative politicians attacked and chipped away at progressive social programs and at legislation that promoted the rights of women and minorities. The political atmosphere of the country in the eighties can be seen as the antithesis of that of the sixties when the Mime Troupe had developed and found their following.

Even though popular opinion had turned against the liberal agenda of the sixties, however, the Troupe continued to use popular theater forms to convey a leftist political message. The right-wing establishment had always borne the brunt of the Troupe's attacks. In the eighties the far-right neoconservative movement became the Troupe's outstanding opponent. In *Factwino Meets the Moral Majority,* their 1982 production, the Troupe sought to discredit right-wing fundamentalism by countering its rhetoric of religious and family values with arguments based in economic, social, and political fact. This represented an initial response to the New Right, emphasizing power through knowledge and information. In this piece and other related pieces, including *Factwino and Armageddonman* and *Factwino: The Opera,* the Troupe created a trickster figure for new times, well suited to debunking conservative rhetoric in an age of disinformation and political whitewashing.

Factwino Meets the Moral Majority is a comic-book-style tale in which a wino is given magical powers by a mysterious character known as the Spirit of Information. These magical powers turn the wino into the superhero, Factwino. This new superhero, however, is very different from superheroes found in comic books and action films. Like his counterparts, he attempts to save the world, but he does so without using force or violence. Factwino's superpower is the power of knowledge. When he is sober, he is able to make people question their own assumptions and the myths they have been fed. Factwino, as a trickster, disrupts the regular course of events in order to reawaken social awareness. Through questioning, Factwino's "victims" become more open-minded and begin to see realities in situations that they had previously denied. Factwino's power is very different from Punch's violent threats; he serves as a vehicle by which relevant facts can enter into political and social discourse. Factwino's more sedate methods of confronting political hypocrisy were perhaps better suited to the political environment of the 1980s.

In one scene Factwino uses his superpowers on a couple attending a

19. *Factwino Meets the Moral Majority* (1981). Armageddonman's Robot (Wilma Bonet) captures Factwino (Shabaka) while her two-headed master Armageddonman (Bruce Barthol, Dan Chumley) gloats. Photograph by Michael Bry.

Moral Majority protest rally. Edna and George, disappointed at the dissolution of their family, have sought solace in Christian fundamentalism. At the rally they testify to the group that their children have been destroyed by "atheistic, communist schoolteachers," "immoral TV programs," "by government interference," "and lured away by the false glitter of hot tubs and narcotics." At this point Factwino, who has been observing the rally, "*can't stand it. He zaps her*" (San Francisco Mime Troupe, *Factwino Meets the Moral Majority* 22). His powers change Edna, who has been speaking, and she begins to ask questions:

Edna: Wait a minute. . . . Do you think the economy might have something to do with it?

All: What?

Edna: I mean, the family farm, like we grew up on, that's gone . . . and the factory jobs are all drying up . . . new jobs, they're for women, I guess 'cause we're cheaper—could these things be affecting the family?

Reverend: No way.

George: Yeah—what kind of future would Clyde have in Iowa?
Edna: Where were you supposed to find time for the kids? I mean, how many families can make it on one paycheck?
Factwino: Not many. Only 17 percent of US households have a mama who stays home while papa goes off to work.(22)

Edna's questioning is contagious and infects George, who also joins in. Only the Reverend who has been selling Edna his religious interpretation of events resists the infection. Factwino, by contrast, takes the opportunity to add some of his own new information that help supports the conclusions that Edna is beginning to draw for herself. During the course of the play other social factors that have added to Edna and George's predicament are elucidated: the couple's son has left Iowa to live in San Francisco because he is gay. Their daughter, "married right out of high school" (21), chose to leave her husband, for which her family has disowned her.

In this scene, Factwino's powers force the couple to look behind the rhetoric they have learned and to see economic, social, and political factors that have contributed to the dissolution of their family. In so doing, they are able to reveal facts from outside the play that support Factwino and the Mime Troupe's position. Throughout the play the act of questioning is portrayed as a superpower that saves the characters from being bamboozled by right-wing propaganda. At the end of the play, in an almost traditional "happy ending," Edna and George are reunited with their son, Clyde, and their daughter, Georgianna. Their questioning has brought them to accept their children's "nontraditional" lifestyles. The Mime Troupe proposes that only by first acknowledging the economic, social, and political realities of the time can people bring about true social renewal.

The Mime Troupe's 1986 summer play, *Mozamgola Caper*, gives another model for tracking down truth in an age of misinformation, this time in regard to the U.S. role in international politics. *Mozamgola Caper* is a good example of how the Troupe's simplistic style allows them to shine a light of political clarity on situations often thought to be too complex for ordinary comprehension. Indeed, one of the Mime Troupe's greatest talents lies in their ability to clear out the distracting details that serve to obscure political issues, to the advantage of a few, and in so doing give spectators an unobstructed view of the bigger political picture, one that reveals where simple truth and justice truly lie. The name of this play itself reflects the kind of confusion that exists in the general public awareness of international affairs, and the tendency to lump unfamiliar places like Mozambique and Angola together.

The plot of *Mozamgola Caper* is itself quite complex. But the piece, like the good spy movies it is based on, brings the spectator with it, through every bit of intrigue and misdirection, in the end moving in a traditional path from confusion to clarification. And, in this case, the clarification of the plot is accompanied by a clarification of the political situation at hand. Political machinations and obfuscations confuse the important issues at stake. These issue only come into focus at the end of the play when the characters responsible for the self-interested manipulations and the confusions they cause are killed off.

This parodic spy thriller tells the story of Regretta, a washed-up African-American spy, formerly known as the "Mahogany Mata Hari." She is enlisted for one final secret mission by her old boss Debarge, the White House special advisor on South Africa. Her mission is to rekindle a romance with an old flame, Luthulu, now president of the fictitious Marxist-led African country Mozamgola, and to find out if he is behind a series of voodoo killings. These killings are the result of several unsuccessful assassination attempts aimed at the world-renowned antiapartheid fighter, Bishop Edmund Tata. Regretta's supposed mission, however, is in reality merely an excuse for Debarge to use her as his pawn in a plan that eventually casts Regretta as the Bishop's unwitting assassin. The play begins with an event for the "Hands Across Africa Party for Peace," at which the Bishop is to make an important speech about the debt crisis in Africa. However, just as he begins, his speech is cut short by an assassination attempt. Bishop Tata is not hurt, but he does not get a chance to make his speech. From the very beginning of the play speech and information are silenced, and important political discussion takes a backseat to secret plots and counterplots. The audience must wait until the end of the play to hear the Mime Troupe's analysis and proposed solution to the debt crisis in Africa. The main substance of the story follows Regretta's search to discover who is behind the assassination attempt that has provoked this political silence.

The process of discovery is not easy. Regretta begins by finding only small clues with the help of a *zanni*-esque figure—a poor, impish, local character called Bongo, known as the Hustler. This character, whom Regretta meets at the airport when she first arrives in Mozamgola, will do almost anything for a dollar:

Hustler: Carry your bags?
Regretta: (Shakes her head) Traveling light.
Hustler: Show you native market?
Regretta: No, thanks.
Hustler: Find you African husband!
Regretta: No
Hustler: Genuine maternity doll!! Guarantee healthy baby in only 6 months!
Regretta: No. You got something for these bugs?
Hustler: Nobody got that.
(Holden et al. 59)

When Regretta finally asks him for what she does want to know, "who's doing voodoo on the Bishop?" (59), the Hustler's answer is, "Oho, you ask five dollar information" (59). The Hustler tells her that he is "the eyes and the ears of the Nation!" and then goes about trying to get the information she wants. In the end he provides the information to her free of charge because he realizes "if I didn't, bad things were going to happen" (70). In true commedia fashion, this politically disenfranchised character who moves through the play invisible to those in power is the one person able to sniff out the truth. Unhampered by the political ties that bind the others he can see the whole situation clearly.

With the Hustler's help and trusting her own instincts, Regretta learns to cut through the masses of misinformation given to her by characters on all sides but most notably by her supposedly loyal boss, Debarge. Debarge, a representative of the U.S. government, manipulates the situation in Mozamgola throughout. He not only deceives Regretta but uses Obeh, Luthulu's rival as well. Obeh thinks that the United States has been backing his war against Luthulu's Marxist government because they want him in power. Debarge finally sets him straight by revealing the extent of the United States' own duplicity:

Debarge: Has it ever occurred to you, in your camouflage chic, that winning the war was the *last* thing we wanted you to do? (*It hasn't*) We learned from Vietnam, Somoza, the Marcos mess—let Marxists come to power. *Then* hit them

> where it hurts, keep them on the ropes, make them look bad—beats spending billions to keep bozos in power, and make ourselves look bad. (64)

Obeh, a character the play depicts as evil and lacking any moral sense, is himself stupefied by this revelation and by Debarge's ability to outdo him in scheming. His response is: "That's so cynical it shocks *me*" (65). Debarge reiterates his position and reinforces the play's critique of the United States' role in foreign affairs in his *Jingo Rap*. He sings:

The whole Third World better learn the rule
If we don't like it, it ain't cool.

Self determination, that's OK
Everybody need an Independence Day
Run your country in you own way
But first you better clear it with the USA. (67)

Through this song the play is able to expand its critiques of U.S. foreign policy to encompass relations with a variety of countries. The song underlines the duplicitous nature of that policy and the fact that covert actions and secret financial backing play a greater role in determining the U.S. government's relationship with foreign countries than most ordinary citizens are told of or are meant to know. The play simultaneously reveals this information and teaches its audience to develop a critical attitude toward other official lines it might hear in regard to international affairs.

It is only at the very end of the play that Regretta is able to put all the pieces together and completely understand how she herself has been manipulated. In a moment of clarity, aided by the information the Hustler has given her, she realizes that the medal the Bishop has just been awarded, that she helped switch, contains a bomb that will kill him. She grabs the medal and dies in a struggle over the bomb, taking Debarge with her.

However, this time the assassination attempt only momentarily disrupts the scheduled events. Luthulu, whose position has been vindicated through the course of the play, decides to carry on with the evening's original plan, in spite of the explosion. With the death of Debarge, who has tried to silence information throughout, there is now no one left to stop Luthulu from speaking. He makes the speech he has prepared on the debt crisis in Africa, a speech similar to the one that Bishop Tata was kept from making at the beginning of the play, and the audience is finally given the straight story. After denouncing the apartheid system in South Africa Luthulu proceeds to denounce what is presented as an analogous global version of apartheid. He states: "We will no longer make payments that are unpayable on a debt that is uncollectible, to those who were the architects of our underdevelopment. After 400 years of economic exploitation, we declare those debts paid in full" (71). He finishes by announcing the "debt moratorium" that he and thirty-four other Third World nations plan to launch.

The Mime Troupe proposes this policy as a vision for the future at the end of the piece. The Troupe also seems to be saying that more than anything else, it is this type of action that the U.S. government is afraid of and has perhaps moved to prevent with covert assassination attempts and secret funding of civil wars. It is not the financial boycott itself that is so frightening, as much as the possibility of Third World countries uniting, without U.S. intervention, and truly taking charge of their own self-determination.

At the very end of the play the issues that are of concern to the people of real African countries are finally allowed to be addressed. The plotting and intrigue throughout the play are obfuscation tactics that serve to obscure the important economic questions. The play goes through a process of clearing these distractions away to reveal a simple truth and a possibility for future action. In this way the Troupe once again provides a model for gaining political clarity in a world that is apparently confusing and beyond the comprehension of ordinary citizens. Revealing information is the first step toward liberation.

Questioning the status quo, making connections between disparate economic, political, and social situations, and using knowledge as a tool to counter political rhetoric had always been part of the Mime Troupe's weaponry against the right. In the 1980s the Troupe emphasized the values of these tactics even more. While their plays continued to dispel right-wing rhetoric, however, it is doubtful whether they actually convinced people to change their ideas as easily as Factwino convinces Edna. In the eighties the Troupe was often criticized for merely preaching to the converted. However, as Harry Elam points out in his insightful study of the role of theaters working for social change, converting new followers is not necessarily the primary function of such theater groups. He writes: "Effectiveness of social theater can not be determined by the ability to convert new followers nor the traditional notion of longevity. Instead, effectiveness should be determined by the ability of plays and theatrical movements for social change to forge an emotional bond between performers and sympathetic spectators that makes those spectators more socially aware and reaffirms their commitment to struggle for change" (3).

Supporting those already engaged in activism and those sympathetic with their views has been one of the Troupe's roles since the sixties. While many today might view them as anachronistic, the Mime Troupe may have actually taken on new importance in their immediate community. The Troupe's performances serve as an opportunity for leftists to reaffirm their ideals and their commitment to a struggle that is still valuable, in spite of the country's change in political direction. The rarer these opportunities become the more important they are. The yearly gathering of Mime Troupe supporters across the Bay Area at the Troupe's annual summer shows provides an occasion to reawaken forgotten ideals and to revisit the possibility that grassroots activism can lead to social, economic, and political change. These events also serve to inspire a new generation: the children of old lefties who come to the show and the young people from the area who discover the Mime Troupe for themselves.

Yet in the sixties authorities like the park commission felt threatened enough by the Troupe's productions to send the police after them, creating the opportunity for a political event. Today the Troupe has won the right to perform outdoors, as well as other battles, and rarely, if ever, elicits the kind of antagonistic reactions from the authorities that they once did. They have become a San Francisco Bay Area institution, perhaps even a national one as well. Some would argue that the Troupe has been absorbed into the status quo, occupying the niche of radical leftist "naysayers." Though their message and tactics are still the same, their opponents have become comfortable with them. By accepting them, the establishment seems to have robbed the work of its former political impact.

Other factors have added to the image of the Mime Troupe as having been coopted by the establishment. One of these comes from the Troupe's increased need for funding and their consequent change in attitude toward government support. In the sixties it was a point of honor for the Troupe that they received no government funding for their work. The Troupe survived then solely on individual donations and on whatever they collected by passing the hat at the end of each show. They feared that if they accepted government funding either government censorship and/or self-censorship would change the political intent of their work. They especially feared becoming dependent on government support that might further compromise their political agenda. The Troupe wanted to be a theater for the people supported by the people.[7]

In his dissertation "The San Francisco Mime Troupe in its Social Context," Lance Jencks shows how the Troupe's financial burdens have greatly increased since their inception. In 1964 the Troupe's yearly expenses totaled $3,400. In just one year that figure rose to $10,000. By 1974 their budget was $100,000 a year (91). In 1984 the Troupe finally gave in to escalating costs and the inability to run the Troupe on donations alone. They accepted an "Ongoing Ensemble Award" for $75,000 from the National Endowment for the Arts. How did the Troupe justify this new attitude toward government funding in light of their past fears? In a 1985 interview, Joan Holden, the Troupe's main playwright, answered the question in this way:

> we *have* definitely changed our position about grants, at least about public money. We have realized that we cannot survive without subsidy. It was a bitter pill for a while because for many years it was our ambition to be entirely independent, supported by the audience. But we can't do more shows than we do; we can't charge much higher ticket prices than we charge. In fact, theater isn't self-supporting anywhere in the world. Going to other countries, going to France, going to Canada, going to England, and seeing what subsidy has done there, brought me around, personally, to where I now regard it as a necessity. If it's a necessity, we don't have to apologize for it . . . No we can't live at the welfare level for the rest of our lives. That is far from compromising your ideals. (Kleb 59)

The Troupe's current situation in regard to federal funding is one that is in some ways tragically ironic. The Troupe over the past few years has had their government subsidies cut 46 percent and must once again rely more heavily on individual donations, but this time not by choice.

In 1987 the Troupe had to contend with another factor that compromised their valued position as outside agitators. The Troupe received a special Tony Award in honor of their years of artistic work and their contribution to the theater. Since the sixties the Troupe had promoted their popular theater as an alternative to Broadway and regional theaters. They criticized the theater establishment for being "apolitical" and for being inaccessible both financially and artistically to lower-income and minority groups. The Tony Award puts the Troupe in the awkward position of

20. Arthur Holden as Rip in *Ripped Van Winkle* (1988). Photograph by Katy Raddatz.

having been honored and accepted by the very theater establishment they had spent years working against.

In the eighties the Troupe found themselves in a very different world from the one that had supported their work in the sixties. America had certainly changed, but not necessarily in the direction the Troupe had hoped. Their acceptance of government funding and a Tony Award were indicative of the compromises the Troupe had to make in response to changing times. A reevaluation of the meaning and direction of their work became necessary. Did popular, festive-revolutionary theater still offer the prospect of supporting or fostering political engagement?

The many contradictions the Troupe has faced in dealing with their current institutional status culminated in the explicitly self-critical production, *Ripped Van Winkle.* Whereas in *Factwino* the Troupe appealed to their audiences through rational argument, *Ripped Van Winkle* more fully emphasized the value of festive-revolutionary spirit for their theatrical project. The play's allusion to the well-known tale "Rip Van Winkle" high-

21. *Ripped Van Winkle* (1988). Rip (Arthur Holden, foreground) wakes from a twenty-year sleep to find the San Francisco Civic Center full of angry homeless people. *Left to right, in the background:* Benny (Ed Holmes), Crazy Lady with Shopping Cart (Sharon Lockwood), Little Fox (Keiko Shimosato), and a Homeless Vet (Mark Christopher Lawrence). Photograph by Katy Raddatz.

lights the sense of disorientation that those who in the sixties predicted an imminent social revolution now feel, living in a country that has, in spite of their own continued effort and conviction, turned in exactly the opposite direction.

The play tells the story of Rip, a hippie activist from the sixties who has, like his namesake, fallen asleep for many years under the influence of some mysterious force. All he can recall of the event is a French woman giving him two purple tabs of LSD. Having closed his eyes in 1968, Rip wakes to find himself in 1988. He does not realize that he has slept for twenty years. The world around him has so transformed, however, that he is convinced he is having a very bad acid trip. Rip finds his old apartment house turned into a chic, yuppie restaurant. The cars on the street seem to have shrunk. A robot voice at the other end of a strange space-age telephone tells him to deposit twenty cents. The people Rip greets as fellow hippies turn out to be San Francisco's homeless. The biggest shock to Rip, however, is his seeing in a mirror that he has grown old. (Rip still has Day-Glo stickers in his pockets that read "Don't Trust Anyone Over Thirty.")

Rip finally realizes that he has lost twenty years of his life and of history. With a rap song entitled "Update Bringdown," an old friend brings Rip and the audience up-to-date on the end of "the Revolution," the failures of the left since then, and the increasing accumulation of political power in the hands of the conservative right. His revelations are met with Rip's utter astonishment and disbelief:

Benny: . . . We took Cambodia, Bombed Hanoi
Lost 50,000 American boys
Cause the war didn't end till '75
And after that, the Movement died.
Rip: '75? '75? *Died*?
Benny: And in Cambodia we backed some stooge
But his ass got kicked by the Khmer Rouge.
Rip: Right On!
Benny: They killed more people than you'd believe
Till they got creamed by the Vietnamese.
Rip: Wait . . .
Benny: Then Nixon sank in a swamp of sleaze
Now the only ones who love him are the Red Chinese.
Rip: Nixon and the Red Chinese?
Benny: . . . And the final nail I'll now pound in
Forgive us Che for we have sinned
It ain't pretty it ain't nice
Ronald Reagan's been elected twice.
[**Rip:** Governor?][8]
Benny: President.
Rip: Y-a-a-a-ahhh! (Holden, Callas, and Barthol 26–27)

The summary of familiar historic events set alongside Rip's reactions brings home not only the inconceivable changes that have taken place in the intervening years but also the incredible optimism that drove the social revolution of the sixties. Rip represents that naive optimism and, in response to these new revelations, points up the direction he and many in his generation genuinely believed the world would take with their efforts:

Rip: I thought, by the time I'm middle-aged, we'd be living in this beautiful country. "Farmers will grow things, city people will make things—we'll trade. We'll dismantle all the corporations. We'll all work—4 days a week. We'll have trains going everywhere—we won't need many cars. We'll only need a very tiny amount of petroleum. We can clean up the rivers. We can save the rest of the redwood trees. Americans will be happy—we can stop proving how great we are. We can let the rest of the world breathe." (28)

From our own contemporary perspective we can't fail to see the naiveté in the ease with which Rip and others thought such things could be accomplished. Rip demonstrates his innocence early on in the play. Still unaware that he's been asleep for two decades, he says of the revolution: "But it's not gonna be victory overnight. It's gonna take two more years at least" (5). What is most agonizing about hearing Rip enumerate the goals of the sixties, however, is that many of them are surprisingly consistent with what the left is still trying to achieve thirty years later. Rip is a character who evokes both the disillusionment and the persistent faith of the left.

Rip's old girlfriend, Susan, provides an opposing perspective on the situation. She, too, is a radical from the sixties but, unlike Rip, she has lived through the intervening twenty years. She has tried to hold on to her ideals while others around her seem to have sold out to the establishment. By maintaining her ideals she feels as if she too has been asleep. She says:

Somewhere, I missed the boat. Someplace I got off at the wrong stop. Sometime, everybody else piled on the train and I didn't even hear the whistle. Everybody was in the Movement . . . then everybody had a baby . . . then everybody got into healing . . . then it gets vague. I was trying to do socially responsible creative work . . . suddenly, everybody else puts their kids in private school, starts remodelling the house they just bought, has a glamor job at a salary they don't even discuss—at least not with me. Is that how you know you've been left in the dust—your friends stop telling you how much money they make? (13)

She voices the feelings of many ex-radicals when she reflects on her life, her thankless devotion to social causes, and her desire for something more. She echoes Joan Holden's plaint that Mime Troupe members "can't live at the welfare level for the rest of our lives. That is far from compromising your ideals" (Kleb 59) when having moved into a swanky new apartment she says: "When a person's past 40, she deserves something different than crumbly plaster, cracked ceilings, and cockroaches. This is how I want to live! Now all I gotta do is pay for it" (7).

In order to pay for her new lifestyle, then, Susan decides to sell out to the establishment. During the course of the play she puts together a public relations event designed to get San Franciscans to feel positive about dredging the Bay and bringing the nuclear battleship SS *Missouri* to San Francisco. In a conversation between Susan and Brad (who is managing her pro-*Missouri* campaign) the Mime Troupe articulates their own position on this timely, local issue, in quick-paced, vaudeville-style, comic repartee:

Susan: You want to dock a battleship loaded with nuclear missiles half a mile from the heart of this city.
Brad: That's it.
Susan: You want to plant a floating atomic timebomb in one of the most beautiful places that still exists on this planet.
Brad: You got it.
Susan: . . . And to make all this happen you want to dredge the Bay floor 50 feet deep, stirring up a century and a half of accumulated toxic garbage, releasing megarems of radioactivity, and finally turning San Francisco Bay into a dead sea.
Brad: We don't just want to do it. We want people to vote for it. (15–16)

The fact that Susan agrees to plan the event in order to reach "Yuppies, gays, the Big Chill generation—people who, if we let them think about it, could vote for peace and ecology" (17), and that she "chilled all the local radical artists" (33) by hiring them for the event is meant to show just how far she and others have surrendered their former ideals. Susan represents one option open to the Mime Troupe in the eighties—selling out—and evokes both the practical and problematic nature of their own compromises.

The first half of the play, though comic, illustrates the pall of apathy and despair that hangs over American radical activism. Yet Rip becomes the means by which the times are reinfused with a spirit of radical protest. He provides an alternative to Susan's attitude of resignation because his ideals have not been slowly eroded by the passage of time and political change. At the end of scene 6, Rip has just realized how long he has been asleep and how thoroughly the world has changed. He finds himself at a turning point. A chorus of homeless sing:

He never thought he would be so alone
What was familiar is now the unknown

Will he survive? Will he find his way home? Nothing really stays the same
But nothing, really nothing seems to change.
Where will he go? What will he choose?
What will he do? What will he do? What will he do?

(28)

Rip is faced with all the questions and doubts that have confronted the sixties radicals since the Reagan-Bush era. The song asks if he too will give up his ideals and sell out to the system. By scene 7, however, Rip has come to terms with his position and has found a positive response to these questions. Rip decides that his radical spirit is needed more than ever in this new environment and takes it on himself to continue the work of social critic. Rip comes to represent the Mime Troupe itself and their determination to persevere in their work.

Rip begins by identifying what he thinks is society's greatest ill, then he moves on to attack it. Rip sees excess consumerism lying at the heart of the strayed values of the eighties. He decides to sabotage the consumer economy at a grassroots level. Shoppers at the "Whole Earth Excess" cashier counter, ready to buy useless items like Swiss garbage disposals, combination pasta maker-food scales, and waterproof telephones, find the telltale traces of Rip's work: Day-Glo stickers on their items that read, "Do you really need this?" "Your purchase today will be toxic waste tomorrow," and "Shopping is the opiate of the '80s" (29–30). The stickers make the shoppers stop and think. They end up forgoing their pointless purchases. Like Factwino, Rip acts as a kind of trickster figure, disrupting the normal course of events and stimulating people to question the status quo.

Rip's second radical plot is to sabotage the pro-SS *Missouri* public relations event that Susan has organized. For this new operation he convinces others to help him. A new vaudevillian regurgitator who is supposed to perform at the event doesn't show up. Instead a Day-Glo note appears, which reads, "The Regurgitator regrets that he will not be able to perform for you today, but there are some things he can't swallow" (34). A comic who does show up tells a series of anti-SS *Missouri* jokes. Even Rambo-Dojo, a band that Susan describes as "absolute fascists" (35), have been converted by "the hippie-looking guy backstage" (36). They sing a new song they have just written for the occasion whose refrain, repeated over and over again, is "Big Mo, Just Say No!" (36). Rip's sabotage turns Susan's event into an anti-SS *Missouri* protest rally in which three thousand people end up walking through the streets chanting, "Big Mo, Just Say No." In Rip's successful sabotage lies the promise of the beginning of a new movement. Rip overcomes the apathy and disappointment that Susan represents, and in the end she too is transformed, rejuvenated, and joins him.

It is too optimistic to assume that a protest movement like that of the sixties could actually emerge as quickly and easily as Rip's does. The play suggests, however, that there is still value in the type of work that activists did in the sixties, and that the Mime Troupe continues to do. For it is only by persevering in such work that the possibility of revolutionary action can emerge. The Mime Troupe and others keep nudging people towards radicalism until the time is ripe for genuine change.

At the end of the play Rip finally discovers what put him to sleep for twenty years. In revealing this mystery, the Troupe offers an analysis of Rip's position, and their own, in a conservative political environment. The unmasking begins when Rip runs into the "French woman" who he remembers having given him the two acid pills twenty years before. When he sees her he asks her who she is: "Liberte: You don't know French painting? The spirit of 1789. Of the Revolution—Liberté. (He doesn't get it) Of Freedom" (43). The woman is the Spirit of Liberty Leading the People, as depicted in Delacroix's famous 1830 painting of the same name.[9] She is the spirit of revolution. In 1830 she was resurrected from her earlier appearance in 1789, and Rip and the generation of political idealists that he represents were her representatives in the 1960s. Liberté goes on to explain to Rip what happened to him: "I have good and bad seasons, like the wine. '68, it was an excellent year. I knew a bad season would come after, and all the good vintage would be consumed. So I bottled some. . . . Not just you—there are many, many, all over the world. And now a better time is on its way. I am letting you out" (43).

The spirit of liberty bottled Rip and his revolutionary spirit like fine wine. She has now decanted him in the eighties when the time is ripe for his return. The play ends with Rip looking for direction from the Spirit of Liberty. "What should I do?" he asks. Her reply: "Shave. And continue—especially with the youth. Au revoir, camarade. The 90's, it looks like a promising decade" (43). Rip brings with him the revolutionary spirit of the past that has been preserved and, like fine wine, has only improved with age. Like the popular theatrical style of the Mime Troupe itself, he embodies the forces of political rejuvenation.

In contrast to *Ripped Van Winkle*, the Troupe's 1991 production, *Back to Normal*, makes a concerted effort to address the issues it presents from a contemporary perspective. In so doing, however, it unintentionally promotes a real nostalgic attitude, one that is truly backward-looking and as a result deradicalized. The storyline of *Back to Normal* involves a leftist radical from the past trying to sustain political activism in the present, and in this way seems to mirror *Ripped Van Winkle*. However, by adopting a contemporary viewpoint on this character and the events around her, the Troupe in effect ends up disempowering her. As a response to the Gulf War, produced the summer following the war, *Back to Normal* also provides an interesting parallel to plays like *L'Amant Militaire*, while making evident the vast differences in the respective political climates surrounding the events. *Back to Normal* takes a broad look at the political complacency of a community that allows itself to be mesmerized into supporting the war.

In this production, and in trying to draw an analogy with the Vietnam War, the Mime Troupe was in a difficult position. The Gulf War was not drawn out the way the Vietnam War was, and the Troupe's summer show already occurred after the fact. The pervasive mood in the country, at the time, was one of elation and national pride. Most people were relieved that the war had ended quickly and that the United States had won with so few casualties of its own. The popular rhetoric and media hype compared Saddam Hussein to Hitler in an attempt to create a parallel with World War II rather than with the Vietnam War. The quick and decisive victory led some to announce that the country had finally gotten over "the Vietnam syndrome," so we could now move on, once again adopting a linear, progressive view of history. A constant attempt to correct the mistakes of Vietnam led people to emphasize the fact that the military troops should not be blamed for participating in the war the way veterans returning from Vietnam had been. Criticizing the war while it was in progress or picketing the welcome-home parades was regarded as simply failing to "support the troops." While the audiences the Mime Troupe played to may have been among the thousands who marched against the war in San Francisco and elsewhere, once the war was over, antiwar demonstrations were no longer an option. Especially when many of the soldiers who served came from local minority communities, groups whose concerns the Mime Troupe has tried hard to address.

In *Back to Normal* Hetty Counts is a leftist who deals in political conspiracy theories on her own late-night radio talk show, "Reality Sandwich," broadcast from her hometown of Normal, California. Her house is overrun with piles of newspaper articles that she has collected over the years in order to gather evidence for her theories. Hetty's grown son, Jamal, who was conceived during a "hot weekend at Monterey Jazz" by, she tells him, one of a possible three different black jazz musicians, has, unbeknownst to Hetty, joined the Marines and gone to fight in the Gulf (San Francisco Mime Troupe, *Back to Normal* 24). Jamal, who has spent his life keeping secrets from his mother—for example, that he was a Boy Scout, then an Eagle Scout, and then joined R.O.T.C.—has led his mother to believe that he is backpacking around the world, just as she did when she was young. However, Jamal's secret military career is revealed when he destroys a land mine and in the process saves the life of an Iraqi. He becomes an instant national hero when his daring feat is broadcast by a Connie Chung-esque reporter.

The episode is seen on TV by the inhabitants of Normal, including an Iraqi diner owner who, since the beginning of the Gulf War, has changed his name (from Farid to Frank) along with his menu (from falafel sandwiches to eggs and bacon); Fumiko, a Japanese-American hairdresser who spent time in an American concentration camp during World War II; a Vietnam veteran; and a mayor who wants to bring industry and tourism to Normal. These people put aside all the economic hardships that have hit their small, depressed town when they watch the exploits of American bomber pilots in the Gulf on television. They are all happy to arrange a hero's welcome for Jamal, who in another effort to distance himself from his mother's values now calls himself Jimmy.

Hetty sees the welcome-home celebration as her opportunity to draw national attention to her theory that George Bush was involved in the assassination of JFK.[10] The moment she begins her public ranting, however, the TV cameras are turned off and security guards drag her from the podium.[11] By carrying out her stunt she completely betrays her son's trust, and he leaves home for good. Left alone, Hetty regrets having devoted her life to political causes rather than to her son and bemoans having been ostracized by the rest of the town. She cries on an oil lamp Jamal has given her, a present from the Iraqi he saved, and a genie suddenly appears, free at last from his bottle. Hetty, of course, gets three wishes in payment for her kind deed and, predictably, wastes two of them on trivialities.

22. The citizens of Normal turn against Hetty in *Back to Normal* (1991). *Left to right:* Hetty (Sharon Lockwood), Delbert (Dan Chumley), Frank (Isa Nidal Totah), the Mayor (Arthur Holden), and Fumiko (Keiko Shimosato). Photograph by Cristina Taccone.

Hetty carefully contemplates how to spend her one remaining wish. At the diner, she watches her son being awarded a medal of honor by President Bush on TV and listens to Bush's speech consisting of half-sentence platitudes: "Our troops: we followed them with prayers, as they punished aggression . . . Operation Desert Storm: dawn of a New World Order of justice and liberty, where might no longer makes right." Hetty unwittingly makes her final wish, exclaiming: "God, I wish you'd can the jive" (32). President Bush then begins to say what is apparently really on his mind, insulting every ethnic group, pointing out the economic benefits he will derive from the war, expressing his contempt for the voting public, and generally being vulgar and grabbing at his crotch. Although Bush could be compared to Factwino at this point, since both are characters who revel in the unadulterated truth, in this instance the image the Mime Troupe presents is a kind of pathetic fantasy. It inspires only disgust, unlike Factwino's enlightening educational jolts that arouse the public's indignation and yearning for action.

This unbecoming presidential display gets Hetty's neighbors to rethink their prior enthusiasm for the war. They are brought back to reality out of the hysteria that had gripped them and begin to remember all their economic woes. Although all the diner regulars agree that the president should be impeached for his indecorous speech, no one takes any action. They all simply return to their personal concerns. Having borne witness to the truth these characters are not inspired to right wrongs. Their lives are not transformed. The characters here are rightly disabused of their patriotic illusions but then are forced to confront a grim but—as the play presents it—unchangeable reality.

In the final scene, Hetty gets a call from Jamal, who has dropped out of the Marines and gone to live in Oakland. In Oakland Jamal has finally begun to see some of the real problems facing the country, and he finally understands what his mother has been fighting for all these years. In a closing sentimental song of reconciliation he makes plans to visit her again. However, all these events packed into the play's final moments come as too little too late, and the family reunion on the horizon at the play's end holds only scant promise for real social change or political renewal.

Although Hetty seems to be carrying on the political project of the sixties, she is a very different character from Rip. She has not really preserved her youthful ideals but has become cynical and eccentric. In fact the play in effect represents her from the perspective of the conservative right. Her views are unbelievable and her rhetoric is unpersuasive. There is little attempt to explain her conspiracy theories in a convincing way or to show what motivates them. Moreover, her concerns focus mostly on issues long past, like the Kennedy assassination, rather than on current problems. More contemporary concerns are addressed only at the end of the play when they should have held center stage throughout. Furthermore, the mother-son relationship is mixed with the political relationship in a way that fails to convey the Mime Troupe's distinctive message. Since parents usually function as authority figures, Hetty takes on the role of a "bad guy" whose eccentric ideas have had a stifling effect on her son. Jamal leaves home because he can't stand his mother any more, and the audience can only sympathize with him. By looking at the situation from a contemporary perspective, the Mime Troupe concedes far too much to the conservative climate of the times, and in so doing, effectively surrenders its own political point of view.

In the end, it is *Back to Normal* that comes to seem nostalgic, much more so than *Ripped Van Winkle,* and it does so precisely because it takes up a contemporary perspective. In drawing on an essentially conservative point of view, the play portrays the mother as a crackpot, precisely because she seems to be clinging to unmotivated, outmoded ideas. In the end, the play must resort to the magic of a genie to bring about its desired result. The cheap shots at President Bush that result seem childish and petty and a poor alternative to attacking the real issues and contradictions behind the war effort. Moreover, the denouement is confusing and simply caters to a sentimental desire to see the family reunited. The audience never sees what Jamal experiences in Oakland, or how those experiences cause him to change his views. The longing for the past, for things to be as they were, is genuinely nostalgic because the whole play, in spite of the Mime Troupe's better intentions, accommodates the political values of the right. The end of the play reveals the complacency of a population continually manipulated by political rhetoric rather than engaging with practical ideas about how to combat that rhetoric and reverse that complacency.

The ending that turns the play around is brought about by the genie and by President Bush, who ends up incriminating himself while under a magic spell. But to hope that solutions will come from the oppressor[12] or through magical means is a way of disempowering people and underrating their ability to bring about change through their own efforts. Even Factwino, whose superpowers were also brought about through magical intervention, did little more than counter inflammatory rhetoric with facts, something that is presumably within the powers of most ordinary citizens. While *Ripped* moved its audience with a vision of rekindling political action, *Back to Normal* simply tries to turn back the clock without rediscovering or reinventing the validity of the radical perspective itself. The play proposes no course of political action, and Jamal's and his mother's reconciliation remains a private affair with no genuine wider political implications.

It is highly ironic that in their attempt to adapt themselves to a new situation, to admit that times are different and that we need a new perspective to meet the challenge of a new age, the Troupe mounted a production that in effect undermined its own convictions. While the times may not always be right for revolution, the impetus for revolution does not itself simply become outdated overnight. It recurs to enliven opposition in each new situation.

Rip is a theatrical metaphor that fittingly describes the Mime Troupe's own situation. An activist group born in the sixties, they continue their political work in a new conservative world. Even though "the movement" is no longer what it was, the Troupe's job is still the same: to question the world we live in and to force others to do the same. This is the role of trickster that they have taken upon themselves. While their popular performances do not have the impact they once did, this is not to say that the basic work of questioning the status quo, turning it upside down through carnivalesque reversals, is itself out of date.

The Troupe attaches relatively little significance to their own changed situation, for instance the Tony Award and the grant from the NEA. Joan Holden has said: "Those are surface changes. I don't feel that I'm coming from a different place than I ever was coming from since I started doing this. I still know who the enemy is, who is poisoning us and starving Africa, who is getting ready to blow up the world if we don't stop them! I know who I want to kill in my plays and who I want to exalt. Who I think deserves to die and who produces the wealth and should have the power. Those things that come from inside you aren't changing" (Kleb 61).

Whether or not the Troupe lives up to their own ideals should be tested in each new production. Either way, the project of supporting revolutionary activity through popular theater is not misdirected. The revolutionary potential of popular forms is ignited only when the proper historical circumstances for revolution exist, as they did in the 1960s. Yet this potential always remains latent within the forms. By keeping the popular forms alive the Troupe is keeping the spirit of revolution alive. When the time is ripe they intend their work to awaken a new generation of activists just as Rip awakened the other characters around him.

Of course there is still a good deal of feminist critique that can be brought to bear on the Mime Troupe's plays. Regretta, the female protagonist of *Możamgola Caper,* embodies the Mata Hari mold. Although she discovers herself in the course of the play, she is originally hired because of her ability to make men fall in love with her. At the end of the play she sacrifices herself, and it is the famous men, Bishop Tata and Luthulu, the country's president, who lead the new political revolution. In *Ripped Van Winkle* our hero is again a man. The women in the play include his ex-

23. Jack Belch (Ed Holmes), king of corporate downsizers, and Alan Greenspan (Amos Glick), in drag, entertain businessmen and political cronies at an exclusive retreat in *Killing Time* (1997). Photograph by Taylor Carman.

girlfriend, who has sold out; her troubled, suicidal daughter; and the allegorical female figure of Liberty. These images appear time and again. When playing with popular images one is always in danger of simply absorbing those images without attempting to reinvent them. But the Mime Troupe plays are always at base parodic, playing on familiar images even as they use them to communicate their own political message. The Mime Troupe never intends to perpetuate harmful images of women or others but to take advantages of familiar, easily recognizable conventions from popular forms in order to provide a frame for political arguments.

What of the Mime Troupe today? This past summer's show in the park, *Killing Time,* followed the Troupe's usual mixture of comic entertainment and revolutionary politics, but it failed to articulate a vision for change in the future. It revealed an utterly pessimistic view of the world at hand. This year's evil megalomaniacal company executive (played brilliantly, as always, by Ed Holmes) dies but is not removed from power. Instead his brain is transplanted into the head of a twenty-something gen-X guy, whose life lacks direction as he goes from one coffeehouse or bookstore job to the next. The CEO lives on through him and continues to carry out his environmentally devastating schemes. The younger generation in this play gives no hint of future transformation and regeneration in a radical direction. Instead, they become the agent by which the evils of the past are carried on into the future. The new world that is born here is simply a replication of the old world, not a radical transformation of it. The play provides no positive model of political action, since the two characters who do fight against the CEO are ridiculed by the play itself and are in the end easily defeated.

Despite widespread recognition today of the excesses and injustices of American political life in the eighties, recent experience has not borne out lady Liberté's optimistic forecast, "the 90's, it looks like a promising decade." The Mime Troupe's pessimism at this point is surely understandable. The NEA funding cut has made the Troupe's current financial situation much more precarious, and the theft in 1996 of their trademark truck was no doubt demoralizing as well. However, cynicism about their own mission tends to rob their plays of their distinctive force. It is instead optimism and a new vision of the future that gives their work its greatest strength. Indeed, as I have argued, just such a vision is what underlies the forms on which they draw. When they can decant the revolutionary spirit in those forms, their work is at its best and has the best chance of inspiring their spectators, even in times of political rest.[13]

The reviews in the local papers continue to debate the success of the summer shows. Depending on the reviewer, this annual ritual of performance is either seen as a sign of the Troupe's continued relevance as part of an ongoing tradition or as a nostalgic remnant of the past put on for the entertainment of disenfranchised activists or now successful, middle-aged, middle-class audiences. The truth is that at their best these shows are both. They are pieces of the past revisited for the present. The San Francisco Mime Troupe productions are strongest when they reawaken old theatrical forms and release the festive-revolutionary spirit dormant within them. They continue to be relevant when they continue to direct this spirit toward specific political issues of the day with the hope of inspiring political change. Their current position as "the most established anti-establishment theater" in America is part of a long tradition of popular theaters working in the name of radical social change. The forms they use are not themselves out-of-date but only need continual political revitalization.

Notes

Introduction

1. San Francisco Mime Troupe member Joan Holden has often described the Mime Troupe in this way in interviews and conversation.

Chapter 1

1. This was especially true in Germany where it was only in the late 1920s and early 1930s that theater groups like Truppe 31 turned to festive forms to convey their political message. Some Russian groups like the Blue Blouses, who inspired Truppe 31, did work more in the genre of popular theater that I wish to describe. The type of work that contrasts most clearly with a festive-revolutionary type of popular theater was done by groups like Das Rote Sprachrohr (the Red Megaphone). Examples of this type of theater can be found in *Théâtre D'Agit-Prop de 1917 á 1932*, Equipe "Théâtre Moderne" from GR 27 of the CNRS, Chief Editor: Denis Bablet, vol. 4 (Lausanne: La Cité—L'Age D' Homme, 1978).

2. The cover reads: "A Panoramic History of Fools and Jesters; Medieval Mimes, Jongleurs and Minstrels; Pueblo Indian Delight Makers and Cheyenne Contraries; Harlequins and Pierrots; Theatrical Buffoons and Zanies; Circus Tramps, Whitefaces and Augustes."

3. Native American clowns are also sacred and perform specific social functions. Towsen explains some of the practices of these clowns and clown societies in the following way: "The Hopi concept of burlesquing the sacred while supporting it is repeated in most North American Indian cultures . . . The clown keeps people in touch with everyday reality while fulfilling the need for a connection with the sacred. While ostensibly mocking the entire performance, he also supports and embellishes it . . . Among the Tübatulabal of California, in fact, the clown's opinions are held in such high esteem that if he criticizes the chief, a new leader is likely to be selected" (Towsen 8–9).

4. For a concise discussion and critique of the Cambridge school, see Schechner, *Performance Theory* 1–6.

5. Examples include "the death of the god or the destruction of a scapegoat, the combat or contentious confrontation, the miraculous mutability reflected in rebirth, sexual substitutions, and physical restorations" (Caputi 39).

6. It is important to note that theater practitioners like Austria's Johann Nes-

troy (1801–62), living neither in the world of Renaissance festivals nor in the Marxist world of Schechter's twentieth-century clowns, were also able to create festive-revolutionary theater using mime, improvisation, and other elements distinctive of popular theater. Nestroy in particular is renowned for the biting satire of the songs he sang in his own plays, adding to them in each performance endless new verses that commented on current social and political issues. For more on the work of Nestroy, see Laurence V. Harding, *The Dramatic Art of Ferdinand Raimund and Johann Nestroy: A Critical Study,* Studies in German Literature, vol. 3 (The Hague and Paris: Mouton, 1974.)

7. For Turner, ritual and performance are social events by which a community overcomes a crisis, some breach in the normal passage of daily life. The process of a ritual helps to recreate what Turner calls *communitas*, a feeling of harmony and coming together within a community. He relates this notion to Csikszentimihalyi and MacAloon's idea of "flow." For a discussion of this in relation to what Turner calls "liminal" and "liminoid" cultures see "Liminal to Liminoid, in Play, Flow and Ritual" in Turner 20–60.

8. In his book *The Origin of Theater,* Ernest Theodore Kirby put forth a different theory, finding the origins of theater not in spring rituals but in shamanistic practices. Kirby describes the shaman as "a 'master of spirits' who performs in trance, primarily for the purpose of curing the sick by ritualistic means." This sort of curative ritual endows the individual with new life. In this context the individual undergoes a sickness, a kind of death, and is finally brought back to life. The cycle of death and renewal here is played out on the scale of the individual rather than the community (E. Kirby 1).

9. It is of course true that Bakhtin, who lived through the Russian Revolution, was well versed in Marxism. However, he attributes an understanding of class struggle to people who had no knowledge of Marxism and finds ample evidence for his position.

10. "It would seem, however, that most mime, from earliest times to the present, has been accompanied by sound of some kind: speech supplied by a narrator, chorus, or the mime performer; percussion sounds produced by striking one part of the body against another on the floor; or the kind of vocal mime Copeau's students experimented with, using pre- and post-verbal warbles and chortles and other expressive sounds that are not words" (Leabhart 2).

11. Use of the term "expressive movement" is also an attempt to distinguish mime, theatrical use of the body in performance, from a kind of dance interested in exploring movement itself. Satisfactorily defining the exact boundaries between dance and mime, however, is always a difficult task. Nonetheless, the terms should definitely be viewed as encompassing different artistic realms, though they obviously overlap.

12. "In 1890 a papyrus scroll was found that contained scripts for thirteen mime plays written by Herondas, a Greek writer who lived in Alexandria around 270 BC (see *The Mimes of Herondas,* trans. Guy Davenport, 1981). These lively,

colourful, and sometimes ribald miniature dramas appear to confirm that in the ancient world at least some performers called mimes spoke, and even memorized texts written by others" (Leabhart 2–3).

13. Interestingly, Ron Davis, the founder of the Mime Troupe, also studied with Étienne Decroux. Davis's early mime work was more akin to the abstract work of Decroux's other disciples. However, the Mime troupe's work changed and evolved away from this style of theater.

14. In chapter 3 I discuss how, even in puppet traditions, in which the human presence may appear to be absent from the performance arena, the human body and its capacities for physical expression are still central to the success of the form.

15. This is true even in the case of pantomime, for it is the physical aspect of objects that is emphasized when pantomiming them, as opposed to their symbolic value. Pantomime through physical action defines the physical nature of objects and environments.

16. Not only are popular performances ephemeral but so are the documents that attest to them. As David Mayer and Kenneth Richards have stated in their proceedings of the Manchester University Symposium on Western Popular Theater: "What no one attending the Symposium disputed is how ephemeral are the documents of 'popular theater'. They vanish quickly and are often irrevocable" (Mayer and Richards vii).

Chapter 2

1. Because of this relationship between theater and politics, theatrical literature has often had a great impact on French political and social life. The Mime Troupe has performed versions of Molière's *Tartuffe,* Beaumarchais's *Marriage of Figaro,* and Alfred Jarry's *Ubu Roi,* pieces that are significant not only as theatrical literature but more so for the social and political unrest that erupted at their respective debuts.

2. Since the 1950s Armand Gatti has both written and directed a wide variety of politically engaged theater pieces. For more on his work, see Dorothy Knowles, *Armand Gatti: Wild Duck Against the Wind* (London: Atholone; Rutherford, Madison, and Teaneck, N.J.: Fairleigh Dickinson University Press, 1989).

3. In 1968 the cultural question revolved not only around the issue of class but also around the related issue of cultural centralization. Most of France's cultural institutions are, and have traditionally been, centered in Paris. This has meant that cultural works are most accessible to people in Paris and the surrounding areas, and that they are most responsive to the needs and tastes of those people. French culture therefore tends to reflect a highly urbanized and usually wealthier sector of society, leaving the rural provinces and their traditions unrepresented. The provinces have historically had little access to theatrical productions, except for touring provincial companies (Molière got his start in one of these), traveling players, and, only more recently, successful Parisian productions that subse-

quently tour the countryside. The traditional lack of permanent theaters is perhaps one reason for the great reliance on local, regional carnivalesque festivals in remote areas. The annual theater festival in Avignon, founded by Jean Vilar in 1947, was a first step toward decentralizing theater in France. When Roger Planchon's Lyon-based theater company was awarded a government subsidy in 1960, it became the first national theater in the French provinces. Theater practitioners like Gatti, after May '68, concentrated on finding new ways to decentralize French theater.

4. Even the great playwright, actor, and king's favorite, Molière, was originally refused a proper church burial on consecrated ground. This was supposedly because his plays, like *Tartuffe,* were considered heretical and not solely because he was an actor. However, there are many other cases of actors being denied church sacraments. Molière was finally buried in the section of Saint Joseph's cemetery reserved for suicides and unbaptized children. For more on the church's relationship to actors see Mongrédien 13–26.

5. Ironically the Prince de Conti had been Molière's benefactor until 1657 when he underwent a religious conversion.

6. "des cérémonies religieuses, des actes véritables de piété envers les dieux." My translation.

7. "bouffons, mimes, pantomimes, danseurs, musiciens, cochers." My translation.

8. "ce précieux moyen de séduction et de puissance." My translation.

9. "transformer ce qu'elle ne pouvait détruire." My translation.

10. Notably, the tradition of April Fools is said to have developed as a vestige of the transition to the Christian calendar in 1564. Whereas before the new year had started in April, after the calendar change only fools still celebrated the new year at that time and were victimized by pranksters.

11. To realize the extent of theater in the Middle Ages one need only read some of the vast body of historical studies based on it such as E. K. Chambers's *Mediaeval Stages* and Henri Rey-Flaud's *Le Cercle magique: Essai sur le théâtre en rond à la fin du Moyen Age.*

12. *Oxford English Dictionary,* s.v. "farce."

13. This is one theory; however, it is difficult to prove actual links between Roman performers and medieval entertainers.

14. Robert Isherwood thoroughly maps out a history of these battles.

15. Also spelled "Lully."

16. One other issue not taken up here but which is of interest is that the divisions that were made among theaters were made according to genres that included opera, spoken drama, and farce. This already outlines the way that theater was perceived. Popular forms needed to develop as a genre in contrast to these other genres where monopolies already existed. Popular theater's genre was eclecticism and incorporated whatever was not already "monopolized."

17. The Opéra held a privilege on performing musical drama, but their finan-

cial situation, which, due to their extravagant productions, was always bad, led them to sell the right to use music in dramas to several fairground theaters.

18. D'Alméras quotes from Champardon's *Les Spectacles de la Foire* in his introduction to *Mémoires de Jean Monnet*: "par ses applaudissements, encourageait les acteurs forains dans la lutte inégale qu'ils soutenaient avec la Comédie-Française." My translation.

19. Pantomime was brought to England by French actors who left Paris and was adopted by English actors like John Rich (1692–1761) who created their own versions of pantomime. It eventually spread to the United States as well.

20. The most famous and accomplished pantomime performer in this new tradition was Jean-Gaspard Debureau (1796–1846). He was renowned for his playing of a Pierrot character (a French offspring of Harlequin) whom he called Baptiste. Marcel Marceau's character Bip is based on Debureau's Baptiste. The governmental restrictions were finally lifted just before Debureau's death, after which his son Charles, and then his student Louis Rouffe, and that student's student, Sévérin, tried to keep pantomime alive.

21. Isherwood proposes that the mixture of styles at the fairgrounds, which incorporated music into spoken drama, evolved into the *opéra-comique* form. Isherwood notes that once this form was taken over by the privileged theaters, its absence at the fairgrounds was the main reason for the demise of the till-then popular fairs of Saint-Germain and Saint-Laurent.

Chapter 3

1. The play was written by then Mime Troupe member Steve Friedman.

2. These figures may well be directly related to the buffoon characters of the comedies of Roman antiquity, or puppet shows that may have existed in the same period. This would lend credence to the theory that itinerant performers kept these comic forms alive after the fall of Rome in puppet shows that were easily transportable and easily hidden from authorities. Some critics, by contrast, believe that the link between the classic forms and the later ones is simply owing to the fact that similar comic characters tend to develop in all cultures. The historical evidence is, as yet, insufficient to establish either claim.

3. In Italy Pulcinella is often portrayed as having many children. Byrom, for example, refers to "a vivid description of a scene performed by the legendary Ghetanaccio in which a drunken Pulcinella returns home to his starving wife and children—apparently numbered 'by the dozen' " (Byrom 21).

4. Byrom counters this argument by showing that the characteristics Speaight claims to be unique to the English Punch were in fact already present in Pulcinella. For instance, in the earliest known Pulcinella text, *Song of Zeza,* Pulcinella has a shrewish wife named *Zeza.* See Byrom 19–23.

5. Speaight says: "Puppets played here long before the Italian motions set the town talking, and comic braggarts strutted on our stages long before Pollicinella

set up his booth at Covent Garden. Punchinello may trace an ancestry as far as Imperial Rome and Attic Greece, but Punch belongs to England" (Speaight, *Punch and Judy* 50).

6. A series of photographs in Paul Fournel's *L'Histoire véritable de Guignol* of Mourguet and Guignol (Paris: Slatkine Ressources, 1981) attests to the accuracy of this story. Earlier Mourguet had also carved another character, Gnafron, who was based on a friend of his and who became Guignol's companion.

7. "Polichinelle l'amuse, mais il ne le satisfait point, car il n'est pas du peuple de chez nous." My translation.

8. Speaight notes that a new wave of regional puppets developed in the nineteenth century with these French puppets. He links the emergence of these new puppets with the effects of the French Revolution throughout Europe:

> It is significant to note that in all the countries affected by the French Revolution, new puppet heroes, local and national in character, sprang up at the beginning of the nineteenth century to supplant the progeny of Pulcinella—Guignol in France, Kasperl in Germany, and many another. Even in northern Italy, the old characters of the Commedia dell' Arte were replaced by a new set of regional heroes. Only in Russia and England, countries which were never defeated by Napoleon—did the Pulcinella character survive in its assimilated form. And in Russia, Petroushka did not survive the Russian Revolution. (*Punch and Judy* 145)

Moreover, the new puppet folk-heroes of the age of the French Revolution differed significantly from their predecessors. Pulcinella was a peasant, with a peasant's rough humor; Polichinelle was a peasant dressed up in court clothes; Punch was a peasant playing the part of John Bull. But the new race of puppet heroes were townsmen, not country men; industrial workers, not peasants; shabbier, sharper, less coarse, more witty (145). These new puppets still represented the lower classes even though the new lower classes were urban factory workers rather than peasants.

9. Here Byrom refers to the commedia characters. Puppet figures, however, were often derived from masked figures and vice versa. Consequently, there exists a variety of puppet figures for the different regions of Italy equal to the variety of masked figures. "It was much the same story throughout Italy: though censorship was officially strict, it was unable to suppress the satirical mockery of Punch, Cassandrino, Rugantino, Arlecchino, Stenterello, Gianduja, Meneghino, and many other impudent marionettes; which is to say it was powerless to control the irrepressible spirit of the people" (92).

10. As European countries developed from groups of principalities into nation-states, they claimed their own identity through many means, including a national language and literature. In so doing, they had to figure out not only how to develop and define their own unique cultural heritage but also how to make that separate and distinct, in the eyes of the lower classes, from the wider European traditions of which they were already a part. The fights that took place between

the fairground theaters in France and the official theaters, covered in chapter 2, resulted partly from this clash.

11. Speaight, again claiming Punch's English heritage, reminds us that many of the unique characteristics the English Punch developed distinguish him from the original Italian Pulcinella: "We must above all, clear our minds of preconceived illusions. The genuine Neapolitan Pulcinella was not, and never has been, hump-backed, nor dressed in bright colours, nor fond of fighting, nor a wife beater" (Speaight, *Punch and Judy* 13). "In fact, he was a comedian not a villain, a hen-pecked husband not a wife-beater, the receiver of slaps not the dealer of blows, the author of puerile vulgarities not a Don Juan, a naughty and mischievous wag not an insensate and indiscriminate assassin" (Speaight, *Punch and Judy* 66). It is perhaps when Punch took on the outfit of the English Jesters that he could be seen as formally outfitting himself to the English imagination: "By about the middle of the century he had discarded his plain white Italian costume and was beginning to wear the red-and-yellow motley of the English jester that has distinguished him ever since" (68). However Byrom argues, and I agree, that these differences aside, the main character of Pulcinella/Punch/Polichinelle has stayed constant: "There was no fundamental difference between the character of Pulcinella and his French and English counterparts: he was a ferocious sadist dedicated to the might of the Big Stick. A rebel in revolt against everything, including Death and the Devil" (Byrom 15). "Pulcinella, like Punch, may not be on the right side of the law, but he is certainly opposed to the Devil; and though he can hardly be called innocent, he is most dreadfully oppressed" (Byrom 18).

12. Punch's voice is created by an instrument known as the swazzle. This small device is held between the teeth and gives a high-pitched squeakiness to the character's voice. Pulcinella, Punch, and Petrushka puppeteers all use this device for the voice of their main character. The device also makes the character's words difficult to understand.

13. He adds: "In no other theatrical medium is this possible. In no other theater can one person perform so many functions at one time" (Baird 101).

14. These effects underline the physical nature of the human body, highlighting Bakhtin's sense of the grotesque in popular forms.

15. The Punch and Judy show is a compilation of small scenes that can be shortened, lengthened, added, or left out according to a puppeteer's needs. A puppeteer can shorten a performance if an audience is unresponsive or lengthen it if they are enthusiastic.

16. There are some exceptions, like the Fujian hand puppets.

17. Quoted from *Penny Magazine*, Apr. 1845.

18. In Italy the puppet shows were almost the only means the lower classes had to express themselves collectively:

> Throughout the golden age of Italian puppet theatre . . . whether the Italian citizen lived under foreign domination or was ruled by a native king as in Piedmont and Savoy, he was

the subject of a tyranny with very little freedom of speech. Almost the only means for the expression of public opinion were the *pasquinate* and the puppet shows . . . The Roman *pasquinate* or pasquinaeds were mordant epigrams and satires, often scurrilous, usually directed against the government or the Pope but aimed with equal facility at any absurdity or abuse. They were named after a 15th. century tailor called Pasquino, who lived in the Piazza Navona during the reign of Julius II and who was famous for his wit. After his death, an ancient classical torso was dug up in the street and set beside his shop. It then became the custom for any protestor wishing to remain anonymous to stick his verses and epigrams on the pedestal at night, following which, copies of these so-called pasquinades would be sold in the cafés and Piazzas. (Byrom 33–34)

Here is an example he gives referring to the French occupation in the nineteenth century:

In times less pleasant and more fierce, of old,
Thieves were hung upon the cross, we're told
In times less fierce, more pleasant, like today,
The cross is hung upon the thieves, they say

(Byrom 34)

19. "Comme pour la plupart des spectacles de marionettes au début du XIXe, le principe textuel du Guignol de Mourguet est l'improvisation. Les canevas qui servent de support au jeu sont de simples prétextes qui sortent pour une part du fonds d'intrigues théâtrale que l'on retrouve dans toute l'Europe et pour l'autre de l'imagination même de Mourguet" (Fournel 87).

20. "Diffuser les nouvelles c'est prendre parti et c'est faire prendre parti à ceux qui n'ont pas droit de regard sur la marche du monde."

21. Fournel gives a quote from an interview with one Guignol puppeteer who makes this state of affairs clear:

Dor: Quand on faisait viser une pièce et qu'on la jouait après est-ce qu'on s'en tenait exactement au manuscrit?

Durafour: Non, jamais on ne s'est tenu au manuscrit, on amplifiait, on diminuait. (Fournel 89)

[Dor: When one had a play looked over and then played it afterward did one keep exactly to the manuscript.

Durafour: No, we never kept to the written text, we added and subtracted.]

22. Talking about one writer of Guignol texts Fournel says: "Vuillerme n'a pas écrit ces textes pour prouver ses talents littéraires ou pour léguer une image de Guignol à la postérité, mais seulement pour le faire passer la barrière préfectorale. L'auto-censure est donc terrible" (89). [Vuillerme did not write these textes to prove his literary talents or in order to leave an image of Guignol for posterity, but only in order to pass the prefectorial barrier. The self-censorship is therefore very strong.]

23. Kelly suggests that the kind of triple censorship that took place with the Guignol texts also took place with "Petrushka," and may account for many of the

similarities we now see within that tradition. As with Guignol, two phases of censorship came before the scripts reached their publishers. Puppeteers would give more polished versions of their shows to philologists who came to record them than they might actually perform. The philologists would themselves make decisions about what they wrote down, "reluctant to record outright smut" (85). The last phase of censorship came from publishers who would hesitate to publish "such crudities as have survived the first two stages of repression" (85). Less inventive puppeteers could then turn to these published texts for their scripts rather than inventing their own (75). This accounts for the general similarity and lack of inventiveness represented in the tradition today.

24. "These comic scenes are not found in the written sources of the puppeteers; they derive from a theatrical tradition which introduces the masked characters into all kinds of plots" (Pasquelino 21).

25. The Russian play of Petrushka was similar to the English Punch and Judy in having developed into a single recognizable story. But here too there was ample room for improvisation. The puppeteer could vary the order in which scenes appeared as well as the ending of each individual scene (Kelly 68).

26. "If the general history of the *Petrushka* show resembles that of the other fairground genres it was, however, less seriously affected by the erosion of the fairground sites in the late nineteenth century . . . But the survival of *Petrushka* had a price—it is increasingly regarded as a text for children. Children had always been among those watching, but by the late nineteenth century it was standard practice to take Russian middle-class children to the performances" (Kelly 54–55).

27. These technological attractions have culminated in the elaborate rides of today's amusement parks.

28. While hangmen represented the law and carried out punishment, it should be remembered that the people who performed these tasks and their families were ostracized from society. They were symbols of control and oppression, but as individuals they exercised no real social or political power.

29. In Punch and Judy nearly everyone gets beaten and killed. Even Punch gets beaten and only half the time survives both the hangman and the devil. But Speaight says of the Clown that often appears in the plays: "Punch always has a merry companion; he may be Scaramouch or Clown or Joey or Mr. Merryman, but one or the other is an essential member of the cast . . . and it is a tradition that he alone of Punch's adversaries does not get killed" (Speaight, *Punch and Judy* 90). This is interesting in regard to the important position of clown figures in popular culture (see chapter 1). Punch is a clown figure, but Clown is even more of one. He is the only one who survives the violence in the play.

30. "While we have tended to blame declining social standards, foreign influences, or base human desires for such vulgarities, I believe, that the vulgar results not from misuse so much as from overuse. I intend to argue that, in the more appropriate colloquial term, *junk* is what results when an adolescent, usually male, audience commandeers the attention of a medium and endlessly rehashes certain

motifs. When the technologies and efficiencies of production make it economical to mass produce an 'entertainment' for young men, 'junk' will result. . . . because they are produced to be mindlessly consumed, they often present an uncorrupted view of the fantasy life of adolescents" (Twitchell 4).

Chapter 4

1. Incidents of mistaken twins occur in theatrical texts at least as far back as Plautus's *Brothers Menachmus.* In some of these plays, however, the use of masks meant that two different actors could play the two different identical characters.

2. Mime Troupe member Sharon Lockwood's depictions of Nancy Reagan and Diane Feinstein are some impressive examples.

3. Minstrels sat on the stage in a semicircle. The Interlocutor sat in the middle, and the minstrels that sat around him were referred to as the "endmen."

4. The nostalgia for plantation life can also be seen as an early appeal to northerners who were already contemplating the abolition of slavery.

5. The minstrel show became such a significant part of American culture that Boskin says: "Prior to the signing of the trade treaty with Japan in 1854, in the ceremonial exchange of presents and rituals, American sailors aboard the Commodore Matthew C. Perry offered a shipboard minstrel show. (The Japanese had presented a demonstration of the ancient ritual of sumo wrestling and ceremonial dancing)" (76).

6. In a symposium at Stanford University sponsored by the Spring Foundation entitled "The Resilient Woman: Strength in the Face of Adversity," feminist scholars from Mary Moore to Carol Gilligan defined resilience and resistance as different tactics by which women dealt with oppressive circumstances while retaining a source of strength.

7. Black minstrel shows also became a means for blacks to enter the world of business as blacks often owned and booked their own companies. This gave them a hand in the shows' financial profits and opened up limited areas of the business world to them. Black minstrel companies, however, often fell into the hands of white managers, who then took control and business advantages away from those who had built the company.

8. When I read a paper based on this material at the "Theatre of the Oppressed" conference in Omaha, Nebraska, in 1995, one listener responded to it saying that it reminded her that she had seen the production and had been picked out of the audience to dance with the minstrels. As an actress, she saw it as an opportunity to ham things up and display her own talents. Her interest in acting on her own agency within the show was not well received by the minstrel actors, who merely wanted to use her for their own theatrical ends.

9. In the original play Legree's murder is almost an accident, carried out by two comic white male characters who are hoping to turn Legree in to the police for a reward.

10. Legree talking objectively about his character in this way happened in an early production of the play. In the later printed version of the script Legree does not break character but speaks as himself within the context of the scene. He says: "Was born dis way . . . grew up dis way, and I intend to die dis way. I am a white man, created in the image of God. God forbid if Satan should ever come to earth, for all you wretched darkies will rise from Satan's furnace like crows, swooping down on white people. But no nigger shall ever rule a white man" (63). In both cases he proclaims that there is no possibility that he will change and embraces his position.

11. On seeing a lock of Little Eva's hair that Tom has with him, Legree is reminded of his own dead mother, whom he treated badly. At this moment there is some chance that Legree is having a change of heart, though in the end he does not become a religious person.

Chapter 5

1. Giordano Bruno (1548–1600) was an Italian philosopher and writer. He wrote the play *Il Candelaio* around 1582. Phyllis Hartnoll describes this play as "a brilliant, mordant piece of work which disclosed the corrupt customs of the time with unabated candour and for that reason was banned" (136). Bruno was burned at the stake in 1600 by order of the Inquisition. According to Hartnoll a 1965 Italian production starring Paolo Poli and Maria Monti was probably the first professional production of this play.

2. Most of the decisions at that time were made by the Troupe's head and founder Ron Davis.

3. According to Harold Jencks, in the 1970s the Troupe made a great effort not only to play in more working-class and minority neighborhoods but also to integrate the company so as to represent a wider variety of ethnic groups in their ranks.

4. The new, reorganized Mime Troupe has experimented with other styles of performance including Brechtian. In 1973 the Troupe did a production of Brecht's *The Mother,* which at least one former Mime Troupe writer and actor, Steve Friedman, believes was one of the Troupe's most successful pieces. In 1996 the Troupe did a piece in collaboration with Borderline Theatre from Tucson, Arizona, focusing on the uprisings in Chiapas, Mexico, called *13 Dìas/13 Days.* This piece mixed Mime Troupe-style comic-mythic characters like Zapata, returned from the dead, along with two drunk folk singers who run into him, with more realistic characters and scenes, and with both fictional and documentary video footage.

5. In the spring of 1997 the Mime Troupe toured a revival of *The Independent Female* in Spanish to an international theater festival in Colombia. Ruth Wikler, a student at Barnard College, toured with them in the role of the Barker. Wikler found that perceptions about whether this play was outdated or not seemed to fall along class lines. In the outdoor venue the mostly lower-class audience, and

especially the women, still related to the story and the characters and felt it reflected their own situation. In an indoor venue that catered to a mostly bourgeois audience the play was not as well received and was considered outdated. The Troupe's biggest fan in this venue was the theater's secretary, who completely identified with the play and sent the Troupe appreciative notes and flowers backstage.

6. The Troupe calls *Frozen Wages* an "Acto" rather than a play. This term was originally used by Luis Valdez a former Mime Troupe member who started El Teatro Campesino, a festive-revolutionary Chicano theater company. Actos are usually shorter than regular plays, use more agit-prop techniques, and are directed toward one specific political issue.

7. In 1964–65 the Troupe received a grant from the San Francisco Hotel Tax Fund. This was a fund set up so that out-of-town visitors, through hotel taxes, would help to fund some of the cultural events that brought people to San Francisco. The Troupe's grant was rescinded in 1965. In 1973 the Troupe fought to again have a grant from that fund. The Troupe reasoned that as one of the city's oldest ongoing theater companies they brought people to the city, entertained them for free in the parks, and were entitled to a share of the fund's proceeds. They fought for this right and were again granted a small yearly sum from the fund in 1977.

8. This line is not written in the script but was included in performance.

9. The image of Liberty leading the people from the Delacroix painting is depicted on the top of the set throughout the play.

10. On the day I saw the show someone at the play was actually distributing flyers promoting this theory. It was never clear just how seriously the Mime Troupe took this point of view.

11. The town's name is, of course, used as a joke throughout the play. When Hetty makes her speech the Mayor wants everyone to know that "this is not Normal."

12. In his Theatre Forum work, Augusto Boal insists that participants who enter a scene in order to change it should start by taking over the role of the oppressed protagonist rather than the role of the antagonist oppressor. As Boal has said in his workshops, we cannot hope to change the oppressor, it is we who must change.

13. The Mime Troupe's optimistic view of the future is perhaps best displayed today in the theater workshops they give for low-income teens. In these workshops Mime Troupe members, outside artists, and San Francisco State students guide teens in scripting, acting, and directing plays that reflect the young artists' own concerns. While all the writing comes from the teens themselves, the plays end up reflecting the Mime Troupe's theatrical aesthetic.

References

Aiken, George, and Harriet Beecher Stowe. *Uncle Tom's Cabin. American Melodrama.* Ed. Daniel C. Gerould. New York: Performing Arts Journal Publications, 1983.

Albert, Maurice. *Les Théâtres de la Foire, 1660–1789.* Paris: Librairie Hachette et Cie, 1900.

Alexander, Robert. *I Ain't Yo' Uncle: The New Jack Revisionist "Uncle Tom's Cabin."* Woodstock, Ill.: Dramatic Publishing, 1996.

Apostolides, Jean-Marie. "La Guillotine Littéraire." *French Review* 62.6 (May 1989): 985–96.

Auslander, Philip. "Toward a Concept of the Political in Postmodern Theatre." *Theatre Journal* 39.1 (Mar. 1987): 20–34.

Babelet, Denis, and Jean Jacquot. "1793, L'Age D'Or." *Les Voies de la Creation Theatrale,* vol.5. Paris: Editions du Centre de la Recherche Scientifique, 1977. 123–278.

Babelet, Denis, and L'Equipe Théâtre Moderne. *Le Théâtre d'Agit-Prop de 1917 á 1932,* Collection Théâtre Années Vingt, vols. 3 and 4. Lausanne: La Cité-L'Age d'Homme, 1978.

Baird, Bil. *The Art of The Puppet.* New York: Macmillan, 1965.

Bakhtin, Mikhail. *Rabelais and His World.* Trans. Hélene Iswolsky. Bloomington: Indiana University Press, 1984.

Barber, C.L. "License and lese majesty in Lincolnshire." *Shakespeare's Festive Comedy: A Study of Dramatic Form and Its Relation to Social Custom.* Princeton: Princeton University Press, 1959. 37–51.

Barrault, Jean-Louis. *Memories for Tomorrow: The Memoirs of Jean-Louis Barrault.* Trans. Jonathan Griffin. New York: Dutton, 1974.

Baschet, Armand. *Les Comédiens Italiens a la Cours de France sous Charles IX, Henri III, Henri IV et Louis XIII.* Paris: E. Plon et Cie, 1882.

Baxandall, Lee. "The San Francisco Mime Troupe Perform Brecht." *Praxis* 1 (1975): 116–21.

Beaumont, Cyril W. *The History of Harlequin.* New York: Benjamin Blom, 1926.

Beck, Julian. *The Life of the Theatre: The Relation of the Artist to the Struggle of the People.* San Francisco: City Lights, 1972.

Benjamin, Walter. "The Work of Art in the Age of Mechanical Reproduction." *Illuminations*. New York: Harcourt Brace & World, 1968.

Berger, Anne, et al. "En Plein Soleil." *Fruits*, 2/3. Paris: Presses Universitaires de Vincennes, 1984.

Berman, Marshall. *All That Is Solid Melts into Air*. New York: Simon and Schuster, 1982.

Bernardi, R. M. *La Comédie Italienne en France et le Théâtre de la Foire et du Boulevard (1570–1791)*. Bibliothèque Théâtrale Illustrée, sous la direction de M. Paul Ginistry. Paris: Schleicher Frères et Cie, 1902.

Berson, Misha. "Cabin Fever." *American Theatre* May 1991: 16–23, 71–73.

Bharucha, Rustom. *Rehearsals of Revolution: The Political Theater of Bengal*. Calcutta: Seagull, 1983.

Blanchard, Kendall, ed. *The Many Faces of Play*. Champaign, Ill.: Human Kinetics, 1986.

Bogle, Donald. *Toms, Coons, Mulattoes, Mammies, and Bucks: An Interpretive History of Blacks in American Films*. New York: Viking, 1973.

Boskin, Joseph. *Sambo: The Rise and Demise of an American Jester*. New York and Oxford: Oxford University Press, 1986.

Bradby, David, and John McCormick. *People's Theatre*. Totowa, N.J.: Rowman and Littlefield, 1978.

Brecht, Bertolt. *Brecht on Theatre*. Trans. John Willet. New York: Hill and Wang, 1964.

Bristol, Michael D. *Carnival and Theater: Plebian Culture and the Structure of Authority in Renaissance England*. New York: Methuen, 1985.

Brook, Peter. *The Empty Space*. New York: PAJ, 1986.

Brown, Frederick. *Theater and Revolution: The Culture of the French Stage*. New York: Vintage, 1989.

Bürger, Peter. "Theory of the Avant-Garde." *Theory and History of Literature*, vol.4. Ed. Wlad Godzich and Jochen Schulte-Sasse. Trans. Michael Shaw. Minneapolis: University of Minnesota Press, 1984.

Byrom, Michael. *Punch and Judy in the Italian Puppet Theatre*. London: Centaur, 1983.

Calinescu, Matei. *Five Faces of Modernity: Modernism, Avant-Garde, Decadence, Kitsch, Postmodernism*. Durham: Duke University Press, 1987.

Caputi, Anthony. *Buffo, The Genius of Vulgar Comedy*. Detroit: Wayne State University Press, 1978.

Carlson, Marvin. *The Theatre of the French Revolution*. Ithaca, N.Y.: Cornell University Press, 1966.

Case, Sue-Ellen. *Feminism and Theatre*. New York: Methuen, 1988.

Chaiken, Joseph. *The Presence of the Actor*. New York: Atheneum, 1980.

Champagne, Lenora. *French Theatre Experiment since 1968*. Ann Arbor: UMI Research, 1984.

Cohen, Gustav. *Etudes d'Histoire du Théâtre en France au Moyen-Age et à la Renaissance*, 6th ed. Paris: Gallimard, 1956.

Cohn, Ruby. "Joan Holden and the San Francisco Mime Troupe." *Tulane Drama Review* 24.2 (June 1980): 41–50.

Cole, David. *The Theatrical Event: A* Mythos, *a Vocabulary, a Perspective.* Middletown, Conn.: Wesleyan University Press, 1975.

Croyden, Margaret. *Lunatics, Lovers and Poets.* New York: McGraw Hill, 1974.

Davis, R. G. *The San Francisco Mime Troupe: The First Ten Years.* Palo Alto, Calif.: Ramparts, 1975.

Dowling, William C. *Jameson, Althusser, Marx.* Ithaca: Cornell University Press, 1984.

Drewal, Margaret Thompson. *Yoruba Ritual: Performers, Play and Agency.* Bloomington: Indiana University Press, 1992.

Duchartre, Pierre Louis. *The Italian Comedy.* Trans. Randolph T. Weaver. New York: Dover, 1966.

Dumont, Frank. *The Witmark Amateur Minstrel Guide.* New York: M. Witmark and Sons, 1899.

Edgar, David. "Ten Years of Political Theatre, 1968–78." *Theatre Quarterly* 8.32 (1979): 25–33.

Elam, Harry Justin, Jr. "Theatre for Social Change: The Artistic and Social Vision in Revolutionary Theatre in America, 1930–1970." Diss. University of California, Berkeley, 1984.

Engle, Gary D. *This Grotesque Essence: Plays from the American Minstrel Stage.* Baton Rouge and London: Louisiana State University Press, 1978.

Enters, Angna. *On Mime.* With drawings by the author. Middletown, Conn.: Wesleyan University Press, 1965.

Etherton, Michael. *The Development of African Drama.* New York: Africana, 1982.

Falassi, Alessandro, ed. *Time Out of Time: Essays on the Festival.* Albuquerque: University of New Mexico Press, 1987.

Feuillet, Octave. *La Vie de Polichinelle et Ses Nombreuses Aventures.* Paris: Collection J. Hetzel et Cie, Petite Bibliotheque Blanche, 1878.

Fo, Dario. *Mistero Buffo/Comic Mysteries.* Trans. Ed Emery. Intro. Stuart Hood. London: Methuen, 1988.

Foley, Kathy. "The Clown Figure in the Puppet Theatre of West Java: The Ancestor and the Individual." *Humor and Comedy in Puppetry: Celebration in Popular Culture.* Ed. Dina Sherzer and Joel Sherzer. Bowling Green, Ohio: Bowling Green State University Popular Press, 1987. 65–78.

Fournel, François Victor. *Curiosités Théâtrales Anciennes et Modernes, Françaises et Etrangères.* Nouvelle edition revue, corigée et trés augmentée. Paris: Garnier Frères, 1878.

———. *Les Contemporains de Molière.* Paris: Didot Frères, Fils et Cie, 1863–75.

Fournel, Paul. *L'Histoire véritable de Guignol.* Paris and Geneva: Slatkine Ressources, 1981.

Fournel, Paul, ed. *Les Marionettes.* Pref. Antoine Vitez. Paris: Bordas, 1982.

Franck, Martine, and Claude Roy. "Le Théâtre du Soleil: Shakespeare." *Photo Double Page,* 21. Paris: Editions SNEP, 1982.

Franck, Martine, Raymonde Tenkine, and Sophie Moscoso. "Le Théâtre du Soleil: Shakespeare 2e Partie." *Photo Double Page,* 32. Paris: Editions SNEP, 1984.

Frye, Northrop. *Anatomy of Criticism: Four Essays.* Princeton: Princeton University Press, 1971.

Gates, Henry Louis, Jr. *The Signifying Monkey; A Theory of Afro-American Literary Criticism.* New York: Oxford University Press, 1988.

Geertz, Clifford. *The Interpretation of Cultures.* New York: Basic, 1973.

Gerould, Daniel, ed. *Melodrama,* vol. 7. Gen. ed. Jeanine Parisier Plottel. New York: New York Literary Forum, 1980.

Gitlin, Todd. *The Sixties: Years of Hope, Days of Rage.* New York: Bantam, 1987.

Goldberg, Rose Lee. *Performance Art: From Futurism to the Present.* Rev. and enlarged ed. New York: Harry N. Abrams, 1988.

Grimsted, David. *Melodrama Unveiled: American Theater and Culture 1800–1850.* Chicago and London: University of Chicago Press, 1968.

Grotowski, Jerzy. *Towards a Poor Theatre.* New York: Simon and Schuster, 1968.

Gruber, William E. *Comic Theaters: Studies in Performance and Audience Response.* Athens and London: University of Georgia Press, 1986.

Hamiche, Daniel. *Le Théâtre et La Révolution.* Paris: UGE, 1973.

Harding, Laurence, V. *The Dramatic Art of Ferdinand Raimund and Johann Nestroy: A Critical Study.* Studies in German Literature, vol.3. The Hague and Paris: Mouton, 1974.

Hardey, Bill. *Bill Hardey's Songs of the Gay Nineties and Other Old Favorites.* New York: Robins Music, 1938.

Hartnoll, Phyllis, ed. *The Oxford Companion to the Theatre,* 3rd ed. London: Oxford University Press, 1967.

Hogan, Patrick Colm. *The Politics of Interpretation: Ideology, Professionalism, and the Study of Literature.* New York and Oxford: Oxford University Press, 1990.

Holden, Joan, Ellen Callas, and Bruce Barthol. *Ripped Van Winkle.* Unpublished manuscript. San Francisco Mime Troupe, 1988.

Holden, Joan, et al. "The San Francisco's *Mozamgola Caper.*" *Theater* 20.1 (1988): 55–71.

Horkheimer, Max, and Theodor W. Adorno. *Dialectic of Enlightenment.* Trans. John Cumming. New York: Continuum, 1987.

Huet, Marie-Helene. *Rehearsing the Revolution.* Berkeley: University of California Press, 1982.

Huizinga, Johan. *Homo Ludens: A Study of the Play Element in Culture.* Boston: Beacon, 1955.

Hutcheon, Linda. *The Politics of Postmodernism.* London and New York: Routledge, 1989.

Huyssen, Andreas. *After the Great Divide: Modernism, Mass Culture, Postmodernism.* Bloomington: Indiana University Press, 1986.

Isherwood, Robert M. *Farce and Fantasy: Popular Entertainment in Eighteenth-Century Paris.* Oxford: Oxford University Press, 1986.

Jameson, Fredric. *Marxism and Form.* Princeton: Princeton University Press, 1971.

———. *The Political Unconscious.* Ithaca, N.Y.: Cornell University Press, 1981.

Jencks, Lance Harold. "The San Francisco Mime Troupe in Its Social Context." Diss. University of California, Davis, 1978.

Jenkins, Ron. *Acrobats of the Soul: Comedy and Virtuosity in Contemporary American Theatre.* New York: Theatre Communications Group, 1988.

———. "Ridiculing Racism in South Africa." *Subversive Laughter: The Liberating Power of Comedy.* Toronto: Free Press, 1994. 79–106.

Johnstone, Keith. *Impro: Improvisation and the Theatre.* London: Methuen, 1981.

Jung, C. G. *Four Archetypes: Mother, Rebirth, Spirit, Trickster.* Trans. R. F. C. Hull. London: Routledge and K. Paul, 1972.

Kaser, Arthur LeRoy. *Kaser's Complete Minstrel Guide: A Collection of Minstrel Material for Every Occasion.* Chicago: Dramatic Publishing, 1934.

Kelly, Catriona. *Petrushka: The Russian Carnival Puppet Theatre.* Cambridge Studies in Russian Literature. Cambridge: Cambridge University Press, 1990.

Kennedy, Emmet. *A Cultural History of the French Revolution.* New Haven and London: Yale University Press, 1989.

Keyssar, Helen. *Feminist Theatre: An Introduction to Plays of Contemporary British and American Women.* New York: Grove, 1985.

Kidd, Ross. *From People's Theatre for Revolution to Popular Theatre for Reconstruction: Diary of a Zimbabwean Workshop.* The Hague: Centre for the Study of Education in Developing Countries, 1989.

King, W. D. "Good and 'B-A-D-D-D-D' Storytelling: John O'Neal's Junebug Jabbo Jones." *Theater* 20.1 (1988): 73–83.

Kirby, Ernest Theodore. *Ur Drama: The Origins of Theatre.* New York: New York University Press, 1975.

Kirby, Michael. "The New Theatre, Performance Documentation." *The Drama Review Series.* New York: New York University Press, 1974.

Kleb, William. "The San Francisco Mime Troupe a Quarter of a Century Later: An Interview with Joan Holden." *Theater* 16.2 (Spring 1985): 58–61.

Knowles, Dorothy. *Armand Gatti: Wild Duck Against the Wind.* London: Atholone Press; Rutherford, Madison, and Teaneck, N.J.: Fairleigh Dickinson University Press, 1989.

Kourilsky, Françoise. *Le Bread and Puppet Theatre.* Lausanne: La Cité, 1967.

Ladurie, Emmanuel Le Roy. *Le Carnaval de Romans: De la Chandeleur au mercredi des Cendres, 1579–1580.* Poitiers/Ligugé: Gallimard, 1979.

Leabhart, Thomas. *Modern and Post-Modern Mime.* London: Macmillan, 1989.

Leach, Robert. *The Punch and Judy Show: History, Tradition and Meaning.* London: Bratsford Academic and Educational, 1985.

Lefebvre, Henri. *Everyday Life in the Modern World.* Trans. Sacha Rabinovitch. London: Allen Lane Penguin, 1971

Lukács, Georg. *History and Class Consciousness: Studies in Marxist Dialectics.* Trans. Rodney Livingstone. Cambridge, Mass.: MIT Press, 1968.

Lunel, Ernest. *Le Théâtre et la Révolution.* Paris: H. Daragon, n.d.

Lyotard, Jean-François. *La Condition Postmoderne.* Paris: Les Editions de Minuit, 1979.

———. *Le Postmoderne Expliqué aux Enfants: Correspondance, 1982–1985.* Paris: Editions Galilée, 1986.

Marcuse, Herbert. "The Affirmative Character of Culture." *Negations.* Boston: Beacon, 1968.

Maugras, Gaston. *Les Comédiens Hors La Loi,* 2nd ed. Paris: Calmann Lévy, 1887.

Mayer, David, and Kenneth Richards, eds. *Western Popular Theatre: The Proceedings of a Symposium sponsored by the Manchester University Department of Drama.* London and New York: Methuen, 1977.

McGrath, John. *A Good Night Out: Popular Theatre—Audience, Class and Form.* London: Eyre Methuen, 1981.

Mémoires de Jean Monnet, Directeur du Théâtre de la Foire. Intro. and notes by Henri D'Alméras. Series, Les Moeurs Légères au XVIIIe Siècle. Paris: Louis Michaud, [1900].

Miller, James, ed. "After the Sixties; The Culture and Politics of Liberation Revisited." *Salmagundi* 81 (Winter 1989): 123–231.

Miller, Judith Graves. *Theater and Revolution in France since 1968.* Lexington, Ky.: French Forum, 1977.

Mimes on Miming: Writings on the Art of Mime. Ed. with historical notes by Bari Rolfe. Los Angeles: Panjandrum, 1979.

Mitchell, W. J. T. *The Politics of Interpretation.* Chicago and London: University of Chicago Press, 1982.

Mongrédien, Georges. *Daily Life in the French Theatre at the Time of Molière.* Trans. Claire Eliane Engel. Daily Life series, 16. London: George Allen and Unwin, 1969.

Muret, Theodor. *L'Histoire par le Théâtre, 1789–1851.* Deuxième series, La Restauration. Paris: Amyot, 1865.

Murray, Timothy. *Theatrical Legitimation: Allegories of Genius in Seventeenth-Century England and France.* New York and Oxford: Oxford University Press, 1987.

Onofrio, Jean-Baptiste. *Théâtre Lyonnais de Guignol.* Pref. Marcel Maréchal. Illus. Eugène Lefebvre. Marseille: Lafitte Reprints, 1978.

Osinski, Zbigniew. *Grotowski and His Laboratory.* Trans. Lilliann Vallee and Robert Findley. New York: PAJ, 1986.

Oxford English Dictionary, 2nd ed. Prepared by J. A. Simpson and E. S. C. Weiner. Oxford: Clarendon, 1989.

Ozouf, Mona. *Festivals and the French Revolution.* Trans. Alan Sheridan. Cambridge, Mass.: Harvard University Press, 1988.

———. *La fête révolutionnaire.* 1936. Paris: Gallimard, 1976.

Pasquelino, Antonio. "Humor and Puppets: An Italian Perspective." *Humor and Comedy in Puppetry: Celebration in Popular Culture.* Ed. Dina Sherzer and Joel Sherzer. Bowling Green, Ohio: Bowling Green State University Press, 1987. 8–29.

Pelton, Robert D. *The Trickster in West Africa.* Berkeley and Los Angeles: University of California Press, 1980.

Penchenat, Jean-Claude. "La Vie d'une Troupe: Le Théâtre du Soleil." *Le Theatre.* Ed. Daniel Couty and Alain Rey. N.p.: Bordas, 1980. 210–25.

Poitevin, Auguste (Maurice Drack). *Le Théâtre de la Foire: La Comedie Italienne et L'Opéra Comique, Receuil de Pièces Choisies, 1658–1720.* Geneva: Slatkine Reprints, 1970.

Proschan, Frank. "The Cocreation of the Comic in Puppetry." *Humor and Comedy in Puppetry: Celebration in Popular Culture.* Ed. Dina Sherzer and Joel Sherzer. Bowling Green, Ohio: Bowling Green State University Press, 1987. 30–46.

Radin, Paul. *The Trickster: A Study in American Indian Mythology.* With commentaries by Karl Kerényi and C. G. Jung. Intro. Stanley Diamond. New York: Shocken, 1956.

Rey-Flaud, Henri. *Le Cercle Magique: Essai sur le Théâtre en Rond a la Fin du Moyen Age.* Paris: Editions Gallimard, 1973.

Reyval, Albert. *L'Eglise et le Théâtre.* Paris: Librairie Blond et Gay, 1924.

Roach, Joseph. "Theatre History and the Ideology of the Aesthetic." *Theatre Journal* 41.2 (1989): 155–68.

Roose-Evans, James. *Experimental Theatre from Stanislavski to Peter Brook.* New York: Universe, 1984.

Root-Bernstein, Michèle. *Boulevard Theater and Revolution in Eighteenth-Century Paris.* Ann Arbor: UMI Research, 1981.

Ross, Andrew. *No Respect: Intellectuals and Popular Culture.* New York and London: Routledge, 1989.

Roters, Eberhard, et al. *Berlin, 1910–1933.* New York: Rizzoli, 1982.

San Francisco Mime Troupe. *Back to Normal.* Unpublished manuscript. San Francisco Mime Troupe, 1991.

———. *By Popular Demand: Plays and Other Works by the San Francisco Mime Troupe.* San Francisco: San Francisco Mime Troupe, 1980.

———. *Meter Maid. Breakout!: In Search of Modern Theatrical Environments.* Ed. James Scheville. Chicago: Swallow, 1973. 111–14.

———. *Offshore.* Unpublished manuscript. San Francisco Mime Troupe, 1993.

San Francisco Mime Troupe and Friends. "Factwino Meets the Moral Majority." *Humanist* 42.4 (July/Aug. 1982): 5–43.

Savran, David. *Breaking The Rules; The Wooster Group.* New York: Theatre Communications Group, 1988.

Schechner, Richard. *Essays on Performance Theory, 1970–1976.* New York: Drama Book Specialists, 1977.

———. *Performance Theory: Revised and Expanded Edition.* New York: Routledge, 1988.

Schechter, Joel. *Durov's Pig: Clowns, Politics, and Theatre.* New York: Theatre Communications Group, 1985.

Segel, Harold B. *Pinocchio's Progeny: Puppets, Marionettes, Automatons, and Robots in Modernist and Avant-Garde Drama.* Baltimore: Johns Hopkins University Press, 1995.

Shakespeare, William. *First Part of Henry the Fourth. The Riverside Shakespeare.* Boston: Houghton Mifflin, 1974.

Shank, Adele Edling. "The San Francisco Mime Troupe's *Americans, or Last Tango in Huahuatenango.*" *Tulane Drama Review* 25.3 (Fall 1981): 81–83.

Shank, Theodore. *American Alternative Theater.* New York: Grove, 1982.

———. "Political Theatre as Popular Entertainment: The San Francisco Mime Troupe." *Tulane Drama Review* 18.1 (Mar. 1974): 110–17.

Shershow, Scott Cutler. *Puppets and "Popular" Culture.* Ithaca: Cornell University Press, 1995.

Sherzer, Dina, and Joel Sherzer. "Verbal Humor in the Puppet Theater." *Humor and Comedy in Puppetry: Celebration in Popular Culture.* Ed. Dina Sherzer and Joel Sherzer. Bowling Green, Ohio: Bowling Green State University Popular Press, 1987. 47–64.

Short, Ernest. *Fifty Years of Vaudeville.* London: Eyre & Spottiswoode, 1946.

Simond, Ike. *Old Slack's Reminiscence and Pocket History of the Colored Profession from 1865 to 1891.* Intro. Robert C. Toll. Bowling Green, Ohio: Bowling Green University Popular Press, 1974.

Soyinka, Woley. "Drama and the Revolutionary Ideal." *In Person: Achebe, Awoonok, and Soyinka.* Ed. Karen L. Morell. Austin: University of Texas Press, 1975.

Speaight, George. *The History of the English Toy Theatre.* London: Studio Vista, 1946.

———. *Punch and Judy: A History.* Boston: Plays, Inc., 1955.

Stallybrass, Peter. *Politics and Poetics of Transgression.* New York: Cornell University Press, 1986.

Stowe, Harriet Beecher. *Uncle Tom's Cabin, or Life Among the Lowly.* Ed. and intro. Ann Douglas. 1852. New York: Penguin, 1981.

Stowe, William F., and David Grimsted. "White-Black Humor." *Journal of Ethnic Studies* 3.2 (Summer 1975): 78–96.

Tavernier, Adolphe. *Guignol des Champs-Elysées.* Paris: C. Delegrave, ca. 1889.

Thompson, Juli A. *Ariane Mnouchkine and the Theatre du Soleil.* Diss. University of Washington, 1986.

Toll, Robert C. *Blacking Up: The Minstrel Show in Nineteenth-Century America.* New York: Oxford University Press, 1974.

———. *On with the Show: The First Century of Show Business in America.* New York: Oxford University Press, 1976.

Towsen, John H. *Clowns.* New York: Hawthorne, 1976.

The Tragical Comedy or Comical Tragedy of Punch and Judy. Intro. and commentary by Charles Hall Grandgent. Illus. George Cruikshank. Cambridge: Washburn and Thomas, 1925.

Turner, Victor. *The Anthropology of Performance.* New York: PAJ, 1987.

———. *From Ritual to Theatre: The Human Seriousness of Play.* New York: PAJ, 1982.

Twitchell, James B. *Preposterous Violence: Fables of Aggression in Modern Culture.* New York and Oxford: Oxford University Press, 1989.

Venturi, Robert, Denise Scott Brown, and Steven Izenour. *Learning from Las Vegas.* Cambridge, Mass.: MIT Press, 1972.

Weimann, Robert. *Shakespeare and the Popular Tradition in the Theater: Studies in the Social Dimension of Dramatic Form and Function.* Baltimore and London: Johns Hopkins University Press, 1978.

Welsford, Enid. *The Fool: His Social and Literary History.* Gloucester, Mass.: Peter Smith, 1966.

———. *The Fool and the Trickster.* Cambridge, England: D. S. Brewer, 1979.

Wikler, Ruth. *Punched by Judy.* Unpublished manuscript. 1998.

Willet, John. *Art and Politics in the Weimar Period.* New York: Pantheon, 1978.

———. *The Theatre of Erwin Piscator: Half a Century of Politics in Theatre.* London: Eyre Methuen, 1978.

Wing, Joylynn W. D. *Techniques of Opposition in the Work of Dario Fo.* Diss. Stanford University, 1988.

Index